New Traditional Games for Learning

A growing interest in the use of games-based approaches for learning has been tempered in many sectors by budget or time constraints associated with the design and development of detailed digital simulations and other high-end approaches. However, a number of practitioners and small creative groups have used low-cost, traditional approaches to games in learning effectively – involving simple card, board or indoor/outdoor activity games. *New Traditional Games for Learning: A Case Book* brings together examples of this approach, which span continents (UK, western and eastern Europe, the US, and Australia), sectors (education, training, and business) and learner styles and ages (primary through to adult and work-based learning or training). Together, the chapters provide a wealth of evidence-based ideas for the teacher, tutor, or trainer interested in using games for learning, but turned off by visible high-end examples.

An editors' introduction pulls the collection together, identifying shared themes and drawing on the editors' own research in the use of games for learning. The book concludes with a chapter by a professional board game designer, incorporating themes prevalent in the preceding chapters and reflecting on game design, development, and marketing in the commercial sector, providing valuable practical advice for those who want to take their own creations further.

Alex Moseley is an Educational Designer and University Teaching Fellow at the University of Leicester, UK.

Nicola Whitton is a Research Fellow at Manchester Metropolitan University, UK.

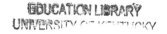

New Traditional Games for Learning

A Case Book

EDITED BY
ALEX MOSELEY
NICOLA WHITTON

Routledge
Taylor & Francis Group

NEW YORK AND LONDON

First published 2014
by Routledge

711 Third Avenue, New York, NY 10017
Simultaneously published in the UK
by Routledge
2 Park Square, Milton Park, Abingdon, Oxon OX14 4RN

Routledge is an imprint of the Taylor & Francis Group, an informa business

Library of Congress Cataloging in Publication Data
New traditional games for learning : a case book / edited by Alex Moseley
and Nicola Whitton.
pages cm
Includes bibliographical references.
1. Educational games.   I. Moseley, Alex.   II. Whitton, Nicola.
LB1029.G3N465 2013
371.33'7—dc23

2013006129

ISBN: 978-0-415-81581-9 (hbk)
ISBN: 978-0-415-81584-0 (pbk)
ISBN: 978-0-203-59751-4 (ebk)

Typeset in Minion Pro
by RefineCatch Limited, Bungay, Suffolk

Printed and bound in the United States of America by
Edwards Brothers Malloy

We would like to dedicate this book to the memory of a lost best friend, Mark Maynard, who always had an eye for fun and playfulness in work and life.

CONTENTS

List of Figures

LIST OF TABLES

ACKNOWLEDGMENTS

From the initial idea to the final touches, putting this book together has been like gathering a group of like-minded friends together in a cosy bar and chatting about our favourite games over a pint or two. It has been a privilege to receive such great ideas and experiences from across the world, and in particular to help some of these case studies reach the wide audience they deserve, with the added hope that they will inspire others. We would like to thank all of our authors for their enthusiastic contributions and collaborations, and particularly for being so helpful and friendly with it: Cheers!

Introduction

ALEX MOSELEY AND NICOLA WHITTON

Games are enjoying something of a golden period at the current time. As mobile/casual gaming competes with the multi-billion pound console game business by capturing new markets (the commuter, or coffee-breaker, or Facebook-updater), and new game forms sprout up every year (immersive and pervasive games in recent years, for example), it is easy to forget that at the core of all these forms is a simple *game mechanic*.

The difference between a good game and a bad game is almost always down to the *core mechanics*: the procedures and rules of a game. They describe "the goal of your game, how the players can and cannot try to achieve it, and what happens when they try" (Schell, 2008: 41). Other elements – such as a strong story, attractive design, or *sub-mechanics* such as chance, conflict or rewards – can make a good game a *great* experience, but if the core mechanics aren't good, no amount of shiny layers will make it enjoyable to play again and again. It is no surprise, therefore, that some of the most re-playable games are board, card or dice games (or digital versions of those games). They stay close to the core mechanics, with little packaging on top, so they have to be good at a core level.

Another area of games enjoying some of the spotlight, and the one we turn our attention to in this volume, is that of *games for learning*. Not any particular type of game, a game used for – or to enhance – learning can be any of the forms mentioned above: there are effective uses of high-end digital games and those of simple card games in education. There are also, as we argued in our previous book *Using Games to Enhance Learning and Teaching: A Beginner's Guide* (Whitton & Moseley, 2012), games for learning that are ineffective or unsuitable on a number of levels: predominantly 'games' that are not games (i.e., are simply simulations, or learning activities); and games that fail to align the learning outcomes with the game mechanics, instead forcing learning into a game, or game mechanics into a learning activity (commonly described as the 'chocolate covered broccoli' idea). Even if learning games are designed properly, for effective digital games the development cost is almost always prohibitive for educational or training institutions.

Attending games and learning conferences around Europe for the last few years, and reading case studies of educational game development in journals, we found ourselves hearing the same kind of problems faced by educators and designers: designing digital games to a standard acceptable to students (or even to meet basic objectives) takes a long time, and requires skilled production teams – at great cost. Even simple web- or mobile-based casual games require some degree of technical expertise. The lure of the digital game has led, we believe, to the proliferation of games that are not fit-for-purpose, because the ability to create these games has been taken away from the teacher.

Once in a while, we came across an individual or team who had eschewed the digital route, and had developed a game for education using more traditional methods: a board game to teach basic genetic theory, or a card game that encourages collaboration among conference attendees. As we explored deeper, we found that these games were often created by teachers, or learning developers, with little or no input from professional designers. In some cases, they were hand-produced and in rough-and-ready form; in others, they included smart artwork sourced from friendly artists, printed on high-quality card.

In at least two cases (*Konkkaronkka*, Chapter 6 and *Healing Blade*, Chapter 13), a successful board game attracted the developers of a digital version interested in its simple, playful mechanics. Traditional games can provide an excellent way to develop a core learning game locally, before then producing a digital form for wider release or more flexible delivery. This lesson emerged, surprisingly, in reverse for Rockwell and Sanchez (Chapter 5) when planning a game to engage attendees with the expertise available at a conference. Setting out to create a mobile phone game (around mobile phone issues), the designers started with a traditional card game approach, and found that the simple approach created more interest and discussion than the digital version would have, and so stuck to it.

In something of a labour of love, we have sought out what we feel are the best – and most representative – examples of this growth in new traditional games for learning. In each case, we've either played (and loved) the games described here, or heard good first-hand accounts from players of the games. In particular, we focussed on examples of cleverly integrated learning-and-mechanics, and on solid practical methods for development and production that would be achievable in most learning contexts.

The case studies cover a range of such contexts: from infant development learning with the cute, playful *Konkkaronkka* board game mentioned earlier (Chapter 6); through secondary teaching with Ottolini and Kramer's interplanetary battle board game to teach fundamental genetic concepts (Chapter 11); to higher education issues explored through Hamshire and Forsyth's *Staying the*

Course and *Accreditation!* games (Chapter 12). There are games for professional learners too: Charlier's use of a clever tile-building game to assess tropical first aid skills among nurses is an innovative new take on assessment of older learners (Chapter 4).

Traditional games escape the tabletop too, and make use of the abundance of natural playful spaces and materials outside of the classroom. Hildmann (Chapter 7) provides an overview of experiential learning games, or *initiative games*, which can unpick complex emotional issues and difficult concepts using discussion tactics around simple active games; while similar learning outcomes are explored using live roleplay techniques in and out of the classroom by Harviainen and Savonsaari (Chapter 10).

When used in this way games are often the catalysts for deep discussion of complex issues, which would be difficult to start in a traditional classroom lesson or seminar. In many countries, the concept of acculturation and a mix of indigenous and immigrant populations are difficult concepts to discuss – loaded with deep-seated attitudes. Männamaa (Chapter 9) developed a fascinating way to encourage such dialogue using a simple metaphor of horses drinking from limited water sources. Cheap to make, but rich in the discussion it leads to, this is a fine example of games leading to results much larger than their size might suggest. Trapani and Hinds (Chapter 3) take this idea further – using a simple off-the-shelf chess game as the catalyst for a range of investigation and inquiry opportunities for their primary school class. Ingleson (Chapter 8) describes a fascinating self-referential game that develops art students' approaches to artist performance while performing as art pieces themselves.

Production issues are discussed in a number of chapters, and range from simple office-based materials that do a fine job, such as Kramer's *Mutation Game* (Chapter 2), which uses coloured card, transparent document wallets and paper CD cases to create a fun and playful experience; through the self-produced one-off works of art such as Ingleson's art game mentioned above; to the creation of a small company to source and mass-produce a game, as described in Mathew's beautifully illustrated medical teaching card game (Chapter 13).

The collection opens with Moseley's simple model for developing traditional learning games that quickly set contexts for deep learning (Chapter 1): and evidence for this follows in the twelve case studies, which we hope will inspire and engage the reader with their creative approach to complex topics using cheap, effective and playful solutions. There is plenty of practical advice in here for anyone wanting to develop their own games for learning – no matter what their budget, skills or previous experience of games.

Ultimately, the best game designs come from experience – both from playing a wide range of games, and from going through game design cycles, testing out good and bad ideas and continually reworking them based on feedback from your players. Take time to play a range of games before designing your own to get ideas for rules, competitive/collaborative/subversive elements, design ideas, etc.

This continual research and development is as true in the commercial world of games design as it is for small developments in education, and two experienced games designers, Alan Paull and Tony Boydell, share their fifty years of experience in the commercial board games world in our closing chapter (Chapter 14). After reading case studies from talented amateurs (in a game design sense) this piece will provide interesting parallels in places, demonstrating that some aspects of game design really are simple to grasp but take a lifetime to master, but help to temper any dreams you might have of making a best seller – or a fortune – from your game idea.

That neatly sums up our aim with this book. We want to inspire, to give ideas and above all to demonstrate how easy it is to design simple traditional learning games for your own setting. We can't promise you riches, but there's a good chance you'll be rewarded by more engaged students and more effective learning experiences.

References

Schell, J. (2008). *The Art of Game Design: A Book of Lenses* (1st edn). Boca Raton, FL: CRC Press.
Whitton, N. & Moseley, A. (eds) (2012). *Using Games to Enhance Learning and Teaching: A Beginner's Guide.* New York: Routledge.

1

Dicing with Curricula
The Creation of a Board Game to Speed up the Course Creation Process

ALEX MOSELEY, UNIVERSITY OF LEICESTER, UK

Setting the Context

In this chapter I will describe the creation of a simple board game. Behind the dice and cards, however, is a complex set of ideas combined with a long history of contextual education theory. Their distillation into a simple, portable game is a process that I believe can be transferred to any education or training setting with effective results. While this chapter focuses on an instructional/course design setting, the principles and advice can be applied to the reader's own context readily, as I will describe in the concluding sections.

To begin, though, I will describe my own local context, and the need that gave rise to the game-based solution; followed by a brief history of the theory that inspired me around the use of contexts and authenticity in education (and, more recently, in educational games). An overview of the design of the board game will be followed by a qualitative reflection on its effectiveness by players of the game, with the chapter concluding with practical advice on using similar approaches in other settings.

My professional role within my institution is that of an *instructional designer.* The field of instructional design:

encompasses the analysis of learning and performance problems, and the design, development, implementation, evaluation and management of instructional and non-instructional processes and resources intended to improve learning and performance in a variety of settings, particularly educational institutions and the workplace.

(Reiser, 2001: 53)

In more compact practical terms, instructional designers work with subject specialists with a goal to produce effective courses that meet a number of different needs.

The first time an instructional designer meets with an academic department to revise or create a new course, the initial meeting is a difficult one. Somehow the departmental staff have to be drawn back from their own concerns, opinions and their current modes of working and asked to take a wider view of the course and how it might best serve the students, academic subject, market conditions and other factors. This process might take an afternoon with receptive departments or might take many meetings and different approaches before all aspects are accepted and valued by departmental staff.

This variable process takes place with every new project, so I and my team identified the need for a useful re-usable tool or activity to help replace, standardise or improve the efficiency of the process.

A particular feature of the problem is that staff need to understand a complex, and in many ways alien, context – including factors and conditions that they would not consider without visualising themselves and their course within this new context. This problem is, of course, not unique to course design; students of any new topic, no matter their level of expertise otherwise, must understand the wider context of the new subject and start to see themselves within it, before their learning becomes easier or more effective. The process described in this paper, and the resulting game-based approach, are therefore useful for any training or education setting involving complex contextual issues, as described in the following sections.

Authentic Contexts: A History

The origins of a theoretical consideration of *context* within education stretch back to the 1960s, when Gilbert Ryle, a philosopher, coined the phrases *thin* and *thick description* to distinguish between an out-of-context and in-context observation by ethnographers (Ryle, 1968). As an example, he describes the difference between a twitch and a wink: while both, on camera, look the same, the meaning and context behind the wink is much more detailed; Ryle goes even further to compare a 'fake wink' and one with actual meaning behind it. A thin description of the fake-winker might be "rapidly contracting his right eyelid" while the *thick* description would be along the lines of "faking a wink to deceive an innocent into thinking a conspiracy is in motion" (Geertz, 1973, p. 6) – much deeper layers of meaning contextualising the apparently simple action.

From another angle, Lev Vygotsky's work on child development led to his *zone of proximal development* (Vygotsky, 1978), which internalised the *context* into learners themselves. For any given individual, the zone of proximal development is the space between his or her current level of development and the level he or she would attain with suitable expert help. Once in this zone, attuned to their own contexts, learners develop more rapidly. Lave and Wenger, in the 1980s and 1990s, developed this theory into communities of learners, engaged in common methods and practices with shared goals or ideals: a *community of practice*. Sharing a strong context will see novice members form a zone of proximity with 'elder' members, and benefit from enhanced and more relevant learning as a result (Lave & Wenger, 1991; Wenger, 1998).

David Kolb described the way in which effective learning makes use of *experiences* – or applying existing knowledge to a real-life context (Kolb, 1984). Drawing on earlier theorists, Kolb constructed an *experiential learning cycle*, which describes a continual loop of testing out knowledge in a real context (applying it), then reflecting on the success or failure of this experience (which generates new knowledge), then re-applying this new knowledge to a real context, and so on through the loop. It is easy to apply Kolb's cycle to our own experiences: playing computer games, for example, often involves trying to complete a level, or fight an opponent, or solve a puzzle. By trying one tack, failing, then trying a new approach, and continuing to try new approaches each time (building on the previous attempts) until we succeed, we are engaging in experiential learning.

Formal education rarely incorporates real-life (or simulated) experiences within the curriculum – and where they do occur, they are usually as special departures: fieldwork, industry visits, etc. – making the link between theory and practice somewhat problematic. How about embedding the *whole* learning process within an experiential context though? This was the aim of *authentic education*, which started to emerge in the early 1980s, but by the 1990s was gaining widespread interest. Shaffer and Resnick (1999) analysed this area to come up with four types of *thickly authentic* educational experience:

a) activities that are aligned with the outside world;
b) assessment that is aligned with instruction;
c) topics that are aligned with what learners want to know;
d) methods of enquiry that are aligned with the discipline.

(after Shaffer & Resnick, 1999: 197–199)

For a learning experience to be *thickly authentic*, all of these conditions have to be met. Shaffer later combined this work with Collins and Ferguson's (1993) ideas of *epistemic forms* and *epistemic games*. They distinguished these as "the difference between the squares that are filled out in tic-tac-toe and the game itself" (p. 25). The *epistemic forms* are the squares or the structure, the underlying context; whereas the *epistemic games* are played out upon it with particular "rules, strategies, and different moves that players master over a period of time" (p. 25).

Shaffer took these ideas and, applying them to the theories of *authenticity* and *communities of practice* already described, suggested that an *epistemic frame* can be used to describe the "practice, identity, interest, understanding, and epistemology" (2005, p. 1) of particular communities. Taking one example,

"Lawyers act like lawyers, identify themselves as lawyers, are interested in legal issues, and know about the law. These skills, affiliations, habits, and understandings are made possible by looking at the world in a particular way – by thinking like a lawyer" (2005: 1) – an *epistemic frame* for a lawyer would then feature all of these aspects. Epistemic frames for other professions, or interest groups, would be different – but all would have rich descriptions of the particular group.

Epistemic frames therefore provide a very useful context in which to base educational activity: if the learning is designed within the epistemic frame, it will all be embedded within the context of the subject or profession the student is working in or aiming towards. Shaffer describes this type of learning by extending the definition of *epistemic games* – activities that use methods, tools and approaches from the profession or subject in order to solve problems that reflect those a professional would have to deal with: "they make it possible for students to learn through participation in authentic recreations of valued reflective practices" (2005: 4). Using the example of lawyers, students might be given a typical real world briefing and asked to run a moot court, being assessed on their professional performance – all activities and assessment fitting within the epistemic frame.

Why a Board Game?

It should be noted that Shaffer's (and Collins and Ferguson before him) notion of an epistemic *game* is not intended entirely literally: the 'game' being merely a set of rules, methods, approaches and strategies. However, Shaffer in particular has applied his ideas to designing playful experiences, or games in the literal sense, to increase engagement and teach concepts within an authentic context (e.g. the game *Madison 2200*, described in Shaffer (2005: 4), although he admits this is strictly somewhat closer to a simulation than a game).

What persuaded me to take a game-based approach to my course design meeting problem, though, was the work of Charlier and Clarebout (2009) who designed and used a board game to formally assess the understanding of key first aid and basic life support concepts; Charlier's chapter (Chapter 4) in this volume describes the design and application of their game. Although focused on assessment (and hence applying knowledge, rather than widening existing knowledge) their game was found to increase mean scores when compared to traditional paper-based tests. The authors speculate that this may be a result of both a reduction of fear/stress (games are "fun, motivating, challenging" when compared to the "fear of examination") but also of peer feedback during the game. An important aspect the authors missed, however, was the context: whereas a written test begins straight away by focusing in on specific problems, the board game eased the participants into the context of a third world country and real-world problems – testing their reactions to contextual events. This swift, effective (given the increased scores) generation of an authentic context, and the consideration of key concepts and methods within it, fits well with Shaffer's model of an epistemic game, which gave me a compelling model for my own particular need.

Designing the Game

I decided on a simple board or card game as a potential solution to my problem. It had to be something that could be reused as often as required, taken along to an initial meeting between an instructional designer and a department, set up quickly with easy rules and within 20–30 minutes aim to set up an authentic context and place the players within the *epistemic frame* of a knowledgeable course designer. By thinking, acting and reflecting within this epistemic frame, the participants could then engage more fully in the remainder of that – and future – meetings.

The aims of the game design were therefore:

- to encourage participants to step back and place themselves in the position of a knowledgeable course designer, looking at the course holistically;
- to give participants an idea of the range of pedagogic, administrative and technical elements available when designing and building a course (the *tools* of the epistemic frame);
- to remind participants that they have to think about their markets and their students' needs, in addition to academic content;
- to give participants a chance to test course designs against authentic situations, without educational, financial or reputational damage;
- to provide a playful/fun experience (to separate it from a simulation, and increase engagement with the process).

Principles for the game came from Schell (2008), who despite focussing on digital games, provides a very useful set of principles and 'lenses' for approaching all types of games. The excellent discussion on numerous game design sites, such as the *Board Game Designers Forum* (2011) and the *Journal of Boardgame Design* (2011), aided in its design. Of no little importance was my own experience of the board games I had played over time – looking at a superficial level at what makes games like *Monopoly, Risk* and backgammon compelling and playful experiences.

The Design Process

Over a number of months I developed a prototype version of the board game. Beginning with the aims, keeping the context in mind throughout, and applying the following standard game design elements:

- random/surprise elements;
- collecting sets;
- competition between players.

I sketched a broad idea out, and prepared a quickly sketched board and cards. This formed the first, heavily flawed, prototype, which was tested locally with colleagues. Feedback from this initial test revealed an over-complexity of rules, confusion over various visual elements and other problems. A second iteration, produced this time with simple graphics and printed on a colour laser printer, was then playtested with a wider group of colleagues – a mixture of game-players and non-game-players. Feedback from these playtests proved invaluable in gradually adjusting the gameplay, points systems, level of fun/excitement, etc. in successive iterations, until I was happy with the overall game mechanics, play time and levels of fun.

To give an example of the kind of problems playtests can highlight: I had tried to embed several elements from the real context within the game as point-scoring opportunities. For the players, this meant that they had to continually match different symbols to one another, and add up values on several cards. In practice, this was too complex for most players to cope with, and detracted from the flow of the game. I therefore removed and simplified the scoring elements, reducing them to two key aspects that modelled the real context well. I also found that the possibility for vindictive/destructive action against another team caused high levels of fun, and so built this into the gameplay with a contextual theme. Further playtesting showed that both of these improvements did indeed improve the gameplay, while retaining the contextual theme adequately.

The Board Game

The resulting game, *Of Course!*, is played as follows:

1. Up to four players can take part in the game, or (better, as it encourages discussion of decisions within the game) up to four groups of 2 or 3 players each.
2. Players roll dice to set up the *demographic* and *resources* for a new course, which are indicated by counters on the demographic and resources boards (see Figure 1.1 and Figure 1.2). These provide a permanent reminder to players of the context they are playing in. They also indicate how many staff and how much money (in units) is available.
3. Players then draw two cards from each of four piles (*Pedagogic Elements, Materials, Administration* and *Assessment*), and by referring to the resources and demographic boards, choose from these any four cards which could go together to form an appropriate course design. They also pick up two *Event* cards, which they save for step (five). Examples of four cards are shown in Figure 1.3.

Figure 1.1 *Of Course!* demographic board

4. Players then score their initial designs: each card has a staff and money value (which, when added up from all four cards, should match the available staff/money units set in step two). In addition, certain cards have bonus points if their symbols match those on the resources or demographic boards (showing a close fit to the allocated context).

5. Players now choose one of their two *Event* cards to play on another player. These will adjust the context of the course or otherwise lower the value of some of the target players' cards. All players can then swap any one of their course design cards for one in their hand to try to reduce the effects of the Event (testing both the flexibility of their initial design, and their ability to respond to unforeseen events). Players then score their designs again, as in (step four).

6. This process is repeated for all players, each one playing an *Event* card, and then going through the process of changing and scoring designs as described in (step four).

7. After all players have played an *Event* card, the players' scores are added up, and the player with the highest score wins.

Figure 1.2 *Of Course!* resources board

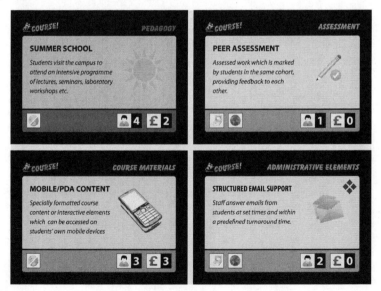

Figure 1.3 *Of Course!* sample set of four cards

This game sequence takes around 30–40 minutes the first time it is played with a group. Further rounds (resetting the resources and demographic boards and running through steps one to six above) can be played, at around 20 minutes per round thereafter. This includes time taken in discussion between team members and across the whole group.

After playing the game, while the players are still firmly within their epistemic frame, the instructional designer can lead them through a reflective stage to "apply the knowledge acquired during the gaming simulation to the real world" (Kriz, 2003: 497). Following this, the normal course design phases can follow (with more engaged, contextually aware participants, hopefully).

Production of Final Versions

Once I had fixed the overall design following the playtests, I needed to create several copies of the board game, and wanted to achieve a professional-looking design (aesthetics proving to be conducive to good initial engagement in the playtests). I created final, high-quality graphics (using colours and free clip art collections in the absence of any personal drawing skills) for the boards and cards. I came up with two options for the production of multiple copies, described below.

1. **Using local resources**: by using my institution's print department, good quality card, and obtaining counters and dice from a local game supplier, I was able to create copies of the board game for around £30 sterling.

   Benefits: easy sourcing; production time as quick as printing times (around 3 days).

   Problems: tricky to source the right materials, and each game must be assembled by hand.

2. **Using a print-on-demand service:** a number of print-on-demand services are available for constituent items (such as business card suppliers for the cards), but I also found a specialist board game print-on-demand service in the USA, Game Crafter (www.thegamecrafter.com), which can produce as few or as many complete boxed games from uploaded designs as required. Each game worked out at around US$20, but postage/import tax outside of the US doubles that figure to around US$45 a game (not too dissimilar to the cost of the locally produced game).

   Benefits: complete, professionally-finished games delivered; easy to set up for international sales to other interested tutors.

   Problems: preparation and upload of materials first time is time-consuming; production time is around 7 days (US) or up to 6 weeks (international, owing to customs clearance). Import charges were also due on the games when shipped to the UK.

I tried both methods, and overall found the print-on-demand service to produce the best looking games with minimal effort, although at slightly higher overall total cost.

Using the Game in Practice: Reflections

I used the board game with two separate academic departments embarking on new course designs; and at a workshop on new course development for academic and administrative staff. A member of academic staff who took part in one of the departmental sessions later reflected on the game's usefulness at a seminar to colleagues; these qualitative reflections were recorded and are denoted in the following section by '(A)'. At the workshop, two instructional designers (new to the game) played alongside the academic/administrative staff, and provided qualitative feedback by email later on the same day; these practitioner reflections are captured below as '(ID)'.

Considering its place in the course design process, the board game is "good early on in the process, before you've got too many ideas set in stone about what you want to do and why" (A). Ideally, the participants should include "the core [course design] team – the course director, research associate, myself [senior lecturer], assistant to the course director and the senior administrator [with an instructional designer]" (A), although this group could usefully be widened "because many [course design] teams are a tight little group, particularly when you're arguing for new resources, getting people outside the teams to help is extremely useful to get a sense of the kind of issues you have to deal with" (A).

The initial set-up and introduction to the rules of the game were mentioned by the instructional designers, noting that:

[the game facilitator] providing initial guidance to all the teams seemed to be fundamental in helping the players quickly understand the game. This guidance entailed describing the purpose of the game, and taking the players step-by-step through the initial set of instructions that covered the set-up and context phases.

On our table, the participants quickly grasped what they were supposed to do and got into trying to arrange the cards into the most optimal course design arrangement that matched the context as well as the resources.

(ID)

Once the game is running, there is a feeling that "it really does demonstrate the inter-relations between different elements of course building and course design" (A); many of these inter-relationships, and the issues around particular combinations of elements, are brought out in discussions between players. A particularly interesting example was described by the instructional designer in the workshop session:

> Right from the start there was a lot of thinking aloud and discussions regarding which arrangements were the best. One particular team got a bit frustrated in a light-hearted way that they could not get the most ideal arrangements for their market which was West Africa. And this light-hearted frustration led to extensive discussions on how they could get around using online access, even though the selected squares on the demo-graphic/market board said they could not. The matter got even worse, when that particular team was handed an events card which stated that there had been a postal strike. When that was applied to the West Africa market, it meant that there would be severe delays in books and other paper-based materials sent to students. As they tried to get round the limitations of the events card, there were discussions about how, in a real-life situation, they could solve this problem . . . and the players started coming up with various ideas such as making more use of [local] agents by sending them the course texts and other materials in PDF files, and getting them to print out and distribute to students in their local areas. Other suggestions included providing the students with tablet computers, and providing students with support via their cell phones. Sometimes, the play aspect seemed to go to the background until they had had a good chat about the issues.
>
> (ID)

This movement from game elements into detailed discussion was also valued by the academic:

> Events come up which cause you problems and you then have to negotiate and deal with, and I think that's useful.
>
> You have to make pay-offs between elements of the course – and that reveals preferences and prejudices within a course team about what kinds of teaching mode you prefer – do you think there should be personal contact on a regular basis between tutors and students or should a lot of the personal contact be done by admin staff? You start to find out what people think.
>
> (A)

This level, and particularly depth, of discussion is not normally reached in a course design process until several meetings in; the game is therefore succeeding in setting contexts very quickly, through a combination of authenticity and sparking discussion through game elements.

An unexpected benefit of the game is the way it allows course teams to discover their own internal ethics, desires and opinions at an early stage – preventing possible larger problems later in the process when it may be too late to change designs or controversial decisions.

One of the core aims of the game was to get the course teams thinking in particular about their core market, and the needs of the students in that market. It was therefore pleasing to hear that the academic participant valued consideration of "the demographics of the student base: can we use that mode of teaching and delivery – does that suit our students? Some courses have very specific focussed groups of students which are similar; others are much broader" (A).

The use of game-based approaches in education is not always met with a positive response (there being an underlying belief by many that higher education should be a 'serious' business), and so the staff attitudes to the board game approach were of particular interest. Across all three formal uses of the game, there were periods of fierce gameplay (particularly during the *Event* card phase, with some players showing vindictive tendencies; and much excitement around the scoring at the end of each round), but was this acknowledged by the players?

> At the end of the game, it seemed to me that the players were more interested in the issues and scenarios that arose as a result of the game rather than who won the game. It seemed that after the players had gone through the first round, playing and winning the game itself became a secondary matter. The discussions on the issues brought up by the game became the players' primary interest and concern; in fact after the first round, when the participants were asked what they would rather do, 'play another round of the game' or 'have a discussion of the various issues brought up by the game', the majority of participants opted to have a discussion about these issues and how it related to their particular situations.
>
> (ID)

It seems the gameplay is mainly of use in engaging staff, and providing them with points of conversation and the contexts to inform these at a deep level, rather than engaging them deeply in the game itself. There is certainly no harm in this, and the game will only ever be used once with a particular group so a deep engagement with the game rather than the concepts would be counter-productive.

The final reflection comes from the academic participant, and forms a useful summary of the findings above:

Obviously it's a bit of an abstract exercise in many ways, but particularly early on it's a very useful exercise: it certainly helped us begin to start to think about what we then might do with online versions of our existing courses rather than just going forward and digitising them. So I think that's how it's helped us, certainly.

(A)

Simple Games for Complex Problems?

The theoretical basis and case study I've presented in this chapter provides an example of how complex concepts in a particular subject area can be introduced to staff through a simple board game, to set up a strong context for future training.

The principles behind this work have the potential to apply much wider. In contrast to other games-based approaches to setting up authentic contexts for learning, which usually feature graphic online resources or other high-end digital simulations, the use of a simple game has obvious benefits for resource- or budget-limited environments.

Drawing on the case study in this paper, and from previous work in this area (Moseley, 2010) I would suggest that any complex area of a subject could benefit from this simple, contextual game approach. Breaking the approach down into simple steps:

1. Think of the context or complex subject: make a list of the key concepts, ideas and environmental issues that you want your students to learn or understand.
2. Go through this list and reduce it down to the most important concepts.
3. For each of your key concepts, think about them in game terms. This might seem difficult at first, but keep things simple and reflect on popular board or card games you played in your youth.
   For example: for a key concept of *mutation* in genetics, use random dice rolls in your game (drilled down to basic concepts, mutation=random); for a key concept of 'profit and loss' in an economics course, your game might include players buying or selling items that gain or lose value; if your key concept is a sense of history, include a timeline or timed events in your game; etc.

The links to game elements don't have to be perfect, and don't worry if you can't think of one for all of your key concepts: a few will be enough.

4. Using some of the game elements you selected in (step three), try to combine them together in a simple game – using a board, or cards, or pen and paper, or mimes, etc. Anything that is easy for you to lay your hands on and create yourself. If you get stuck for ideas, try playing some simple off-the-shelf board or card games (*Monopoly* or *Cluedo* are good epistemic games, for example). Keep the rules as simple as you possibly can: the best games are quick to learn, but take a long time to master.

5. Playtest your ideas on family or friends – you will soon find out which game elements are fun, and which aren't; which concepts work, and which don't.

6. Amend your game design based on the playtest, and add a layer of narrative or story to further embed it in the context.

7. Produce a prototype, and playtest this with two groups: friends and colleagues who already play games (if possible), and friends or colleagues who don't. Note any problem areas or suggestions from players, and test them after playing to see if they picked up the key concepts from your original list in (step two).

8. Make the necessary changes, create a new prototype, and then return to (step seven). Once you have a game that you are happy with, and which is generating some fun or engagement during playtesting, you can produce your final version and start to use the game in a real education or training environment.

In this way, simple games-based approaches to teaching difficult concepts or contexts can be created by any educator or trainer, resulting in low-cost yet re-usable and effective resources. The ability to create *epistemic games* in this way, without the usual development timescales, budgets and expertise, is compelling.

References

Board Game Designers Forum (2011). Blog. Available at: http://www.bgdf.com/ (accessed 19 September 2012).

Charlier, N. & Clarebout, G. (2009). Game-based assessment: can games themselves act as assessment mechanisms? A case study. *Third European Conference on Games Based Learning*, FH JOANNEUM University of Applied Sciences, Graz, Austria, 12–13 October 2009.

Collins, A. & Ferguson, W. (1993). Epistemic forms and epistemic games: structures and strategies to guide inquiry. *Educational Psychologist* 28/1 (January 1): 25–42.

Geertz, C. (1973). *The Interpretation of Selected Cultures*. New York: Basic Books.

Journal of Boardgame Design (2011). Blog. Available at http://jbdgames.blogspot.com/ (accessed 19 September 2012).

Kolb, D.A. (1984). *Experiential Learning: Experience as the Source of Learning and Development*. London: Prentice-Hall.

Kriz, W.C. (2003). Creating effective learning environments and learning organizations through gaming simulation design. *Simulation & Gaming* 34/4: 495–511.

Lave, J. & Wenger, E. (1991). *Situated Learning: Legitimate Peripheral Participation*. Cambridge: University of Cambridge Press.

Moseley, A. (2010). Roll, move two steps back, and admire the view: using games-based activities to quickly set authentic contexts. *Fourth European Conference on Games Based Learning*, Copenhagen, Denmark, 20–21 October 2010.

Reiser, R.A. (2001). A history of instructional design and technology. Part I: A history of instructional media. *Educational Technology Research And Development*. 49/1: 53–64. Available at: http://www.springerlink.com/content/8284v653u0641h87/ (accessed 19 September 2012).

Ryle, G. (1968). *The Thinking of Thoughts*. The University of Saskatchewan University Lecture series, Vol 18.

Schell, J. (2008). *The Art of Game Design*. Burlington, MA: Morgan Kaufmann.

Shaffer, D.W. (2005). Epistemic games. *Innovate* 1/6. Available at: http://www.innovateonline.info/index.php?view=article&id=79 (accessed 19 September 2012).

Shaffer, D.W. & Resnick, M. (1999). 'Thick' authenticity: new media and authentic learning. *Journal of Interactive Learning Research* 10/2: 195–215.

Vygotsky, L.S. (1978). *Mind and Society: The Development of Higher Mental Processes*. Cambridge, MA: Harvard University Press.

Wenger, L. (1998). *Communities of Practice: Learning, Meaning, and Identity*. Cambridge, UK: Cambridge University Press.

2

The *Mutation Game* – A Versatile Educational Tool

CAS KRAMER AND NICOLA SUTER-GIORGINI, UNIVERSITY OF LEICESTER, UK, KAREN MOSS, NOTTINGHAM TRENT UNIVERSITY, UK, EOIN GILL AND SHEILA DONEGAN, WATERFORD INSTITUTE OF TECHNOLOGY, IRELAND

Introduction and Aim

A mutation is a change in the DNA of an organism. Mutations happen very often, and are mostly repaired by sophisticated cellular mechanisms. If a mutation is not properly repaired the resulting change in the DNA does not have any effect on the individual or its offspring in the vast majority of cases; occasionally the changed DNA may have a negative or positive consequence. However, the word 'mutation', and even more so the word 'mutant', carry highly negative connotations. Why is that? Mutations can indeed cause disease, but mutations are also one of the driving forces of evolution.

As part of 2WAYS, a two-year EU-funded project to better communicate the science behind European-funded life science research (EUSEA, 2012), we aimed to create an educational tool that would be able to:

- better communicate the science behind mutagenesis;
- illustrate that mutations can be both good and bad;
- illustrate a number of evolutionary processes ('evolution in action').

Creating a Versatile and Cheap Educational Tool

We decided we wanted to create an educational tool that would be mainly used in schools and colleges, and could potentially also be used in public engagement events with the general public. Furthermore, our resource-to-be should be simple and free or cheap, probably a game, and it should be interactive and fun, yet educational and 'scientifically correct'. Having decided all that, the *only* thing we needed to do was to create it. Such was our challenge . . .

We therefore made stepwise game design decisions to home in on what became the *Mutation Game*, in its first version also known as the *Evolution Game*.

- First, we made a deliberate choice not to enter the route of creating a computer-based game, even though these may have educational potential. Instead, we thought an interactive board game would be the way forward: first, as the teacher (or a game facilitator) would be able to direct the topic and area of study; and second, this would encourage interpersonal interaction between the participants, help to improve students' group working skills, and open up excellent opportunities for 'peer-learning'.

- Two game boards immediately sprung to our minds: the classic *Monopoly* and *Snakes and Ladders*. With our own challenge in the back of our minds we contemplated what we could perhaps utilise from the above games. From the former, it was its circular board (so no visual 'end' to the game) and picking up cards that had consequences; from the latter it was the unexpectedness of 'snake' or 'ladder', which adds an extra emphasis on luck. From this we decided the following: we would go for a circular board without a strict beginning or end, as evolution is a continuous process without a real beginning or end. We would obviously opt to use dice to go around the board, but wanted to create an extra level of uncertainty to emphasise the importance of luck and random events. We decided to use decks of cards whereby sometimes nothing happened, sometimes something good and sometimes something bad (e.g. similar to the 'chance' cards in *Monopoly*). This, of course, fitted in nicely with our aim to illustrate that mutations may have different consequences. In general, we carefully considered and chose our game design elements to match all of the educational messages we wanted to convey.
- Our next decision was to keep it simple! The simplicity of the game would not only help its versatility (see below), it would also allow us to create a cheap game. Keeping it simple would mean having a small number of basic game rules; uncomplicated rules would be beneficial when making the game available for free online downloading. For this, we already had a well-established vehicle, Genetics Education Networking for Innovation and Excellence's (GENIE's) VGEC, the Virtual Genetics Education Centre (2012), a hub of evaluated online genetics resources for educators and learners that frequently has 10,000–20,000 hits per month.
- We aimed to make our game as versatile as possible. The use of decks of cards seemed to be ideal in this respect. We envisaged that by using different sets of cards created for different levels of knowledge, we would be able to reach different audiences. Also, the text on the cards had to carry an accurate scientific take-home message, and should be written in such a way so as to ensure continued engagement by the players. Moreover, new cards could be added or removed at a later stage without difficulty. This would allow for the use of completely

different sets of cards on different topics while using the same game board. We decided to base the first version of our game on 'mutation and evolution' while a second version could be based on 'mutation and disease', for instance. As mentioned above, keeping the game board and rules simple would benefit its versatility greatly.

- Finally, we wanted to incorporate visual aspects into the game in order to accommodate different learning styles (Honey & Mumford, 1982). We did not want to just describe evolution; we were also keen to show evolution happening in front of players' eyes!

Game Description

And so, one sunny Sunday afternoon in early 2010 the first version of the *Mutation Game*, also known as the *Evolution Game*, was born after a rather long period of labour!

The game is set on an alien planet and aims to show 'evolution in action' in a very short period of time. It is based on a small number of very straightforward rules and the use of sets of mutation and events cards. We have opted to utilise the well-established board game principle where players move around a simple, circular board using a die. Going around the board, like going around in the 'circle of life', two major things happen: 1) the DNA of species on the planet pick up mutations (mutation cards) and 2) things happen to the species on the planet and/or its environment (*events* cards). Unlike competitive board games like *Monopoly*, the *Mutation Game* does not have any winners or losers.

The *Mutation Game* is played with 4–6 teams; each team consists of 1–4 players who represent one imaginary species on the alien planet. Each game also needs at least one knowledgeable facilitator, either an individual with *Mutation Game* experience or an individual briefed beforehand (we have used the help of teachers, teaching assistants, academics and postgraduate students). We feel that the use of a facilitator is essential to keep the basic rules simple. However, this does not mean that the *Mutation Game* is restricted to a simple scientific level. The game lends itself perfectly to the explanation and illustration of more complex biological concepts, such as speciation and competition.

At the start of the game all of the species (up to six) are very similar in physical appearance (Figure 2.1), possess a number of identical traits (like 'the ability to run' and 'being healthy') and have a population of equal size. Within minutes of the start of the game 'evolution in action' can be observed, both in obvious changes in physical appearance like body shape and colour, as well as more subtle changes like having developed smaller eyes or a pair of pointy ears. At the end of the game all species show quite substantial differences in both physical appearance and population size.

While the game is quite flexible with respect to the number of players (from a minimum of 3 or 4 players, up to a full class of 24 players), both the room size

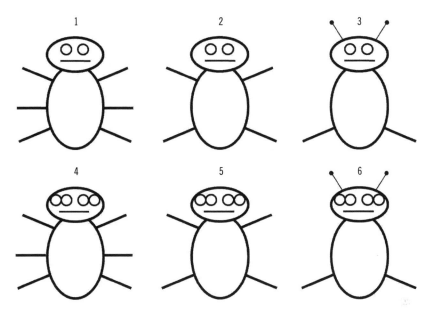

Figure 2.1 *Mutation Game:* players

and age of the audience play quite important roles when deciding how many students to have per game. First, when the game is played with over 16s (and definitely when it is played with undergraduate students) we recommend that teams of two players should be used; and when the game is played with under 16s teams of 2–4 players may be used. Second, if the room is small, reduce the maximum number of players per game accordingly. Students will be less engaged, and will learn less from the experience, if the allocated learning space is not suitable (Ramsden, 1988; Biggs, 2003). While teams can consist of single individuals, the game works better if each team comprises at least two people. The two-person minimum is recommended because if a species reaches a critical population size, speciation occurs and the team splits up to continue playing the game as two subspecies.

Finally, another very flexible feature of the *Mutation Game* is its duration. The fact that the basic concepts of the game have been kept very simple allows for the possibility of a very short time span; if needed, a minimum time period of 25 minutes is quite feasible (5-minute explanation plus 20 minutes playing the game). However, a time span of 45–50 minutes is preferred. If time allows it is good to allow for at least a 5-minute recap at the end (also refer to 'How to Play'). As the game aims to reflect real-life evolution, without a real beginning or end, it is quite easy to stop the game after an agreed number of rounds or an agreed time period. By stopping the game evolution

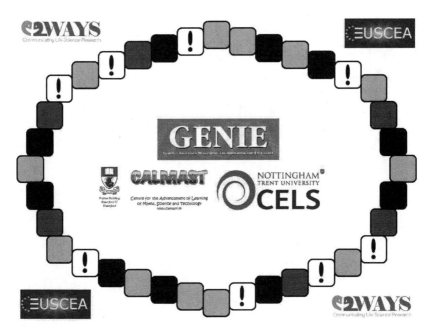

Figure 2.2 *Mutation Game*: game board

is 'frozen in time', and students are then given the task to assess how their species has changed.

The following materials are needed to play the *Mutation Game*:

- One *Mutation Game* board (A1 size; Figure 2.2);
- Laminated A4 sheet with species starting cartoons (see Figure 2.1);
- A deck of 64 Spontaneous Mutation cards (printed on yellow card; for examples see 2.1);
- A deck of 40 Induced Mutation cards (printed on yellow card with <+>; for examples see Table 2.1);
- A deck of 40 Minor Events cards (printed on blue card; for examples see Table 2.1);
- A deck of 24 Major Events cards (printed on card with <!>; for examples see Table 2.1);
- Population cards (50, 100, 500; printed on red card);
- Various population traits cards (printed on red card; e.g. disease, weak, resistant, smelly, infrared, underground);
- Laminated body shapes (normal, large, extra large);
- Coloured A4 sheets (white, yellow, red, green, blue);
- A4 population traits sheets (darker skin, hair, fur);
- Laminated population tables (one per species);

- Plastic wallets (one per species, plus some extra);
- Non-permanent markers;
- Tissues (for adjustments of characteristics);
- Coloured counters (one per species, plus some extra);
- One die.

Table 2.1 *Examples of* Mutation Game *cards*

Card type	Card colour	Examples of text on the card
Spontaneous Mutation	yellow	Your DNA has picked up several mutations that have resulted in your species having developed two long rabbit ears.
		Your DNA has picked up a small mutation within a gene, but this has not affected its function.
		Your DNA has picked up several mutations that have resulted in your species becoming blue. Pick up a skin colour sheet and place behind the body shape sheet, replacing the white sheet (or any other skin colour sheet).
		Your DNA has picked up several mutations that have resulted in your species having more hairs. Pick up a hair sheet and place between the body shape sheet and the skin colour sheet. If your species already has hairs, your species is from now on covered in thick fur. Pick up a fur sheet and replace the hair sheet.
Induced Mutation	yellow with \<+\>	Your DNA has picked up several mutations that have resulted in your species becoming more resistant to infectious diseases and general illnesses. Pick up one RESISTANT card.
		DNA that is involved in making sex cells (sperms and eggs) has been damaged. Your species will produce less healthy offspring. Pick up a MAX 50 INCREASE card; the increase in population for your species will from now on be limited to a maximum of 50 only! If you already have a MAX 50 INCREASE card, the increase in population for your species will from now on be zero; your population size cannot grow anymore! Pick up a NO INCREASE card.
		Your DNA has picked up several mutations that have resulted in your species having a longer body. Pick up a new body shape sheet.

Continued overleaf

Table 2.1 *Continued*

Card type	Card colour	Examples of text on the card
		Your DNA has picked up a small mutation within a specialised gene, which has resulted in your eyes now having 'infrared-vision,' which enables you to see in the dark. Pick up an INFRARED card.
Minor Event	blue	As a species you have exposed yourself to more and more sunlight by changing your eating behaviour. More sunlight is not good if your skin colour is pure white; if your species is white, pick up a WEAK card. More sun also means more ultra violet (UV) radiation, which means more induced DNA mutations – pick up ONE Induced Mutation card.
		As a species you have developed 'strong smells' to find mates. This strategy works well, and you will have an increase in population. Pick up a SMELLY card to show that your species has now become permanently smelly!
		In the area of the planet where your species lives, the local climate is changing and outside temperatures are rising dramatically. As a consequence your species is struggling and will decrease in population; if your species have hairs or thick fur your species will even halve in population!
Major Event	white with <!>	Due to changes in the planet's atmosphere there is an increased exposure to UV for all. More radiation means more DNA mutations – TWO Induced Mutation cards for all!
		New predators have evolved that love to eat a 'nice bit of leg'. Species with more than four legs will halve in population! Species that can only swim will not be affected.
		New dangerous predators have evolved. All species need to be extra careful. Species with small (pinprick-size) eyes or no eyes will halve in population; species with one, two or three normal eyes will decrease in population; species with four or more eyes will increase in population.

Mutation Game: **How to Play**

At the beginning of the game the facilitator will explain the small number of basic rules (see below). The *Mutation Game* board consists of 36 squares of 4 different colours (white, blue, yellow and red) arranged into an oval shape (see Figure 2.2). Players move clockwise around the board by throwing a die. Teams start the game on a white square of their choice.

There are six basic rules:

1. Every time a team passes a YELLOW square, its species picks up a spontaneous mutation (a yellow card); the team reads the card out loud and follows its instructions (for examples see Table 2.1).
2. If a team finishes its turn on a YELLOW square, its species picks up an induced mutation (a yellow card with <+>); the team reads the card out loud and follows its instructions (for examples see Table 2.1).
3. If a team passes or finishes its turn on a RED square, its species reproduces; the population increase depends on the species' population size and fitness (the team follows the rules according to the population table provided).
4. If a team finishes its turn on a BLUE square, its species experiences a minor event (a blue card). The card's consequences only affect that species; the team reads the card out loud and follows its instructions (for examples see Table 2.1).
5. If a team finishes its turn on a WHITE square with <!>, the planet experiences a major event (a white card with <!>) and its consequences can affect all species; the team reads the card out loud and all teams follow its instructions (for examples see Table 2.1).
6. All the actions connected to the team's throw should be carried out in order, e.g. if a team passes a red square, then a yellow square and then finishes its turn on a white square with <!>, the order of actions to be taken by that team will be: RED (increase in population) – YELLOW (pick up a *Spontaneous Mutation* card) – WHITE with <!> (pick up a *Major Event* card).

If more than one game is played simultaneously (we played six games simultaneously at Utrecht University in the Netherlands, five games simultaneously at the University of Leicester in the United Kingdom (see Figure 2.4), and often two classrooms simultaneously in a school setting), it works best to let one person introduce the above basic rules, often supported by a short five-minute PowerPoint presentation.

Once the basic rules have been explained the game facilitator divides the participants into teams; ideally every team will consist of two people, with up to a maximum of 6 teams. Each team is then allocated a species and is asked to replicate the characteristics of its species onto the plastic wallet containing a

Figure 2.3 Secondary school students playing *Mutation Game*

standard body shape. Each team acquires a coloured counter and chooses a white square with <!> on which to start. After that, it works best to let the students 'discover' the game by themselves. Within minutes 'evolution in action' can be observed and once that has happened the students will be fully engaged! (See Figure 2.3 and Figure 2.4.)

Other, more complex rules, such as competition battle and speciation, may be explained by the game facilitator at a later stage when the need for these occurs during the game. Alternatively, these situations may be ignored when the game's time span is very short. Furthermore, it is also the facilitator's role to highlight and explain happenings using the appropriate language for the audience concerned. For instance, when talking about a competition battle (two teams hitting the same square) the facilitator should use a phrase like 'competing for the same niche' when talking to undergraduate students and a phrase like 'competing for the same food and space' instead when talking to secondary school students or the general public. Moreover, the fact that DNA mutations can have both positive and negative effects should also be repeatedly emphasised during the *Mutation Game*.

The timing of the end of the game is arbitrary and should be controlled by the game facilitator. We normally stick to an agreed time period ("We don't have 40 million years, we have only 40 minutes to see what evolution can do to

Figure 2.4 First year undergraduates playing *Mutation Game*

our species . . .") or an agreed number of rounds. At the end of the game the facilitator can announce that evolution is 'to be frozen in time' and then the group will look at what has happened. Teams are asked to assess the physical characteristics of their species and its population health and size. A recap of the main issues that have arisen plus a comparison of the species in their current state (see Figure 2.5) compared to the beginning of the game (as depicted in Figure 2.1) is recommended. When more than one game is played simultaneously, we normally bring the whole group together and compare species 1 of one game to species 1 of the other game. This normally is a fun and engaging part of the game and the importance of physical separation of populations of the same species may be emphasised at this point.

Outcomes

Since March 2010 the *Mutation Game* has been played in four different countries: United Kingdom, Ireland, Belgium and the Netherlands. In December 2010 the *Mutation Game* beat sixteen other entries to win the 'Grand Jury Award', an international Science Communication Award from the European Science Events Associations (EUSEA). Although the game is not, as yet, publically available it has been played well over 100 times, with

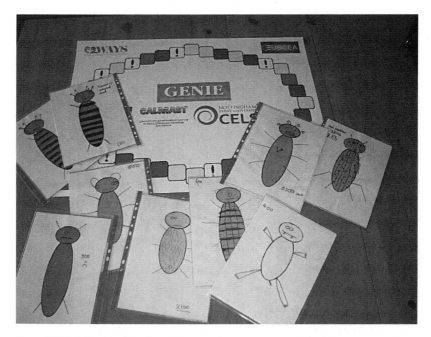

Figure 2.5 Evolution in action observed

participants ranging from secondary school (13–16-year-olds) and post-16 (16–18-year-olds) students, to undergraduate and postgraduate students and the general public. With the *Mutation Game* we have shown that a board game can be fun and engaging as well as educational – not only for science-orientated participants but also for non-science participants. Both educators and learners agree that the *Mutation Game* is educational and fun; while one teacher commented: "My students have learned considerably more in 45 minutes than I could have taught them . . .", quotes from students included "it's fun, I didn't want to stop. I want to play it again!", "it's like Monopoly, but better as it's about Biology!" and "This is by far the best teaching I've ever had here in Leicester!"!

The *Mutation Game* was originally designed to be played in a classroom with one or two secondary school year groups and one teacher as game facilitator. The game works very well in that set-up, both for mixed gender as well as single sex groups. However, from the very first trials, it was clear that the *Mutation Game* had great potential for audiences of all ages, so we expanded its use into post-16 education, with great success (Kramer & Donegan, unpublished results). It was apparent that there was no need to change the level of communication on the cards for the different age groups, as an appropriately trained facilitator can easily adjust the scientific take-home messages from the game to suit the knowledge level of the audience. Therefore, we decided to take the game one level up into Higher Education in 2011/2012, as we believed that, as an engaging, educational tool, the game had great potential to help students take ownership of their learning (Prosser & Trigwell, 1999). Again the *Mutation Game* lived up to expectations, and the game has now been incorporated in the first year curriculum of Biology students at Utrecht University and of Biological Sciences students and Interdisciplinary Science students at the University of Leicester. We did not change the text on the cards, but instead we are making sure that we always use fully trained game facilitators. We use the *Mutation Game* as a tutorial starter and have extended the session by adding pre- and post-questionnaires and a work session where undergraduate students need to compare and contrast evolution in the game with real life (Kramer, Gretton, Donegan & Persoon, unpublished results).

The *Mutation Game* has proven to be a highly versatile educational tool. It is possible to easily adjust the game dynamics to meet the needs of most audiences and many different classroom set-ups. The flexibility of the game with respect to numbers of players and allocated time span has already been discussed. The starting population size of each species is another variable that can be easily adjusted and can affect the outcome of the game quite dramatically; starting with a small population size (1,000 or less) increases the likelihood of species extinctions; starting with a larger population size (1,500 or more) increases the likelihood of speciation. In addition, adjustment of the contents of the decks of cards gives the game an unforeseen level of opportunities for game modification and fine-tuning. If, for instance, it is preferred to emphasise physical changes, then the number of resistant/disease cards can be reduced within the deck increasing the chance of picking up cards associated with changes in physical characteristics. Another example would be, if the game is to be played for an extended period of time, the number of cards that reverse certain changes can be increased or new cards could be introduced to the deck (like 'losing body colour' or 'reducing body length'). A computer simulation of the *Mutation Game* is currently under development to investigate this and to help predict ideal starting parameters for different preferred game conditions (Kramer, Moody & Schmid, unpublished results).

One unexpected outcome was that the game often sparked different levels of artistic expression with the game participants. The game itself only requires very basic visual expression of some characteristics to show 'evolution in action', such as the acquisition of a pair of ears. While some participants were indeed very minimalistic and clinical in their visual expression, others were highly elaborate and imaginative. For instance, one undergraduate student had drawn his species to have a shield and sword to symbolise the acquisition of disease resistance, a trait that is normally shown within the game by simply having a 'resistant' card. Personalisation of the game at that creative level enables even more levels of teaching and learning.

Further Developments and Future Prospects

The success of the first version of the *Mutation Game* has sparked much interest for a diverse range of people. While the game will be made freely available online in due course, talks are underway to market the product as an educational tool for use in schools and colleges. For this purpose, the game cards and rules will be translated in a number of languages for wider distribution within Europe. Current plans include French, German, Spanish, Dutch and Italian versions of the game. Even though the cards in English (as they are, or translated on the spot by the facilitator or a translator) work well with school-aged children, it is believed that translated versions of the game will have the potential of a much wider reach within school communities. A good example of this is the exciting collaboration between the University of Leicester in the UK and the Nara Women's University in Japan. Postgraduate students from the latter will be translating the *Mutation Game* into Japanese as part of their transferable skills training within their university degrees. The translated game will then be used in Japanese schools as part of the Nara Women's University outreach programme.

It is clear that the versatility of the *Mutation Game* lends itself to a great variety of adaptations. In fact, the *Evolution Game* was created as a first version of the *Mutation Game*, as mentioned before. A second version of the *Mutation Game*, again fully based around mutations and mutagenesis, is in the early stages of development. Here, we are using the same basic game concepts and the same board, but instead of creating a fun, educational tool we are developing the game as a revision tool to aid the learning of undergraduate medical students. Moreover, other versions of this game can easily be envisaged with the emphasis on different topics, using the game concepts developed in the *Mutation Game*.

Acknowledgements

The authors wish to acknowledge the financial support from the European Science Events Association (EUSEA) under the 2WAYS initiative. We also would like to thank Lisette Cartier van Dissel and other willing volunteers who piloted our game, for the many useful comments and suggestions.

References

Biggs, J.B. (2003). *Teaching for Quality Learning at University*. Society for Research into Higher Education. Open University Press.

EUSEA (2012). *2WAYS, Communicating Life Science Research*. Available at: http://www.eusea.info/Projects/2WAYS (accessed 7 December 2012).

Honey, P. & Mumford, A. (1982). *The Manual of Learning Styles*. Peter Honey: Oxford.

Kramer, C. & Donegan, S. Unpublished results.

Kramer, C., Gretton, S., Donegan, S. & Persoon, H. Unpublished results.

Kramer, C., Moody, E. & Schmid, R. Unpublished results.

Prosser, M. & Trigwell K. (1999). *Understanding Learning and Teaching: The Experience in Higher Education*. Society for Research into Higher Education. Open University Press: London.

Ramsden, P. (1988). *Studying Learning: Improving Teaching*. Kogan Page: London.

Virtual Genetics Education Centre (VGEC), University of Leicester (2012). *Virtual Genetics Education Centre*. Available at http://www2.le.ac.uk/departments/genetics/vgec (accessed 7 December 2012).

3
THREE BOYS AND A CHESS SET

FIONA TRAPANI, UNIVERSITY OF MELBOURNE, AUSTRALIA, AND ELIZABETH HINDS, ST JOSEPH'S PRIMARY SCHOOL, MERNDA, AUSTRALIA

This case study presents chess as a context for learning in an Australian primary school classroom with students aged 9–12. It is offered as a model to signpost a way forward in using games as situated learning spaces. Elizabeth is a learning advisor (LA) at St Joseph's and, at this time, Fiona was a science helper in the studio, working fortnightly with students whose passion projects were centred around science.

Once Upon a Time, There Was a School . . .

Welcome to St Joseph's, a Catholic primary school in the outer suburbs of Melbourne, Victoria, Australia.

Our story begins in 2010, when St Joseph's was in its second year of operation. This school was set up by a group of educators who were passionate about building a vibrant learning community and who set out to re-define what learning in a Catholic primary school could look like. Through this innovative approach it aimed to give students a genuine voice in their learning. It drew on inspiration gleaned from Discovery 1 school in New Zealand (Discovery 1 School, 2012) and the success story of The Grange in the United Kingdom (The Grange School, 2012). It was, and still is, centred on current pedagogy that places the child and their passions, interests and needs at the centre of the learning. St Joseph's continues to be a place where students were encouraged to "Dream, Believe, Create" (St Joseph's mission statement, 2010) and realise that anything is possible.

This school even looks different. Instead of classrooms, there are studios and outdoor learning spaces. There are no doors between studios, but alcoves in open spaces (see web references at end). There are homegroups instead of classes, learning advisors (LAs) instead of teachers and everyone addresses each other using their first names. There are no long lists of rules, just 'Trust', 'Respect' and high expectations in work and behaviour of both the adults and the children working in this environment.

Each year the school has an annual theme with which to "Dream, Believe and Create". The theme for the year 2010 was 'Splash'. This was interpreted by the teachers and students in a number of ways. Students were encouraged to think about making a 'splash' at their school. Students thought beyond themselves to consider the legacy they may leave at the school and how they could make lasting change in their community. The following case study explores an example of 'shaping' educational opportunities based on student interest and passion, with LAs guiding, questioning and extending students' ideas and learning opportunities. The project described in this chapter, initially involving three students, developed over 18 months. It started with a game of chess and a conversation about how these students might use this game to make a 'splash'.

Case Study

'Games are the most elevated form of investigation.' Einstein

The principal had organised a number of games to be brought in as stimulus materials for students to explore and respond to. One of the games that had been bought was a chess set with giant pieces. Three boys made a beeline for this set, and were excited about the strategy and competition elements of chess.

"So, what could we do with these?" asked a learning advisor as she was observing the children unpacking the pieces and setting up a game.

Her question was met with a reply from a boy who was usually pretty quiet, "I'd like to start a chess club." This boy, Albert (pseudonyms used for children throughout) who suggested the idea, was in grade 4. He really liked chess, and had played it at home with his parents and siblings. His older brother and sister had been part of a chess club in the past.

"That's a cool idea" was the consensus from the two friends he had been playing with. Albert had been teaching them different strategies and they were intrigued.

"So who wants to help out?" asked the learning advisor, addressing the general group around her.

"I will!" said Ben.

"Me too!" Carl chimed in.

And at that precise moment, a passion project, the school chess club, began.

Passion and Pedagogy

"How can you get deep, rich, learning out of that?" one might ask. "Chess is a great game, but how can it become a context for learning?" We only need to look towards some of today's thinking about twenty-first-century learning and skills for guidance.

Enabling children to engage in the learning process by exploring their passions and interests, setting up opportunities for innovation, problem solving, communicating ideas and collaborating with others (Dede *et al.*, 2005) are just a few of the things that we have been seeing, reading and hearing about for a while now.

As educators we understand that project-based learning and personalisation can unlock engagement, promote curiosity and motivate learners (Robinson, 2010). We encourage students to work through challenges and problem-solve (Gerver, 2010) as we believe these are important qualities to develop in our children every day. It is what students will need in order to be successful in future workplaces, as when you look at today's workplace, skills including an ability to problem solve and work collaboratively are sought by employers (for example, Valve Corporation, 2012). Add this to the research that is being done on gaming and links to learning (Gee, 2003; Salen, 2008; Squire, 2011, Whitton & Moseley, 2012) and it becomes clearer that using the context of chess presents some amazing opportunities for students to learn these skills and develop understandings about things beyond "these are the rules and here is how you play".

It is not surprising that the project that ensued went way beyond these three students simply playing chess. Their learning journeys took them to a number of 'places', including finding out the obscure origins and historical uses of chess, teaching other students how to play chess, and engineering a whole upper school human chess game. Each of the sections below outlines the main steps in six-month blocks for this journey. We have also included student and teacher reflections on this project at the end of this chapter.

Before we go further, it is important for us to explain how project-based learning works at St Joseph's. When students discover, or share, a passion or interest, it becomes a vehicle for engaging the learner in the process of inquiry. At St Joseph's we call this a 'spark'. A lot of time is spent discussing what a feasible 'spark' is with the children so that they can see that it needs to be a BIG concept that is also PURPOSEFUL at the same time.

Once a student has his or her 'spark', he or she has a 'conference' with a learning advisor, who will use his or her professional knowledge and understanding of pedagogy and curriculum to tease out questions, ideas and experiences to make the work being undertaken rich and purposeful. To put this in a context that is more accessible for the children we use a 'spark sheet', outlined in Table 3.1.

We have divided the process of inquiry into four sections: play, discover, think and use. Learners constantly move between each phase of the learning process and not in a prescriptive sequence. Sometimes a student might go back and forth between the play, discover and think stages before they come up with a genuine purpose to USE their learning. Over the course of this project we actually developed three different spark sheets.

Table 3.1 *Spark sheet learning process*

Play:	Discover:
Look at from many points of view	**Find new information**
Write questions and wonderings	Consult one of these sources:
Use the five senses	Ask an expert
	Research on a website
Explore in a different way	Read a book
Have a go	Watch a video
Watch someone	Find a magazine
Get familiar with	Look through a fact sheet
Do it!	Use a 'resource detective'
Expect to make mistakes	
Use your hands	**Organise information**
Find a friend	Say it in your own words
Share	Record/Show where you found it.
Ask opinions	Create a list of topics
Get excited	**Choose one of three ways to collect information**
Practice, . . . practice again!	Take notes
	Take a photo or Video
	Brainstorm or mind map
	Record sound/interview
	T Chart or CCC
Think:	**Use:**
Set goals for how you:	**Do something with your learning**
Work with others	Practice, Practice, Practice!
Organise your time (timeline)	Draw/Paint
Plan your learning	Write
	Act
How will you know when your	Talk
Spark is complete?	Computer presentation
	Write and present music/song
Review and celebrate	Make something
Self assess your goals	Other
Complete a mini-test	
Create/Check against criteria	**Go Further**
Share with others (Celebration of	Venn diagram
Learning)	ECG graph
	Scales organiser
	Cause and effect bridge
	Thinkers' keys
	Blooms
	PMI
	Sentence starters
	Ranking ladder

Stage 1 From Little Things . . . (February 2010)

After the initial idea of a chess club was suggested and accepted by all involved, it was time to develop a 'spark' (see Table 3.1) and plan some learning activities around the idea of chess club. The boys began by discussing their plan to play chess in a local competition with an LA. Their initial learning goal involved getting a chess club running and entering into chess competitions, providing the context for the think and use components of their project.

Before they could think about meeting their goals however, the boys had to play with the notion of a chess club and discover what was needed to make their goal a reality. Through conferencing with an LA, the boys realised that first and foremost, they had to let other students know about chess club and find out who was interested in learning to play chess. The boys began by negotiating time with the other LAs to talk with their homegroups about their experiences with the game.

From this research, the boys discovered that many other students didn't really know much about chess. They decided that they needed to write a presentation to inform the students and school community about chess. Some wonderings that the boys had at this point were: how can we teach other kids about chess? How can we get them interested in chess club? Where did chess come from? What is the point of it?

Another challenge that presented itself at this stage was how to document all of their work in one place. It was at this point the homegroup and their LA were exploring the use of Web 2.0 tools, particularly Google Docs. The boys' homegroup LA was aware that keeping workbooks and filing sheets of paper were not these students' strengths and were looked upon by the boys as being tedious. Together with another LA, these two staff members worked with the boys to set up a Google document as a wiki-type space to guide them in researching the history of chess.

The boys were asked to explore websites that learning advisors had located, and use graphic organisers such as a cross-classification chart, and an information report, to summarise their findings. This enabled the students and the staff to collaborate in an online space as everyone could add to the document at their convenience. This helped the students develop research skills and find out many interesting chess facts. From an Information Skills and English/Literacy point of view, the students had to learn that interpreting and summarising information was different to simply cutting-and-pasting it. It also enabled the students to become familiar with the structure of an information report and the importance of validating or cross-checking information. This formed the main part of the discover phase of the boys' project.

After this initial research was complete, the children put together an information report in the form of a slideshow to present to the school community at a Celebration of Learning (school assembly). They had to make it easy for young children to understand, and also enticing to students of all ages.

From this presentation, additional students began to meet regularly as part of chess club with the aim of playing a local competition. As part of their work, the boys had to negotiate appropriate times to organise and run workshops with their homegroup LA, as well as LAs of the other homegroups in the school. They had to advertise their workshops, organise schedules and sign up sheets. They were responsible for keeping track of the time and for making sure that they were well prepared.

This presented a huge learning curve for the boys, as far as communication and organisation skills were concerned, along with organising timetables and schedules. But the enthusiasm from the rest of the school was there. Lots of children were eager to play in a chess tournament and volunteered to play. The boys negotiated the hurdles of timetabling and organising equipment successfully, and at last they were ready. The first round of workshops arrived and the boys put their plan into action, but, unfortunately many students didn't know how to play and wouldn't listen to the boys' instructions. This was a disaster for the boys.

Instead of giving up, the boys listened to the feedback that was given to them by other members of staff and asked some of their peers for ideas. They knew the other students were still enthusiastic, so the boys re-visited the learning process through conferencing and realised that it was time to call in the 'big guns' by contacting an 'expert' to talk to the chess club.

One of the LAs found an organisation called 'Chess Kids' and suggested that the boys have a look at it. After reading through the information on the website, the boys decided to register their interest. They contacted this organisation and arranged for an expert to come to school and work with students. They also re-organised the students into smaller groups at more regular intervals, so they could play chess and teach it at the same time.

As a result of this, the boys realised that they needed to educate the school community about the function of each game piece and how to move it around the board. This became an activity for the "Use" part of their project. The boys created a series of posters, explaining what each piece was called and how to move it around the board, in language that was accessible to everyone. These posters were displayed in the Learning Spaces close to where chess was being played. In undertaking this task the boys also had to learn about how to set up a uniform layout for their posters, the impact of visual graphics upon the reader and how to write simple explanations. They designed a simple template that could be used easily on a computer and on an iPad. As part of this process they had to print posters in different sizes, with different fonts, and ask their peers for feedback.

Stage 2 . . . Big Things Grow . . . (September 2010)

Within six months, the boys had met their first set of learning goals: to teach others and prepare a team to participate in an interschool chess tournament. Other students were still excited about chess, and more sets had been bought and donated to the school to support the students in playing. The first ever iPads had arrived at the school, with the students in grades 4, 5 and 6 (ages 9–12) leasing them in a one-to-one technology program and with them came iBooks and apps all about chess. As other students were still interested and wanted to improve their understanding and knowledge of the game, the boys considered how they could extend this project.

While in LOTE (Languages Other Than English) Italian workshops the boys had talked with their Italian LA about chess. She shared with them photos and stories about chess being played in town squares in Italy, and how it is played with 'big' pieces. She talked with the boys about similar games played in Asian cultures. The boys were excited by this 'big' idea. They began looking for different ways they could make their own giant chess pieces and sought out staff members such as their Visual Arts LA for ideas and opinions. They were back into Play mode again! They experimented with different materials and looked into the costs related to purchasing more sets of giant-sized chess pieces. It was time to get creative and to think outside the box.

During their next conference Albert, Ben and Carl started to explore the idea of making a 'human' chess game. Their classmates could be the pieces and they could all play outside. They thought it would help everyone to learn and see how each piece worked within the context of the larger game and it would be something a whole homegroup could play together. The boys thought that it would be a great way to bring a bit of Italian culture into the school and realised that people would be more excited about raising money for human chess equipment instead of more chess boards. Little did they know it would be another eight months before they would see it played out.

Stage 3 . . . And Grow . . . (February 2011)

So just how do three, now grade 5 (10-year-old), boys organise a human chess board and 32 people to play as pieces? It was a massive undertaking, and learning occurred that wasn't expected. For example, building a board:

- How big do the base squares need to be?
- What sizes of pavers are available and how much will they cost?
- What space is needed to accommodate these pieces?
- How will the 'pieces' know who they are and to where they can move (especially as the students are used to playing the full game: having only one set of moves is a different perspective)?

- What will the pieces look like?
- What is the best way to direct the 'pieces'?

This was a springboard for an intense period of learning centred on Mathematics, Thinking and Design. The boys had to figure out the cheapest way to make this game a reality. They discussed a number of ideas with each other and in conferences with LAs. Someone finally came up with the idea of using bibs for each piece after playing a game with netball bibs during a Physical Education workshop.

When another project group was at a local hardware store sourcing the cost of materials for a garden shed and greenhouse, they spotted chequer board linoleum, carpet squares and carpet materials that they thought would be affordable for the chess club to use. They took photographs of the materials and recorded the prices to show the boys when they got back to school.

The boys then set about estimating how many squares they would need to purchase or make and how big they would need to be, so that they could figure out which material would be the most suitable to use for the chess board. This involved the homegroup LA organising workshops exploring area and perimeter. The students were asked to create square metres out of newspapers and to evaluate the size of their ideal chess "square" in relation to this model. The boys then experimented with making squares of differing sizes to figure out how small they could go. They did this in a variety of ways, taping outlines to the floor, drawing with chalk on concrete and cutting paper to ideal sizes. They had to find out what a right angle was and how to make one.

In the end, the boys obtained a few lengths of carpet material to cut squares from. Once again, they had to measure how much material they had and work out the ideal size of each square to cut from it, allowing room for errors. With help from various LAs the boys learned how to measure out, mark and cut squares from this material using tools safely and making sure that they were a consistent size. The task of creating the chess board took the students through all phases of the Spark's Learning Process.

As far as the labelling of the pieces, or bibs, were concerned that was another learning curve again. The boys had to figure out how large to make the image of each piece and the size of the font for the English and Italian labels. They also had to figure out which colours to use for each set because creating black posters on white paper was going to be too expensive. The boys also had to work out what the ideal bib size would be and as a result learned about the dimensions of paper sizes. They decided to print everything out on A4 white, enlarge it onto A3, and then copy it onto two different colours. This involved a lot of adult assistance so the boys could learn how to use the photocopier without wasting reams of paper.

Once the set of bibs was printed the next hurdle was how to make them easy to put on and remove and durable enough to use more than once. The boys decided to laminate each bib, as they had seen LAs do this for other things before, and to make shoulder straps and waist straps like a netball bib. Wool was the first material they tried for straps, but it didn't work the way they thought, so in the end one of the LAs handed the boys a length of elastic cord to use. The boys had to figure out a standard length for each piece, total how much was needed and prepare the set of bibs.

This process definitely took longer than the boys had originally planned. They hadn't anticipated the many smaller details that would be involved in executing what seemed like a simple idea at the time. There were many times where there was active problem solving, with LAs and students working as a team to figure out how to resize the carpet squares when it was found that the carpet purchased had a different width to what was originally planned. This step alone took over six weeks.

Now that the chess board was ready and could be used inside regardless of the weather, the boys turned their attention to the next problem: movement of the pieces. The boys wanted to use a grid reference like in computer chess, but they realised the pieces would be standing and this reference system might not be easy for everyone to see as there was no overhead view; they talked again with their LA and discussed other options for movement. Quickly they saw that left and right would be confusing. At the time, there was a focus in Mathematics workshops on space and location. The LAs designed activities for the grade 4, 5 and 6 classes (aged 9–12) to work through, enabling them to learn the compass points with reference to the school grounds. After working through these activities, and through conferencing, the boys realised that using the compass points to direct the pieces could work really well. The grade 4, 5 and 6 students worked on consolidating their understanding of the compass points of North, South, East and West for a few weeks before the human chess game was to be played. In addition, the boys were reviving student interest in chess as there had been a Christmas vacation in between the creation of the chess board and the completion of the chess pieces. Excitement was building!

Finally, the end of term (May/June 2011) approached and the game of Human Chess was scheduled. All of the students were very excited, and the boys were glad that they had organised an inside game as it was a wild, wet, winter Melbourne day outside. It took about 15 minutes for students to get organised for the game, with the carpet squares being laid out in formation, labels given to the 32 'student pieces' playing and getting in position. Albert, Ben and Carl were able to get the attention of all the 'student pieces' and showed them the compass point directions as they related to the board. Labels were put up on pillars in the Learning Space to help with those who weren't quite sure. The first game of Human Chess at St Joseph's began!

Initially 'student pieces' were all standing, but it was difficult for them to see the game play and difficult for the leading students to see all labels. They decided to ask the 'student pieces' to sit down on their squares and the game began. Turn taking was clear to the leading students, but not so clear to the players and onlookers (who were also noisy), so an LA got out a bell to strike when a turn was completed.

As the game progressed 'student pieces' were moved successfully using compass points, and only the 'knight' pieces were a little confusing to place. As 'student pieces' were jumped, they removed themselves from the board and sat along-side the board on small benches called 'chatterboxes' to watch the game play out. After 30 minutes of intense gameplay, these students were a little restless and, as they were often calling out to the student leaders the play/moves they would make, the LAs intervened and allowed these students to return to their studio to do another task. As an onlooker I (Fiona) was surprised that these restless students went straight to the games cupboard and got out chess sets to play; they had obviously enjoyed being part of this game and were excited to continue playing and control their own pieces. The chess "Masters" were so good that both sides had reached a stalemate, and the game was stopped after an hour of play.

Reflections on Learning

St Joseph's Primary School emphasises teaching the whole child in response to the child's specific passion and needs. In this section of the chapter we would like to share the reflections on learning from both the students and the LA. We have used student quotes and short profiles to give a sense of the growth of these students through the learning opportunities provided using passion-based learning. As you read this it is worth pondering the Einstein quote at the beginning of this chapter: how have Albert, Ben and Carl demonstrated varied and deep investigations using chess as the context?

Student Profiles and Reflections

Albert: "We learned how to measure, area and perimeter, got better at measuring and playing chess. Being an expert and talking to people helped my confidence."

Albert was the generator of this initial idea. He was new to the school and experienced challenges with his learning. He was quietly spoken and not confident speaking in front of a group. By the end of the project he had built some great friendships and had become much more confident when speaking to others in formal and informal contexts. He discovered from his peers that he is good at explaining things in simple, easy to understand terms and has revealed a great sense of humour. He is more confident with organising himself and expressing his opinions and ideas. This project provided many opportunities for him to apply his favourite subject, mathematics.

> Ben: "Organising an expert helped my confidence, I used this to organise the basketball program this year."

Ben was one of Albert's friends. When the project began, this was a new friendship. Ben was quiet and would often sit back and listen rather than participate in group discussions. He would often agree with everyone else even though he may have had a different opinion. This student could work well, but needed to become more confident with collaborating, negotiating and working with others. He didn't appear to take many risks with his learning.

By the conclusion of this project, he had developed better organisational skills. Ben became better at negotiating with others and developed his capacity for leadership through learning to co-ordinate and manage others. To do this he had to take a lot of risks and, at times, tell his peers to increase their efforts. He was the person who kept things moving, and he understood Albert really well.

> Carl: "We learned how to use Google docs. We had to work on how to explain the pieces to the other kids, and work with the little kids."

Carl was also in the friendship group. When the project began this student was also new to the school and was starting to find his own place within it. Carl has a gregarious nature and is an eternal optimist. At the time this project began he also loved games and would play them any chance he could get. The strategic elements of chess really appealed to him as he is good at thinking on his feet.

Carl loved school but didn't always realise the importance of being account-able for his learning and meeting deadlines. This project presented some challenges for him because although he loved working with others, he had to learn to do his part and to take feedback on board. During this project he was like a cheerleader, encouraging his friends through hurdles and obstacles and, along the way, learned how to give clear and honest feedback. He improved his public speaking skills and learned the importance of listening to others, as well as teaching. Carl was a student who also loved all things related to technology.

Learning how to use an online space was a significant part of his learning journey along with communicating his ideas more clearly to others.

Learning Advisor Reflection

It was during more recent discussion (2012) with these students about their learning last year (2011) that their interest was re-ignited. Pondering the beginning point of 'making a splash' the boys began to think about how this project could continue after they move to secondary school. During this discussion they identified several students from lower year levels, between grade 2 (age 7) and grade 4 (age 9), who were involved in the chess club and that they thought showed leadership skills. Revisiting this learning was a visible source of pride and these students were eager to help others share their passion too.

The boys have decided to organise more Human Chess games and set up chess boards on a more permanent basis. There is a new area of the school grounds that has been handed over to the children to design and at this stage, the grade 5 and 6 students would like to create an outdoor chess board using pavers or mosaic tiles that they create themselves to leave behind as their ongoing legacy once they move on to secondary school. The original home-group LA for these boys is teaching grades 3 and 4 this year and has plans to ask the boys to teach her students how to play Human Chess using the compass points and/or grid references before the year is out. Staff and students realise that chess needs to remain as an ongoing learning context.

Conclusion

In summary, this case study shows how students were encouraged and supported to grow their ideas in rich, authentic ways. 'Three boys and a chess set' used the school's philosophy and a focus on twenty-first-century skills to develop three projects that sustained the students' interests and efforts for 18 months. 'Spark sheets' were used as a simple and clear framework to plan each stage of this project as it grew. This game-centred approach has gone beyond hijacking a game for a one-off learning episode, and has used a game to develop an extensive and meaningful curriculum for these students. Students are able to reflect upon their own learning and with very little prompting, and are able to list a number of learning highs and lows from this project. They have begun to develop recommendations for other students to further develop this project, making even more of a 'Splash'.

Who knows what the next group who pursue a chess-based passion project will come up with? We do know that each child has different ideas, goals and passions. The next group to take this on will bring with them different experiences and goals. As LAs we will rethink and help them to shape their project differently. We can't wait to see what they come up with.

References

Dede, C., Korte, S., Nelson, R., Valdez, G. & Ward, D. (2005). *Transforming Education for the 21st Century: An Economic Perspective*. Chicago, IL: Learning Point Associates.

Gee, J.P. (2003). *What Video Games Have to Teach Us About Learning and Literacy*. New York, NY: Palgrave Macmillan.

Gerver, R. (2010). *Creating Tomorrow's Schools Today*. London: Continuum International Publishing Group.

Robinson, K. (2010). *Changing the Education Paradigm*. Ted Talk/YouTube. Available at: http://www.youtube.com/watch?v=zDZFcDGpL4U (accessed 18 October 2012).

Salen, K. (2008). *The Ecology of Games* (1st edn). Massachusetts Institute of Technology (MIT) – The John D. and Catherine T. MacArthur Foundation Series on Digital Media and Learning.

Squire, K. (2011). *Video Games and Learning: Teaching and Participatory Culture in the Digital Age* (1st edn). New York, NY: Teachers College Press.

Valve Corporation (2012). *Handbook for New Employees*. Chapter 4. Available at: http://newcdn.flamehaus.com/Valve_Handbook_LowRes.pdf (accessed 18 October 2012).

Whitton, N. & Moseley, A. (2012). *Using Games to Enhance Learning and Teaching*. New York, NY: Routledge.

Weblinks for Schools

Discovery 1 School (2012), NZ: http://www.discovery1.school.nz (accessed 18 October 2012).

School in Action (watch from 2 minutes 38 seconds): http://www.youtube.com/watch?feature=player_embedded&v=OzqfbpTD3ZQ (accessed 18 October 2012).

St Joseph's Catholic School Mernda, School Mission Statement (2010): http://www.stjosephsschool-mernda.org/general/school-philosophy (accessed 18 October 2012).

The Grange School (2012), UK: http://www.grange.org.uk/ (accessed 18 October 2012).

Village Environment: http://www.stjosephsschoolmernda.org/village-news/ (accessed 18 October 2012).

4

GAME-BASED LEARNING AS A VEHICLE TO TEACH AND ASSESS FIRST AID COMPETENCIES

NATHALIE CHARLIER, KATHOLIEKE UNIVERSITEIT
LEUVEN, BELGIUM

Did you know that most cardiac arrests occur outside the hospital setting where, in most cases, the general public will be responsible for providing initial basic life support (BLS)? In case of an accident, injury or sudden illness, a bystander rather than a medically trained person is often first to be present at the scene (Van de Velde *et al.*, 2009). First aid (FA) training is essential in preparing the general public for an initial response to such situations. Incorporating FA training in the school curriculum would maximize the number of potential first aiders in the community.

Studies have shown that teachers are able to train pupils successfully in cardiopulmonary resuscitation (CPR) (Toner *et al.*, 2007). With this in mind, training the whole school population can be considered a feasible option for disseminating the importance of acquiring CPR skills. Nevertheless, many secondary schools do not provide first aid and CPR training due to rather logistical barriers such as lack of classroom time, and lack of time for teacher training in CPR instruction or for implementing the training in the classroom (Reder & Quan, 2003).

This chapter focuses on the design and implementation of a board game to teach and assess first aid competencies of secondary school and university students. I'll lead you through three experimental studies we have set up to evaluate the validity of the designed board game. First, I'll provide a theoretical background discussing (i) the challenges of organizing training and assessment of first aid competency, (ii) the appearance of learners' test anxiety in summative assessment and (iii) suggestions to overcome these issues.

Organizing First Aid Training

In designing a first aid programme for secondary school students, one of the most important challenges is to conceive a project that best fits (i) the teenagers' personalities and expectations, and (ii) the available resources of the particular school where it will be applied. Related to the first recommendation, the concept of game-based learning has been growing for many years now. Regarding the second recommendation, alternative training methods that are economically and logistically feasible need to be explored. Although most teachers acknowledge the need for first aid education, they cannot be expected to embrace first aid education if they are limited by financial constraints hampering the implementation of effective learning methods, such as simulations.

In addition to learning about first aid, it would be beneficial for schools that teachers are informed about effective methods to teach first aid resulting in teachers having the competence and confidence they need to implement first aid training in their schools.

Organising First Aid Assessment

A major challenge in medical education and first aid in particular is the assessment of competency (knowledge, skills and attitudes (KSA)). The testing of technical skills requires methods and assessment instruments that are somewhat different than those used for cognitive skills. Simulations – manikin simulations, standardized patient simulations and computer-based simulations – are increasingly being used in medical education to ensure that examinees can demonstrate integration of prerequisite KSA in a realistic setting (Norcini & McKinley, 2007). However, a major drawback of computer-based simulations is that in most cases they do not provide the opportunity to conduct a real physical examination or to demonstrate motor skills, such as first aid (Garret & Callear, 2001; Bergin et al., 2003). Complex manikins are used to realistically simulate clinical cases, but here users are restricted to conducting physical examinations other than those for which the manikins are designed for (Gordon et al., 2001). Specially trained actors – referred to as "Standardized Patient" (SP) – portray patients with particular health concerns and are able to answer the full spectrum of questions about their condition (Eagles et al., 2001). However, because of the high costs for training, students are not exposed to a large number of cases and the encounters are often only used for summative assessment and not as formative learning activities (Hubal et al., 2000). As a consequence, alternative assessment methods that are economically and logistically feasible need to be explored.

Assessment and Test Anxiety

Assessment of learning is an integral part of education: (a) formative, to provide support for future learning; (b) summative, to provide information about performance at the end of a course; (c) certification, involving selecting by means of qualification; and (d) evaluative, a means by which stakeholders can judge the effectiveness of the system as a whole (Hornby, 2003). Although extensively studied in research, assessment of student learning and knowledge remains a contentious topic in education. While high-quality assessment can facilitate learning, poor-quality assessment can discourage high-quality learning or even be harmful to students (Chen, 2010). Furthermore, since test scores are so important for academic and career development, students are naturally under tremendous pressure to achieve high test scores.

Test-anxious students have a higher risk of being retained and having lower test scores; they even have an elevated risk of dropping out of school (Peleg, 2009; Vitasari et al., 2010). On top of that, test anxiety inhibits students from performing to their full potential (Hancock, 2001; Onyeizugbo, 2010). Among high school and college students, test anxiety is a common and potentially serious problem. Up to 30 per cent of students experience high levels of test anxiety (Bradley et al., 2007; McDonald, 2001; Orbach et al., 2007). Girls are significantly more affected by test anxiety then boys (McDonald, 2001; Ollendick et al., 1989; Putwain, 2007).

Game-based Assessment

Because test anxiety has many adverse effects on the lives of students, and the accurate assessment of their academic achievement, it is important for teachers to create favourable testing conditions. Games, for instance, are fun, motivating and challenging, suggesting that students – in this enjoyable environment – might tend to 'forget' they are being assessed in a high stakes test and might suffer less from test anxiety resulting in emotional and physical rest (Desrochers et al., 2007). Games are able to promote a positive attitude toward learning and school (Durkin & Barber, 2002), mainly because of their intrinsically motivating character (Annetta et al., 2009; Fengfeng, 2008; Papastergiou, 2009). These positive effects may suggest that games have an added value in assessment by reducing test anxiety and by creating the opportunity for students to perform at their utmost capability.

In the following section, I'll present the game and its context and I'll describe three experimental studies:

- a study using the board game to teach new learning content,
- two studies in secondary education focusing on summative assessment:
  - one study evaluating the validity of the board game as assessment instrument,
  - one study focusing on test anxiety.

The Board Game

Rationale and Initial Development Phase

As mentioned above, organizing a first aid training that is appealing for students and feasible for teachers is a challenge. In Belgium, BLS and first aid training is part of the cross-curricular attainment targets. A drawback of these targets is their permissive character in contrast to the compulsory subject-related targets. This often results in a limited timeframe for teachers to work on contents such as first aid and BLS. In addition, while cross-curricular themes are setting objectives for the whole school, only a few teachers have background knowledge regarding these cross-curricular contents. To overcome these issues, we launched in 2009 a search for a game covering first aid competency with the following criteria: the game had to be (i) in line with the specific curricular objectives and subject matter pertaining to the Belgian secondary school curriculum, (ii) suitable for secondary school students, (iii) inexpensive to purchase and (iv), if digital, able to run on older computers. At the moment of our search, no first aid board game nor digital game was available that suited at least the first criterion. As a result, we decided to develop our own educational game. Critics might wonder why we opted for a board game instead of a computer game. Simply constructed board games like ours provide potential benefits to learning: they are inexpensive, easily adapted or flexible without the need of programming knowledge. Furthermore, no special technical skills are needed to implement board games in secondary schools.

In our game, we wanted to apply principles that (i) allowed us to organize assessment in large-size classes in an easy and logistically feasible way and (ii) minimized the impact of test anxiety on the performance of the student. Therefore we opted to apply the concept of peer assessment and feedback. Peer assessment is a process wherein peers evaluate each other's work, usually along with, or in place of, an expert marker (Topping, 1998). Peer assessment can be used as a tool for social control, for assessment, for active participation, and as a learning aid for how to assess (Gielen, 2007). Using peer assessment has potential benefits for the student being assessed and the assessor, for instance sharing the observation or reading burden among multiple assessors since students are considered to be 'surrogate' or 'assistant' teachers (Forbes & Spence, 1991). Concerns, however, exist on the validity and reliability of peer-generated grades and the literature is inconclusive. Nevertheless, these concerns should not be a barrier to implementing peer evaluations, provided that appropriate scaffolds are applied, e.g. providing guidelines, checklists or other tangible scaffolding to students, and introducing decision making by teams instead of individual peers, etc. (Cho et al., 2006). Peer assessment can also prove to be helpful in terms of providing feedback. Peer feedback can confirm existing information, add new information, identify errors, correct errors, improve conditional application of information and aid the wider restructuring of theoretical schemata (Butler & Winne, 1995). Although peers are not experts in the domain, their feedback can be a trade-off against expertise in terms of being understandable, timely, frequent, extended, individualized and reassuring (Cole, 1991).

The Board Game

The board game was designed in line with a standard work written by emergency medicine experts. Several trials testing the game and the pedagogical method were conducted beforehand to optimize the playfulness of the game and the presentation of the content. This latter is presented by means of question cards targeting low level of knowledge (by means of true/false or short answer questions) and high level of knowledge (by means of open essay questions), as well as questions demanding a (simple or complex) skill demonstration.

The game board is played by groups of three or four competing students or student teams. It represents a landscape of a developing country built by the players as the game progresses. The game starts with a single terrain triangular tile face up and 69 others shuffled face down for the players to draw from. On each turn a player draws a new terrain tile and places it adjacent to the tiles of the progressing landscape in such a way that it extends features on the tiles it abuts: swamps must connect to swamps, fields to fields, seas to seas and bushes to bushes (Figure 4.1). After placing the new tile, that player chooses a blue, red, green or brown card with a true/false, short answer, performance and open essay question respectively. This question is read aloud by a competitive peer player. If the answer or performance is deemed as being correct by the peers, the player keeps the question card. If not, the card is placed aside. As soon as a player has collected a blue, a red and a green card, he is allowed to station a first

Figure 4.1 Five tiles showing features

Figure 4.2 Transferring a first aid post of one of the players (yellow) into a hospital

aid post. Building is only allowed on a specific feature on the tile marked by a white square (Figure 4.1). If this feature is present on the newly placed tile, the player may opt to station a first aid post in exchange for the three collected cards. In a later round the player can transform his first aid post to a hospital in exchange for a brown question card (Figure 4.2).

Players are able to sabotage one another by natural disaster. Six of the 70 tiles display a malaria epidemic, a bush fire or a tsunami (Figure 4.1). They can be used to destroy a first aid post of a competitive player (Figure 4.3). Hospitals cannot be destroyed by disasters.

At the end of the game, all first aid posts (1 point) and hospitals (3 points) placed by each player are counted. The player collecting the most points wins the game.

Figure 4.3 Destroying a first aid post by the natural disaster 'malaria'

Test–retest Phase

- *Board game*: initially, the game was played without the element of natural disasters. As of the first trials, it became quite clear that young adults desire for competition and sabotage within the game environment. As a result we searched for a game element in which the strategic competencies of the players could be deployed. We came up with three types of disasters destroying a first aid post of a competitive player with the extra challenge of matching the type of disaster with the landscape element. In addition, we adapted the conditions to build a hospital. Players are only allowed to replace a first aid post by a hospital if they can place a newly drawn tile directly adjacent to the tile containing their previously built first aid post. In this way, players can sabotage each other by placing their tile adjacent to a tile containing the first aid post of a competitive player.
- *Pedagogy*: Since we implemented the game as an assessment instrument, we needed to take into account the validity of the game (do we measure what we want to measure?). The question items on the coloured cards covered all course material delivered during the intervention and were direct translations from a standard work written by emergency medicine experts (European First Aid Manual (EFAM): http://efam.redcross.be/). Second, we opted to assign one type of question to each coloured question card. By collecting different coloured cards for building, different cognitive levels [from reproductive and constructive (red and blue cards) to problem-solving (brown cards)], as well as motor skills (green cards) are being assessed (Bloom, 1956).

Since assessment was performed by peers, a scoring form depicting correctly and wrongly answered/demonstrated cards was needed (Figure 4.4). At the end of the game, we were able to objectively measure the peer assessment by counting all cards answered (correctly or wrong) by each player.

Game-based Learning as a Vehicle to Teach First Aid Content: A Randomized Experiment

Overview

Goal: to evaluate the learning effectiveness and motivational appeal of our board game for acquiring first aid knowledge

Setting: general secondary education; 120 students from the eighth grade

Procedure: learning first aid by a game or by a traditional lecture:

- knowledge measurement by a prior-knowledge test, a post-test after the intervention and a short-term retention test eight weeks later
- motivation measurement by means of a questionnaire.

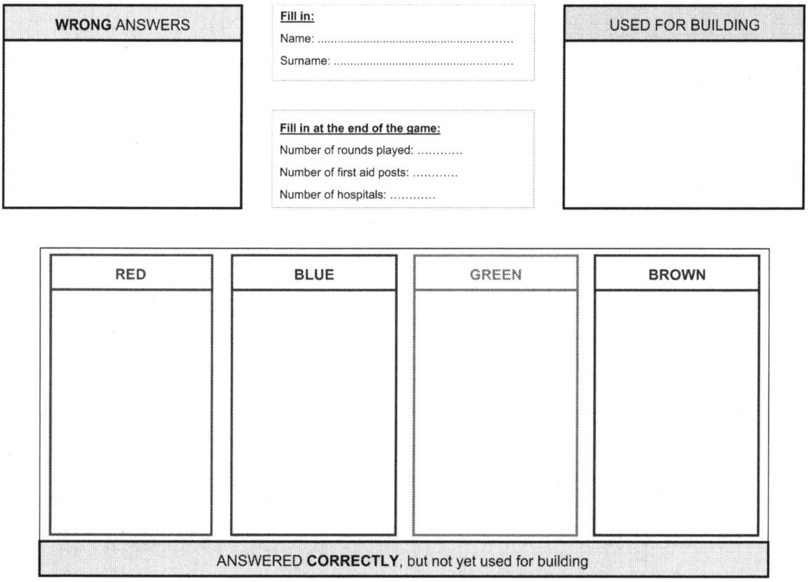

WRONG ANSWERS	Fill in: Name: .... Surname:	USED FOR BUILDING
	Fill in at the end of the game: Number of rounds played: .... Number of first aid posts: .... Number of hospitals:	

RED	BLUE	GREEN	BROWN

ANSWERED **CORRECTLY**, but not yet used for building

Figure 4.4 Scoring form for each player

Our first study aimed at assessing the learning effectiveness and motivational appeal of our board game for acquiring first aid knowledge. We compared this to a traditional approach in the form of an interactive lecture giving a PowerPoint presentation, encompassing identical learning objectives and content but lacking the gaming aspect.

The study was carried out in general secondary education (science programme): a total of 120 students from four class groups of the eighth grade of a Belgian public school (middle SES, mainly Caucasian) participated. Fifty-five (46 per cent) students were female and 65 were male. The intervention took place over an eight-week period.

Measuring Learning Effectiveness

To analyze a learning curve, we measured the first aid knowledge of the students prior to the intervention (prior-knowledge test), immediately after (post-test) and eight weeks later (short-term retention test). We developed a paper-and-pencil test that consisted of ten multiple choice questions. To assure comparability between the three measurement occasions three questions were identical, two questions were identical in content but were rephrased and five questions were different in content but similar in level of difficulty. A scoring key for all items of the written tests was designed in advance.

Measuring Motivational Appeal

To investigate students' opinions on playing games in the classroom, we conducted a short survey consisting of four items at the end of the retention test: "To what extent were you motivated to learn? To what extent did you gain knowledge on first aid? Did you find the first aid class (game or lecture) interesting? Did you enjoy the first aid class (game or lecture)?" The first two items are rated on a 5 point scale (from 1 = strongly disagree to 5 = strongly agree); the last two items are answered with yes or no.

The Intervention

Following the prior-knowledge test, all students of the four class groups received an identical introductory lecture of 20 minutes by their respective teacher. General principles, such as 'What should I do in the event of an accident, during an accident and after an accident?' and 'Misconceptions' were discussed and an overview of the content of the first aid lesson was given. Subsequently, the four groups of students were split: two classes with 62 students in total used the gaming application and the other two with 58 students in total used the traditional lecture method.

- In the game condition, the teacher initially explained the rules of the game (one teacher per class group). Beforehand, the board game was given to both teachers allowing them to master the rules. Both teachers had expert knowledge on the content of the course. Their task consisted of assisting the students with the questions/discussions where needed. Since the first aid game was new to all students, a test round of five minutes was played in order to master the rules and the course of the game. Subsequently, groups were given 50 minutes to play the game. Each game group consisted of four players, randomly divided by the teacher. In this condition, first aid knowledge was acquired by means of group discussion following each question using the information/answer on the card.
- In the lecture condition, students were taught – on the same content as in the game condition – by means of an interactive class during 60 minutes. Each teacher used an identical PowerPoint presentation with video fragments and pictures.

Knowledge Results

Compared to the prior-knowledge-test scores, we observed – immediately after the intervention – significant increases in knowledge scores as a result of both game play and the lecture. This confirms the statement that games, encompassing curricular objectives, are believed to be effective learning aids (Papastergiou, 2009).

We then compared the learning gains of both groups and found that the mean differences between post- and prior-knowledge-test scores for the lecture group significantly surpassed those for the game condition suggesting that the lecture group outperformed the game group.

Two months after the experiment, the mean retention score of both groups decreased significantly compared to the post-test results. Although the lecture group obtained a significantly higher learning gain compared to the game group immediately after the intervention, two months later we observed in this group a higher loss in knowledge. However, while the students' level of knowledge decreased over a period of two months it remained significantly higher than the initial knowledge prior to the course.

Survey Results

Two months after the intervention, we handed out a short survey investigating students' opinions on playing games in the classroom. Most students (86 per cent of the game group, and 82 per cent of the lecture group) indicated that they were motivated to learn. Most students agreed that they gained knowledge from both the game (70 per cent) and the lecture (76 per cent). Between the game and lecture group, we found no significant difference for motivation and knowledge gain. Most students found the introductory class interesting (66 per cent of the game group, and 82 per cent of the lecture group).

The factor enjoyment resulted in a significant difference between both conditions. While most students (83 per cent) enjoyed learning first aid by playing a board game, only a minority of the students (21 per cent) in the lecture condition enjoyed the class.

Conclusion

The goal of this study was to investigate the effectiveness of a board game as a tool for learning first aid with a focus on learning gain and enjoyment. We demonstrated that a game approach to teach first aid clearly resulted in a significant knowledge gain in secondary school students immediately after the experiment and two months later. However, when we compare the game group with the traditional method group, we found a smaller learning gain in the game group. An important difference between both methods was that more students of the game-playing group indicated that they enjoyed learning first aid.

Our results suggest that – although self-instruction by a board game alone was sufficient to teach first aid knowledge to secondary school students – traditional lectures are more effective in increasing student knowledge of first aid, while educational games are more effective for student enjoyment. The lecture method may be particularly useful in learning concepts for the first time, whereas the game may have a potential benefit in stimulating initial interest, or as a review method for previous instruction.

From this case study we recommend alteration or combination of these teaching methods to make learning first aid and other health-related topics both effective and enjoyable.

Game-based Assessment: Making Assessment Fun

Overview

Goal: to evaluate the validity of our board game as assessment-instrument of first aid knowledge

Setting: vocational secondary and post-secondary education related to the health sciences; 303 students

Procedure: summative assessment by means of a game or a traditional test, both based on peer-assessment:

- prior-knowledge test
- game-based assessment or paper-and-pencil test.

To provide us with more insight in the applicability and suitability of using a game as assessment instrument, we set up a study in secondary education. We opted for a vocational school setting. This target group (which is, for various reasons, rarely addressed in educational research) is important because of reported problems on learning, such as lower levels of motivation and the potential attractiveness of gaming for this target group. In this particular study we limited our assessment to knowledge only (demonstration of skills was excluded) due to practical and logistical reasons. In a previous study, however, with a lower number of students and in higher education, we assessed both knowledge and motor skills by means of a cross-over design (Charlier, 2011).

A total of 303 secondary (grade 11 and 12) and post-secondary (level 5) school students (237 women and 66 men) of 11 schools in Belgium participated. The mean age was 19.8 years old (SD=6.63). All students were enrolled in a first-aid (FA) related course being part of their school curriculum, i.e. vocational education related to the health sciences (such as nursing, child care, or pharmacy assistant). The full study took place over one and the same school year.

The Intervention

To investigate prior knowledge, we set up a pre-test at the start of the FA course. This paper-and-pencil test consisted of two true/false, four short answer and three essay questions. The following weeks the FA module was given by their regular teacher, who had given an FA course at least once before this study. The content of all FA courses was in line with the attainment targets and was derived from the standard work of the Flemish (Belgian) Red Cross.

At the end of the FA course, we randomized the students of each class into two groups, receiving the game-based assessment (163 students) or the traditional test (140 students) within the same class time but in two separate rooms. Given the fact that students received only one of both assessments, we used identical questions in the traditional and game-based assessment.

- In the game condition, students were randomly assigned to four-member groups. We started with explaining the rules of the game. Then, a test round of 10 minutes was played in order to master the rules and the course of the game. Subsequently, groups were given exactly 45 minutes to play the game. We instructed the players to finish the last round to ensure an equal number of answered questions by each player within their own group. The outcome of the game (number of first aid posts and hospitals) was not used as assessment score, due to a factor of luck (i.e. the chance of drawing a tile with a white square) and sabotage (by natural disaster). Instead we generated a summative individual score by comparing the amount of individually collected question cards (representing the level of acquired knowledge) to the number of play rounds. The final decision had to be made via consensus by three peers, increasing the objectivity of the peer-assessment.
- The traditional test group was supervised by their class teacher. Students were given exactly 45 minutes to take the paper-and-pencil test individually. The test consisted of six true/false, seven short answer and five essay questions, assessing their knowledge on FA. At the end of the exam, all copies were collected and randomly redistributed among the students. Each student assessed the written test of a peer using a mark of 0 or 1 for each item, which was consistent with the scoring procedure in the game.

Results

During the timespan of 45 minutes, students played an average of 9.48 rounds, answering an equal amount of questions within their group. Compared to our previous study (Charlier, 2011) where students played 12 rounds in 90 minutes, students were able to play faster due to the exclusion of skill demonstration. In both groups, we found a significant increase in knowledge gain after the FA module.

Mean scores of the game-based assessment did not significantly differ from those of the traditional test, suggesting that the board game can serve as a valid alternative assessment instrument.

Regarding gender differences, we found no significant difference in learning gain between boys and girls, nor in the game-based assessment nor in the traditional test. Also, girls in the game-based group obtained no significant different post-test score than girls in the control group. We observed the same for boys.

In this study, several factors may favour the choice of the board game over the traditional exam.

While traditional tests are most likely to induce a high degree of stress/anxiety resulting in a poor performance, games can be fun, motivating and challenging and therefore able to dispel some fear of examinations (Desrochers *et al.*, 2007).

In this study, winning the game is not necessarily equivalent to an excellent performance in the assessment. Players who don't like playing games and who have no insight or strategy could have performed poorly in building their first aid posts and hospitals, resulting in a low game result. To avoid this we opted to disconnect the results of the game play from the assessment score.

Furthermore, using a game format creates the opportunity of assessing large-size classes simultaneously. Peer assessment might be an alternative for overcoming costly and time-consuming assessment methods. To overcome concerns of reliability, observation matrices, extensively used during training, served as skills assessment instruments. Also a final decision was made by at least two peers to increase accuracy.

Conclusion

Changing assessment practices and the role of students and teachers in this, is a challenge in education.

Our results showed no significant difference between the mean post-test scores of the game-based assessment and those of the traditional test, confirming our previous observation that the board game might provide an effective means of assessing student knowledge at the end of a practical course.

Due to the use of a larger population we were able to also study specific student characteristics, such as gender. We found no difference in learning between boys and girls, suggesting that the board game is widely applicable and outcomes are not gender-sensitive.

Game-based Assessment and the Effect on Test Anxiety

Overview

Goal: to evaluate the impact of our board game as assessment-instrument on test anxiety

Setting: vocational secondary education related to the health sciences; 296 students

Procedure: summative assessment by means of a game or a traditional test, both based on peer-assessment:

- test-anxiety measurement by means of a questionnaire, weeks before and immediately after the intervention
- game-based assessment or paper-and-pencil test.

Test anxiety has extended consequences, not only for the mental and physical health of students, but for their entire educational career and expectations for the future. This study aims to investigate for the first time whether test anxiety in the summative assessment of first aid knowledge can be reduced by using a game instead of a traditional exam as assessment instrument.

The study was conducted in vocational education related to the health sciences: a total of 296 secondary school students (231 women and 65 men; grade 11 and 12) of 17 classes of 10 schools participated. The mean age was 17.42 years old (SD=1.18). All students were enrolled in a first-aid related course being part of their school curriculum.

Measuring Test Anxiety

In order to investigate the effect of a game-based assessment on test anxiety, we set up a baseline test to measure the test anxiety level of a student in a standard test environment. During a lesson prior to the first aid module, we subjected the students to an unannounced paper-and-pencil test, immediately followed by a test anxiety questionnaire (TAI; Spielberger, 1980). This test is a validated instrument and uses a twenty-item self-reporting psychometric scale that is developed to measure individual differences in test anxiety specifically in secondary school and college students. It contains propositions such as: "I feel confident and relaxed while taking tests", "During tests I feel very tense" and "During tests I find myself thinking about the consequences of failing". Completing the test only takes 10 minutes. The TAI uses a scale, ranging from 1 = 'almost never' to 5 = 'almost always'. The higher the score on the TAI (between 20 and 80 points), the higher the level of test anxiety.

At the end of the intervention, i.e. the assessment, all students completed the TAI for the second time.

The Intervention

All students followed the first aid lessons during several weeks (number of weeks depended on the program of each of the 17 classes). During the last lesson of the first aid module, we prepared an unannounced, summative assessment. We did not inform the students on the format of the exams until the assessment took place.

In preparation to the assessment, we asked each teacher to enumerate the learning content in order to adjust the questions in the board game and in the traditional test to the content of each course.

Based on their test anxiety level measured by the baseline test, we subjected the students to a game-based assessment (161 students) or a traditional paper-and-pencil test (control condition; 135 students), consisting of an equal number of high- and low-anxiety students. We used identical questions in the traditional and game-based assessment.

- *Game-based assessment group:* Students of the experimental group were instructed to choose three other peers to play the game. After explaining the rules of the game, a rehearsal round was played to get familiarized with the board game. Then, we gave all groups exactly 45 minutes to play the game and we instructed them to complete the last round before finishing the game.
- *Traditional test group:* Students were given exactly 45 minutes to complete a paper-and-pencil test individually. The test consisted of six true/false, seven short answer and five essay questions, covering all course objectives and comprising the different levels of the cognitive domains (Bloom, 1956). At the end of the exam, all copies were collected and randomly redistributed among the students. Each student assessed the written test of a peer using a mark of 0 or 1 for each item, which was consistent with the scoring procedure in the game.

Immediately following the assessment, the test anxiety level was remeasured by means of the TAI.

Results

Overall, we found a significant reduction in test anxiety when taking the game-based assessment, while no significant difference was found for the group being assessed by the paper-and-pencil test. However, some factors could have beforehand implied an increase in test anxiety. Anastasi's (1981) test sophistication hypothesis posits that familiarity with the test (i.e., amount of prior experience) reduces confusion and test anxiety. Since the implementation of games in summative assessment occurred rather rarely and was new to the participants in this study, the unknown aspect could have caused more test anxiety. Second, oral exams can be anxiety provoking (Furnham *et al.*, 2011). In the game-based assessment condition, students were assessed orally by their peers, while in the traditional test the assessment occurred by a written paper-and-pencil test. Students in the game-based assessment condition had limited time to consider and formulate their answers, while in the traditional test students were able to choose which questions to answer first within a larger timeframe. Test anxiety could have been enhanced due to the presence of peers or moderate levels of arousal created by the time pressure (Mendl, 1999).

Comparison of the characteristics of both assessment methods might reveal some factors that contribute to the positive effect on test anxiety in this study. A first and main difference between both conditions is the game-factor. While playing games, students might suffer less from test anxiety resulting in emotional and physical rest. In this enjoyable environment, students might tend to 'forget' they are being assessed in a high stakes test. In addition, using a game as assessment instrument was new and might have had a positive effect on the motivation of students. Second, while in the traditional test condition students work individually and quietly, the game-based assessment creates a social situation in which students – although assessed individually – cooperate. The atmosphere resembles that of collaborative testing, i.e. an assessment approach that allows students to work in teams while taking an examination or performing a task. Many studies showed that a team situation may lend itself to participants experiencing less anxiety, increased pleasurable arousal or enhanced motivation due to competition between players (e. g. Desrochers et al., 2007; Meseke et al., 2009; Zimbardo et al., 2003).

We observed that both low and high test-anxious students benefited more from the game-based assessment than from the traditional test. The anxiety level of the low test-anxious group reduced when taking the game-based assessment, while an increase in TAI-score was found for low test-anxious students in the traditional test group. The change in test anxiety level was significantly different between the low test-anxious students in the game-based assessment and those students in the paper-and-pencil test. We observed the same pattern for high test-anxious students.

Previous research showed that girls are significantly more affected by test anxiety then boys (McDonald, 2001; Putwain, 2007). Our results confirm this finding: girls obtained a statistically significant higher test anxiety score than boys on both TAI. Test anxiety of both boys and girls significantly reduced following game-based assessment, while no significant reduction was measured following the traditional test. No significant difference in test anxiety reduction, however, was found between girls and boys within each condition, indicating that the effect of game-based assessment in our study is not gender-related.

Conclusion

This study shows for the first time that games in summative assessment induce a positive effect on test anxiety. We found a significant reduction in test anxiety when taking the game-based assessment, while no significant difference was found for the control group. Both low and high test-anxious students benefited more from the game-based assessment than from the traditional test. A similar observation was made for boys and for girls. Since games in summative assessment are able to induce a positive effect on test anxiety, we can recommend a wider use of games in education, not only as learning aids, but also as assessment instruments.

General Conclusion

In this chapter we have discussed some of the issues teachers might face when teaching in health sciences education and in skills education in particular. Financial and/or logistical barriers such as lack of classroom time hamper the implementation of first aid training in many schools. Board games, designed in line with the school curriculum, proved not only to be a valid alternative to train and assess first aid competency, but also for engaging teenagers and young adults in learning new content. I hope that I have offered some useful information, based on our experience from our experimental studies and my own teaching, and that I have inspired you to adapt some of the principles within your own classroom.

References

Anastasi, A. (1981). Coaching, test sophistication and developed abilities. *The American Psychologist*, 36, 1086–1093.

Annetta, L.A., Minogue, J., Holmes, S.Y. & Cheng, M.T. (2009). Investigating the impact of video games on high school students' engagement and learning about genetics. *Computers & Education*, 53, 74–85.

Bergin, R., Youngblood, P., Ayers, M.K. *et al.* (2003). Interactive simulated patient: experiences with collaborative e-learning in medicine. *Journal of Educational Computing Research*, 29, 387–400.

Bloom, B.S. (1956). *Taxonomy of Educational Objectives, Handbook I: The Cognitive Domain*. New York, NY: David McKay Co Inc.

Bradley, R.T., McCraty, R., Atkinson, M., Arguelles, L., Rees, R.A. & Tomasino, D. (2007). *Reducing Test Anxiety and Improving Test Performance in America's Schools*. Results from the TestEdge® National Demonstration Study, California: Institute of HeartMath.

Butler, D.L. & Winne, P.H. (1995). Feedback and self-regulated learning: a theoretical synthesis. *Rev Educ Res*, 65, 245–81.

Charlier, N. (2011). Game-based assessment of first aid and resuscitation skills. *Resuscitation, 82/4*, 442–6.

Chen, C. (2010). The implementation and evaluation of a mobile self- and peer-assessment system. *Computers & Education*, 55/1, 229–236.

Cho, K., Schunn, C.D. & Wilson, R.W. (2006). Validity and reliability of scaffolded peer assessment of writing from instructor and student perspectives. *J Educ Psychol*, 9, 891–901.

Cole, D. (1991). Change in self-perceived competence as a function of peer and teacher evaluation. *Dev Psychol*, 27, 682–8.

Desrochers, M.N., Pusateri Jr, M.J. & Fink, H.C. (2007). Game assessment: fun as well as effective. *Assess Eval High Educ*, 32, 527–53.

Durkin, K. & Barber, B. (2002). Not so doomed: computer game play and positive adolescent development. *Journal of Applied Developmental Psychology*, 23, 373–392.

Eagles, J.M., Calder, S.A., Nicoll, K.S. & Sclare, P.D. (2001). Using simulated patients in education about alcohol misuse. *Acad Med*, 76, 395.

Fengfeng, K. (2008). A case study of computer gaming for math: engaged learning from gameplay? *Computer & Education*, 51, 1609–1620.

Forbes, D. & Spence, J. (1991). An experiment in assessment for a large class. In R. Smith (ed.) *Innovations in Engineering Education*. London: Ellis Horwood, pp. 97–101.

Furnham, A., Batey, M. & Martin, N. (2011). How would you like to be evaluated? The correlates of students' preferences for assessment methods. *Personality and Individual Differences*, 50/2, 259–263.

Garret, B.M. & Callear, D. (2001). The value of intelligent multimedia simulation for teaching clinical decision-making skills. *Nurse Educ Today*, 21, 382–90.

Gielen, S. (2007). *Peer Assessment as a Tool for Learning*. Ph.D. dissertation, Katholieke Universiteit Leuven, Belgium.

Gordon, J.A., Wilkerson, W.M., Shaffer, D.W. & Armstrong, E.G. (2001). Practicing medicine without risk: students' and educators' responses to high-fidelity patient simulation. *Acad Med*, 76, 469.

Hancock, D.R. (2001). Effects of test anxiety and evaluative threat on students' achievement and motivation. *The Journal of Educational Research*, 94, 284–290.

Hornby, W. (2003). Assessing using grade-related criteria: a single currency for universities? *Assessment and Evaluation in Higher Education*, 28, 435–454.

Hubal, R.C., Kizakevich, P.N., Guinn, C.I., Merino, K.D. & West, S.L. (2000). The virtual standardized patient. *Stud Health Technol Inform*, 70, 133–8.

McDonald, A.S. (2001). The prevalence and effects of test anxiety in school children. *Educational Psychology*, 21, 89–101.

Mendl, M. (1999). Performing under pressure: stress and cognitive function. *Applied Animal Behaviour Science*, 65, 221–244.

Meseke, C.A., Bovée, M.L. & Gran, D.F. (2009). Impact of collaborative testing on student performance and satisfaction in a chiropractic science course. *Journal of Manipulative and Physiological Therapeutics*, 32/4, 309–314.

Norcini, J.J. & McKinley, D.W. (2007). Assessment methods in medical education. *Teach Teach Educ*, 23, 239–250.

Ollendick, T.H., King, N.J. & Frary, R.B. (1989). Fears in children and adolescents: reliability and generalizability across gender, age and nationality. *Behaviour Research and Therapy*, 27, 19–26.

Onyeizugbo, E.U. (2010). Self-efficacy, gender and trait anxiety as moderators of test anxiety. *Electronic Journal of Research in Educational Psychology*, 8, 299–312.

Orbach, G., Lindsay, S. & Grey, S. (2007). A randomized placebo-controlled trial of a self-help Internet-based intervention for test anxiety. *Behaviour Research and Therapy*, 45, 483–496.

Papastergiou, M. (2009). Digital game-based learning in high school computer science education: impact on educational effectiveness and student motivation. *Computers & Education*, 52, 1–12.

Peleg, O. (2009). Test anxiety, academic achievement, and self-esteem among Arab adolescents with and without learning disabilities. *Learning Disability Quarterly*, 32, 11–20.

Putwain, D.W. (2007). Test anxiety in UK schoolchildren: prevalence and demographic patterns. *British Journal of Educational Psychology*, 77, 579–593.

Reder, S. & Quan, L. (2003). Cardiopulmonary resuscitation training in Washington state public high schools. *Resuscitation*, 56, 283–288.

Spielberger, C.D. (1980). *Test Anxiety Inventory: Dutch Version and Mannual*. Menlo Park, CA: Mind Garden.

Toner, P., Connolly, M., Laverty, L., McGrath, P., Connolly, D. & McCluskey, D.R. (2007). Teaching basic life support to school children using medical students and teachers in a 'peer-training' model. Results of the 'ABC for life' programme. *Resuscitation*, 75, 169–175.

Topping, K.J. (1998). Peer assessment between students in colleges and universities. *Review of Educational Research*, 68, 249–276.

Van de Velde, S., Heselmans, A., Roex, A. *et al.* (2009). Effectiveness of nonresuscitative first aid training in laypersons: a systematic review. *Ann Emerg Med.*, 54/3, 447–457.

Vitasari, P., Wahab, M.N.A, Othman, A., Herawan, T. & Sinnadurai, S.K. (2010). The relationship between study anxiety and academic performance among engineering students. *Procedia Social and Behavioral Sciences*, 8, 490–497.

Zimbardo, P.G., Butler, L.D. & Wolfe, V.A. (2003). Cooperative college examinations: more gain, less pain when students share information and grades, *Journal of Experimental Education*, 71, 101–125.

5

A GAME OF PHONES – DESIGN, DEVELOPMENT AND DELIVERY CASE STUDY

KRIS ROCKWELL HYBRID LEARNING SYSTEMS, USA, AND ALICIA SANCHEZ, CZARINA GAMES, USA

Introduction

The idea of using traditional, non-digital games as learning tools is certainly not new. While the idea of games for learning has recently centred on the popularity of video games, traditional games such as board games have served in the classroom for decades. This chapter will detail a design process that evolved into an unlikely game for a mobile learning conference. The resulting game leveraged traditional game elements in a way that could provide a meaningful learning experience and focus on the technology the game was meant to showcase, without using the technology. The results of the design were surprising, but the success of the end project was unquestionable.

Project Goals

A Game of Phones was the result of an opportunity to design and deliver a game for mLearnCon 2011, the E-Learning Guild's annual conference for mobile learning. The game developed would be the official game of the mLearn 2011 conference, which typically attracts approximately 500 professionals from corporate, government and academic sectors. We took this project on as a grand challenge for ourselves, as the conference organizers offered no compensation for creating and delivering the game. Instead of compensation, we saw this as a chance to provide a game to the conference attendees that would demonstrate our unique perspectives on the integration of a game with a conference while not creating the typical conference game that so often equated to scavenger hunts. As designers of games for education, we knew that we wanted to build a game that had learning application, and we wanted the game to be aligned with the conference's vision. As a serious game, this game wasn't specifically designed to be fun, although we hoped people would have fun playing it. Instead this game was designed to meet several specific objectives that we felt represented the spirit of the conference.

Our primary objectives for *A Game of Phones* were derived from our assumption that the conference attendees were coming to mLearnCon to a) learn what their colleagues were doing with mobile learning, b) tell their colleagues what they were doing with mobile learning, and c) learn more about how mobile learning could benefit their respective organizations. Our secondary objective for the game was to help conference attendees create a common vernacular for various elements of mobile learning that were a source of confusion in our personal observations. Finally, we wanted to incorporate our game with the conference, and not just create a game that was played at the conference. This meant that we needed to create a game that embraced the spirit of mobile learning and that would have real utility for players after the conference when they returned to their workplaces.

As no compensation was provided for creation and delivery of the game, we realised that we would be embarking on a rogue game development effort that likely would require the commitment of our nights and weekends as well as chipping in funds for the eventual production and development. We saw this as a challenge that we were anxious to tackle as opposed to a hindrance and made the decision early on to design a game based on our objectives and goals that did not take any budget constraints into consideration, with the intention of taking our brilliant unconstrained design and scoping into the game we would ultimately deliver at mLearnCon. We also hoped to create a game that would have some commercial viability and that the costs associated with the project could be considered marketing and would be recouped in new business opportunities.

Initial Design

While we felt that we had seen lots of examples of unsuccessful conference games, in our initial design process we did seek inspiration from a game that we felt had been very successful. The game, named *The Meta Game*, was created by Local No. 12 and was deployed at the annual Game Developers Conference in 2011. What separated this game from all of the mediocre games we had seen or even been involved in was that it was designed to spark intellectual conversation and debates between conference attendees about a topic they all loved ... games. The game was comprised of a stack of approximately 10 notecards and a sticker worn on the conference badge that identified any individual as a *Meta Game* player. Some of the notecards simply held the name of a video game ranging from new titles to true video game classics; others included a statement such as "which is more engaging" or "which encompasses the true spirit of play". The game was played casually, with one player challenging another to a "duel" of sorts. One of the players selected a statement card, and both then selected a game title from their stack that they felt was the strongest example for a debate. After hearing each player's argument, either one player conceded or bystanders were asked to decide a winner. The winner's prize was the game title card that the losing player had played. Throughout the conference we were impressed by the voracity of the debates, and the players' desire to engage in conversations surrounding the philosophical aspects of games.

With this game fresh in our minds, we were determined to create a game that had the same type of impact at the conference. We wanted to get people talking, something that so often we go to conferences to do, but wind up not doing enough of. While *A Game of Phones* obviously reflects some similarities to *The Meta Game*, the design process was not as obvious as this. The conference we were designing this game for was, after all, a mobile learning conference. It was assumed by all, including ourselves, that we would create and deliver a mobile game.

From our perspective, in order to win any game, you should be able to demonstrate mastery and understanding of the concepts employed within the game. Our initial idea session resulted in a concept that we believed to be a great starting point for this development initiative. We would start with the real-world problems that the attendees of the conference would typically be presented with on the job in their mobile learning efforts. We turned quickly to LrnChat (Learn Chat), a weekly Twitter meet-up in which topics were presented for 140-character discussions. The LrnChat organizers were generous enough to allow us to propose the topics for discussion for one of their weekly gatherings. We introduced our project goals as collecting real-world challenges that the LrnChat participants faced in their workplaces and asked them to provide us concrete examples either in LrnChat or offline.

With a greater sense of the types of problems that our practitioners of mobile learning were facing in their work lives, we were free to consider the variety of game constructs that could be used to provide the attendees with meaningful learning experiences. We philosophically believed that every game design starts on paper. A napkin, a sticky note, a scrap of wrapping paper, somehow every single game design first moves from its creator's mind onto paper. Every learning challenge collected from LrnChat was initially put onto notecards, and then sorted into types of problems and categories. Redundancies were eliminated, and we found ourselves easily able to categorize the challenges based not on the type of problems, but instead on the types of solutions.

At this point, we started writing down our own potential solutions to these types of problems. What emerged were categories of possible solutions. This went on for a few weeks in an iterative process considering each challenge and the various types of solutions to those problems, but interestingly this was not a collaborative effort. Both of us worked in isolation, still searching for the metaphor that would tie this game together and make it a "real" game.

We eliminated solution-related redundancies and quickly created two additional categories of cards that represented two elements that were pervasive throughout the potential solutions. Those two categories were Hardware and Technology.

In this early state, our framework was that we would have challenge cards, hardware cards and technology cards, and that each challenge could be met through a combination of hardware and technology cards. With this strawman, we continued to search for a game paradigm that might fit our goals.

Iterations

With our initial content collection complete, we turned to the design of the game. Certainly any game featured as the official game at a mobile learning conference must be a mobile game, right? And while we felt this could lead to great learning experiences, how would we tie this into the conference? There had to be a common thread that made the game more relevant to the conference than just occupying the same space. We set off individually again to consider modalities for the delivery of this game, one that wouldn't distract or dissuade what we believed was learning in its most basic form. Upon regrouping, we had a few ideas that we felt could lead us to the right solution.

The first design idea was to create an online version of the game, available via native or web-based application on mobile phones that allowed all conference attendees the ability to select a card and challenge another registered player to a "match". Once the other player accepted the "match", each player would select the cards that would be the best potential solution. If the players selected the right solution, then they would collect points. In order to keep people playing, each player would be awarded points for participating in a match, but winners of matches or matches in which both players selected the right answer would receive more points. At the end of the conference, the player with the highest score would be our grand champion. From the programming perspective, this could be easily accomplished as each challenge would be associated with technology and hardware cards that represented the "school house solution".

First Playtest

One afternoon, we found ourselves sitting in a bar prepared to enter into our first real test of the validity of the content we had gathered to date (Figure 5.1) and the initial design concept we had conceived. We felt that ensuring that the game was based on realism would help the attendees understand the immediate applicability of the game. So we took two sets of our notecards and decided to validate the challenges and their solutions by independently selecting the hardware and technology cards that would be relevant for

Figure 5.1 Initial playtesting with demo decks

each one. We randomly selected a challenge from one deck of cards, each read it, and it was at that point that the game became clear. We had each spent time with the challenges, and had each developed our own solutions to each of them.

The very first challenge card we turned over was, "You've been asked to design a mobile option for new student orientation on your college's campus".

We then took turns presenting our potential solutions. One of us presented the Hardware Cards "Smart Phones" and "Tablet Computers", along with the Technology Card "Native App" and the solution of having an interactive map that the users could use to determine location and facilities.

The other of us presented the Hardware Card "Feature Phones", the Technology Cards "Geolocation" and "SMS" with the solution of sending the user short text messages based on location.

This came as a particularly interesting revelation, as we both fully expected that we would have revealed the same solution. For each challenge we had individually mentally constructed a "correct" answer and we each believed that the other would clearly reach the same conclusion. This was the pivotal moment in our game design process. We were both wrong.

After the initial shock wore off, we were both able to see the value in each other's approach, and were able to have a constructive conversation regarding the two approaches. In the end, we decided that one of our solutions might be most appropriate and moved onto the second challenge, but the course was set. After reviewing each challenge and discussing our potential solution, we both realized that there was a level of authenticity that we had not predicted in this design exercise. We both left that bar a little smarter, and we had something special that we could move forward with. Unfortunately, at this point, our technology plans were blown out of the water. If no "correct" answer existed, we would be facing increasingly complex programming, which would drive up development costs significantly. Additionally, we didn't feel that players would be able to express their ideas using their mobile devices if forced to type in their solutions. The ability to discuss the merits of each proposed solution would be lost. Most importantly, however, we feared that the level of enjoyment would be harmed by a level of asynchronous gameplay, postponing the satisfaction and curiosity of players and possibly detracting from their learning.

Second Playtest

Determined to keep this effort moving forward, we gathered some friends who happened to be in town attending a conference for a second playtest. This time we proposed some minimal instructions: 1) Randomly select a Challenge card and show it to another player; 2) Use the Technology and Hardware cards to help you form your potential solution; 3) Present your solution to the other player and hear their solution; 4) Discuss the two potential solutions and decide among yourselves which one has the highest probability of success.

Our fearless playtesters, lured by promises of beer and games, took their task very seriously as we watched quietly from across the table (Figure 5.2). It took only one round to replicate the findings that we had reached in our first playtest. Each player created a story that surrounded their potential solution and presented it. They each listened to their 'opponent's' potential solution and were immediately involved in a discussion discussing the merits and shortcomings of each other's solutions. They were impressed by the potential solutions presented by their counterparts and often remarked that "they hadn't thought of that". After many rounds of play, we were convinced that we had a solid learning experience that was enjoyable and that met our learning objectives and goals.

One unexpected finding in this playtest, however, was that players often found themselves debating what the potential solution cards really meant. What exactly was a feature phone, what counted as a web app, and how was a smartphone different from a palm device? Our goal of establishing a common vernacular for the concepts in a new area such as mobile learning would save a lot of time and frustration for players; therefore we ensured that each Hardware and Technology card included a definition and an example.

Figure 5.2 Playtesting with volunteers

At this point, however, we still wanted to demonstrate a meaningful use of technology as a critical element of the game. Our next big idea came in the same place we turned to for our content collection. If we could use Twitter during the conference to include both attendees and non-attendees who might be interacting with the conference from afar we could engage an even larger audience in our game. We tossed around ideas of having the players involved in casual "matches" tweet their Solution cards and an abbreviated use case story in order to allow attendees and virtual participants to vote on the winner of each match. This could be linked into an app, allowing for an external scoring mechanism to be maintained.

Third Playtest

Our third playtest involved only the two of us, and was geared towards testing the possible inclusion of Twitter-based voting. We created new match numbers that could be used for each match that two players could engage in. We engaged in representing our potential solutions to each challenge including the Technology and Hardware cards in our solutions within 140 characters, the Twitter character limit. Our results were not encouraging. It was excessively hard to reduce our solutions to such limited space. Using more than one tweet could wreak havoc on the system that would be designed to capture the matches in order to create an external scoring system and high score board. Most importantly, we did find that a critical element of gameplay was lost, the post-solution discovery phase, in which players critiqued each other's solutions and created new solutions together. At this point, we knew that we would not be able to integrate technology for mLearn-Con.

We were short on time and money and needed to move forward with our design, but in the end those factors mattered little. We felt that we had created a powerful learning experience and we couldn't find a way that technology made the experience better. This was an opportunity to not only help people learn how to use technology in learning, but to actively demonstrate that, sometimes, technology wasn't necessary. So we hoisted our heads high and decided to practice what we had always preached. This game would be mobile, in as much as a deck of cards could be slipped into your pocket and taken anywhere. But it would never require a plug or a charge.

Our final goal for the game was to create a meaningful tie between the learning game and the conference. We didn't want the game to be a great game that happened to take place at a conference, but instead we wanted to make sure that the conference was relevant and present within the game play. At this point, we had three categories of cards: Challenges, Technology and Hardware. We realized that there was an additional level of grouping that we knew we could leverage. This formed the fourth and final category of cards used in play, which were Speaker cards. The name was deceiving, however, as those cards really represented implementation types. For example, a solution might be:

> I would create a performance support tool, that was a native app usable on a tablet or a smartphone, that allowed my sales managers to access inventory and pricing data in real time.

or

> I would create a game that as a web app that could be used on a feature phone, allowing students to take and upload pictures of relevant architectural features found in our city.

It was this typology of the mobile learning solutions into implementation types such as performance support tools or games that created the Speaker card category. We scoured the mLearnCon schedule, found an expert presenting in each implementation type and immediately requested permission to use their image on a card that represented their area of specialty. We decided that it would be most interesting to have a core deck, one in which all of the playing cards requisite for play (i.e., Challenges, Hardware and Technology) and the most frequently used implementation types or Speaker cards (including Games, Alternate Reality, and Performance Support Tools) were present and then have the speakers of several implementation types distribute their own cards during their sessions during the conference. Sessions in which Speaker cards would be distributed were marked on the conference programe and in signage at the event. We hoped that this could create a separate economy of gameplay in which Speaker cards began to represent a collectible card, enabling this game to be customized for this and future conferences.

Production

With the design process wrapping up, we faced the very real problem of creating 500 low-cost decks for distribution at the conference. Our initial research into the printing of card decks indicated that there was an industry for creating customized playing cards. While most of the customizations were specific to the back of normal poker deck playing cards, we were able to locate a printer who was willing to custom print both the front and the back of standard playing cards. We quickly realized that deviating from a standard 54 card deck (typically 52 playing cards and two information or joker cards) would be costly both in the price of printing separate cards and the price associated with packing the decks into some sort of container such as a box.

We again went back to our cards and decided that we could accomplish a 54 card deck, which would consist of 21 Challenge cards, 8 Technology cards, 4 Hardware cards, 11 Speaker cards, an Instruction card and a Logo card. We included two blank cards for each card category except for Speaker cards. This allowed players to include their own challenges, hardware and technologies as the rapidly changing workplaces evolved. The use of a 54 card deck meant that in order to provide the most flexible gameplay options, each player would need their own deck of cards in order to play. The final card types can be found in Figure 5.3.

The rules were strategically varied in our stages of playtesting. Our final rule set emerged as follows:

1. One player randomly selects a Challenge card and shares it with all of the players.
2. Each player selects 1–2 Technology cards and 1–2 Hardware Cards that represent their strategy.

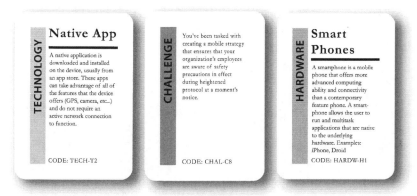

Figure 5.3 *A Game of Phones* card examples

3. When all players are ready, reveal your cards and take turns presenting your strategies to each other as if you were presenting your idea to your boss.
4. Decide among yourselves who wins; solicit help from non-players if you can't decide!

Implementation

We arrived in San Jose (California, United States) for the mLearnCon conference to meet our preshipped, sight unseen 500 decks of cards. After separating the Speaker cards that were to be distributed at mLearnCon sessions, we began distributing the decks to attendees by positioning ourselves next to the conference registration desk. We advertised several sessions of gameplay during the conference, and on the last day of the conference planned to hold a tournament in which the grand prize was a customized *A Game of Phones* Kindle.

Many of the conference attendees were bemused by the decks of cards and our description of the game. Some simply stated "[B]ut I don't have a smartphone, I can't play?". We spent the greater part of two days explaining, playing sample games and confirming that the game was in fact solely a deck of cards.

Our first game play session at the conference was not heavily attended, but the few faithful players who showed up on the first day helped spread the word of the learning benefits of the game and later sessions grew in popularity. While we did see a few casual games in the conference hallways, we didn't see mainstream adoption of the game. Instead, it appeared that the game was often left in the attendee's hotel rooms along with the rest of the conference materials and giveaways to be reviewed and considered later.

On the final day of the conference, we hosted the main tournament (Figure 5.4). We enlisted judges and followed a round robin tournament format.

Figure 5.4 mLearnCon tournament

Thirteen rounds of play culminated in a final showdown for the grand prize. The conversations were meaningful and many players who had been eliminated in earlier rounds stayed to hear the top players craft their stories of their solutions with true flair. Finally, a single player emerged as our champion, and was recognized as such at the closing session to the applause of the entire conference.

We declared success that day, but were more than pleased when the many attendees who had not engaged in the game at the conference returned home and were able to play the game themselves and at their workplaces, often ordering additional decks of cards so that they could host their own workplace tournaments and use the cards to solve their own mobile learning challenges.

Adaptations

In the creation of *A Game of Phones*, we inadvertently created architecture for a powerful gameplay framework that could be applied to virtually any content that would benefit from person knowledge sharing. We have found application of the framework for product knowledge, decision-making support, strategic planning, idea sharing, discussion primers, cognitive decision support systems and vocabulary support in almost every field including medical, academic,

Figure 5.5 Example cards from version 2

sales and general business processes. The power of this game comes from the satisfaction of two basic human needs: curiosity and recognition. When we are interested in a process (an assumption that we must make about our players), we want to hear what others are doing and we want to share our own stories. This game enables both of those needs to be satisfied.

Always keeping an eye on commercially viable applications for *A Game of Phones*, an opportunity shortly arose to sell the decks of cards in the bookstore at another conference. We realized quickly that *A Game of Phones* version 1.0 wouldn't be viable, because it was too closely linked with the mLearnCon speakers. We went back to the design board and added an additional element of play that evolved from play observations made during the tournament and subsequent play sessions. We noticed that players liked to add variations to the game in the form of limitations on the Challenges. A challenge to create new hire employee training to help employees memorize the ingredients for dishes on a menu might have very different potential solutions if the limitation of having only $200 and two months were imposed on potential solutions. Therefore, *A Game of Phones* version 2.0 was realized, removing the Speaker cards and implementing Constraint cards in their place (shown in Figure 5.5).

Conclusions

The game design process embarked on in the development of *A Game of Phones* was a learning process for all involved. In order to create the best game we could, we had to first eliminate the real constraints and then let go of the expectations that were so integral to our initial conceptions of the game. By designing a game with no budget constraints, we inadvertently also did not design a game that was more costly than warranted. We allowed ourselves the latitude to build a game that might have warranted a hefty price tag, and if we had, we would have been forced to downscale the game significantly. We also allowed ourselves to be lured, but not led, by technology. We are big fans of technology. Finding out that technology didn't add great value to the game might have been tolerated in the final design, but in our case, finding that technology actually detracted from the learning was justification enough to step away. The playtesting phases of our paper design were critical to determining the game play, and we recommend that it is never too early to start testing out ideas. Our focus on our objectives and goals instead of technology allowed us to follow the path most beneficial for this game, albeit the path least expected.

Acknowledgements

Thanks to the eLearning Guild for hosting this game at mLearnCon 2011; to Kevin Thorn for the card cover art; to David Kelly, Dr Jane Bozarth, and Trina Rimmer for being our playtesters; and to Aaron Silvers, Brian Dusablon and Jason Haag for serving as tournament judges.

6

FROM IDEA TO PRODUCT – A BOARD GAME FOR PRESCHOOLERS

PÄIVI MARJANEN AND ILKKA MÖNKKÖNEN, LAUREA UNIVERSITY OF APPLIED SCIENCES, FINLAND

Introduction

The purpose of this chapter is to describe and critically analyze the process of designing and developing a low-cost board game for preschoolers. The description follows the steps of developing the board game *Konkkaronkka* from a prototype to the end product.[1] Plans of further development of the game are also discussed. The project was carried out as a Research and Development (R&D) activity at Laurea Hyvinkää, which is one of the seven units of Laurea University of Applied Sciences (polytechnic) in the Greater Helsinki Region of Finland. Our unit is specialized in training nurses, experts in social services and professionals in business administration.

The board game is a joint effort of multiprofessional teams consisting of both teachers and students of various fields of study in our unit – and a neighboring institute. In addition, kindergarten teachers of two day care centers and other professionals working with young children have been consulted. The project is practice-based. The idea of a new board game sprang up as a response to the needs of the kindergarten teachers of a day care center, who needed a tool for teaching communication skills and socio-emotional skills especially to preschoolers who were in need of special education.

We begin our chapter with a short description of the board game. In the next section we discuss the choices we have made while developing the game. Finally, we discuss the project as part of research and development activities in our unit.

The Board Game *Konkkaronkka*

Board games have retained their popularity among young children even in the era of computers. Games are an excellent way to relax and spend unhurried quality time with friends. While playing and having fun, children practice hand-eye coordination and manual dexterity. The games teach children valuable social skills, such as sharing, waiting and taking turns. The players explore colors, numbers and shapes. While playing they learn to communicate with each other. Playing always involves a chance of surprise, since the course of playing cannot be determined beforehand (Callois, 2001: 8–9). It is no wonder that board games are so popular.

Various taxonomies have been constructed in order to categorize the almost infinite multitude of games (e.g. Kelly *et al.*, 2007; Amaro *et al.*, 2006; Ogershok & Cottrel, 2004). Some of the board games have been planned especially for pedagogical or educational purposes (Dondi & Moretti, 2007). Caillois' classification of games into the four categories of *agon, alea, mimicry* and *ilinx* is based on the central characteristic of the game under consideration. Some games, such as football and chess, involve skill and competition (*agon*), while others, for example the games of dice, are based on chance (*alea*). There are also games in which the role of simulation (*mimicry*) or vertigo (*ilinx*) is dominant. The last mentioned type refers to games in which "one produces in oneself, by a rapid whirling or falling movement, a state of dizziness and disorder" (Callois, 2001: 12). Some of the educational or pedagogical games, which aim at developing the emotional and physical skills of the players, such as the board game *Konkkaronkka*, appear to be of mixed type.

The board game *Konkkaronkka* was developed for pedagogical and educational purposes in day care groups which consisted of four- to seven-year-olds. The game aims to promote the players' socio-emotional development and support their body management. Instead of competing with each other the players try to act together, in order to achieve a common goal. During a playing session they form a kind of community. They must be ready to collaborate and negotiate with each other. The idea behind the playing sessions may be illustrated by McMillan's theory of the sense of community. McMillan views the sense of community through four dimensions: spirit, trust, trade and art (McMillan and Chavis, 1986). 1) A *spirit* of belonging together implies the boundaries that delimit "us" from "them". The boundaries make a sense of emotional safety possible and contribute to a sense of mutual confidence among the players. Normally there are no other children or grown-ups nearby during a playing session. 2) *Trust* relates to an authority structure in a community. Mutual understanding about the norms and rules in the community is a prerequisite for the players to know what they can expect from each other. The players may know each other, as, for example, in a day care group. In a day care group the role of the educator is also important. 3) *Trade* refers to the choices and mutual exchanges the players make. Through interaction the players discover that they can benefit from being and acting together. 4) The dimension of *art* refers to community stories, which represent the values and traditions of the community. Such stories may include slogans, rituals, common rhymes, songs and narratives.

The Game Design

The layout of the game is traditional, as shown by Figure 6.1. The board consists of 28 steps, green, yellow or gray, arranged in a circle, a dice and the playing pieces. In addition, there are two packs of cards which indicate various tasks the players have to perform during the game. By performing the tasks given, the players are rewarded with a block of a picture puzzle that they place in the open space in the middle of the board. The aim is to complete the six-block-picture-puzzle collaboratively.

The rules of the game are simple. The players, from two to four in a session, roll the dice in turn and move the piece forward on the board according to the numbers cast. If the piece ends on a green square, the player lifts a card, which shows the task he or she has to perform, for example, stand on his or her left leg. Some of the tasks are complicated and call for negotiating and collaboration among the players. If the players cannot read the text on the card, the educator, who intervenes in the play as little as possible, helps them. A successful performance of the task is rewarded by a block of the picture puzzle. If the piece ends on a yellow step the players have to remove one of the blocks from the puzzle and return it to the educator. If the piece ends on a gray step the turn goes to the next player without any task performed. The players may choose

Figure 6.1 The board game *Konkkaronkka*

between two different puzzles. The game ends when the picture puzzle has been completed and all the players have come to the middle of the board.

There are two packs of task cards, one for the "emotional skills game" and another for the "body game". Emotional skills refer to children's ability to deal with, express and control their emotional states. The tasks that the players have to perform, such as "Say something friendly to your partner", "Why does everyone need friends?" or "Give examples of bullying", refer to social relations, identification, expression and processing of feelings together with empathy and self-consciousness. The players learn that all feelings are meaningful. During the play they also learn to listen to their co-players and wait for their turn. Emotional self-regulation is an important aspect of coping with daily life in society, where socio-emotional difficulties seem to have grown more common and severe. A child's motor clumsiness often co-occur with difficulties in social relationships, attention problems, learning difficulties and poor self-esteem (Ahonen, 1995: 249–256). The task cards of "the body game" have been planned to help the players control and perceive their body. Examples of such tasks include "Stand on your toes", "Put your ear against your partner's shoulder" or "Move and make a hissing sound like a snake". The tasks must not be too difficult to perform. By supporting various developmental areas and showing empathy and warmth towards the players the educator can support the players' overall development and help them avoid difficulties in school or society.

From Idea to Product

The development of the board game *Konkkaronkka* was started in our unit four years ago – and the process is still going on. The German version of the game has been tested, but it still needs refinement. At the moment we are looking for students who would translate the task cards into English and Estonian. At times we have come along nicely, but there have also been periods when the process has lain dormant.

Various groups of business students and students of social services, particularly those with plans of becoming kindergarten teachers, have contributed to the development of the game during the different phases of the process (Table 6.1). The assignments they have conducted as part of their study program have varied from telephone contacts with the representatives of working life to research work.

In this section we will describe some of the highlights of the process. We will also give two examples of the research conducted in our unit. Our description proceeds chronologically.

In the Beginning There Was a Need for a Board Game, 2008–2009

The idea of planning a board game in our unit came out of the blue in autumn 2008, when we were starting an optional one-year course for students of social

Table 6.1 From an idea to the end product

	2008	2009	2010	2011	2012
product development	voluntary course, prototype of the game	assessment of the prototype	productization, test product, 2. prototype	end product, international versions of the game	international versions of the game
research		bachelor's thesis	usability lab with kindergarten teachers assessment of commercialization	second research with children	
multiprofessional participants	students, working life partners	working life partners, multiprofessional student team	consultants, multiprofessional student team		business and administration students

services. The aim of the course was to think up new ways of improving the quality of daily life of various groups of people, such as the handicapped and the elderly living in residential homes and of children attending preschool in a day care center. Two students had concluded with the staff of a kindergarten that new kinds of tools were needed in order to tackle the emotional and social problems of the children. As a response, they constructed a simple version of a board game, and offered it to the staff as a solution to the problems. The game had proved successful.

This "duo" obtained so much positive feedback from the staff of the day care centre that they decided to go on working with the board game, to carefully analyse the feedback they had received from the staff and make the game even better. Finally, they constructed the first prototype of the board game *Konkkaronkka*. In order to learn more about pedagogical and educational games, they chose early socio-emotional development and the *Konkkaronkka* game as the subject of their bachelor's thesis (Heinikoski & Muhonen, 2009). The theoretical part of their thesis relied on Lev Vygotsky's (1978: 84–91) ideas of social interaction as a basis of learning.

In the empirical part of their thesis the students made an attempt to explore how the board game supported learning in a special education group during early childhood. They gathered the data through interviewing two teachers, a kindergarten teacher and a teacher of a group of children with special needs. They also gathered additional data by observing eight playing sessions. Observation was targeted on social and emotional skills of the players and the empathy they showed during the playing sessions. The method used in the analysis of the data was qualitative content analysis. The results suggested that the children of this group could be taught to pay attention to and accept differences in a heterogeneous day care group by playing a board game. The players had learnt social skills, such as sharing, waiting, taking turns and showing empathy towards each other. Some of the tasks the players had had to perform during the playing sessions had encouraged them to approach each other, even tap another player on the shoulder. Touching each other and hugging had become spontaneous ways of showing feelings among the players during the playing sessions. The initiative of playing the board game had mostly come from the children, which was an indication of their motivation to play the game. The longest session had lasted 20 minutes.

The Product Was Born, 2010

The feedback obtained from the day care center staff encouraged us to go on with the process. It seemed that there could be a gap in the market for an educational board game meant to develop social and emotional skills. We thought that our potential customers would be the numerous day care centers and kindergartens, both municipal and private, all over the country. But something was still missing. We did not have any product for sale or a sales system. The partly hand-made, black-and-white prototype had to be processed into a product.

In order to tackle the problems ahead the developers of the game expanded their team with two business students. They had studied marketing and knew how to productize new ideas. In order to make the board game look nice and attractive, two students from the design degree program of the neighbouring university were invited to join the team for some time. They helped plan the layout of the board, the task cards, the form of the pieces and the picture puzzle. While this multiprofessional team worked with the productization of the idea, a group of professionals working with children were asked to assess the game in what we called usability labs. While playing the game they made notes and critical comments. Through these sessions we received valuable feedback about the layout, the rules and the texts of the task cards, which the team took into consideration.

There was still an obstacle in our path towards a product: shortage of money. Our unit would finance only part of the process. Since the services of the printing house would be expensive, sponsors were needed. Finally we managed to get funding (5,000 €) from the Finnish Funding Agency for Technology and Innovation (Tekes). After a few months of working the effective teamwork was rewarded with a product ready for sale.

Research and Plans for the Future, 2011–2012

The board game was launched in spring 2011. Marketing was organized by a group of business students, who arranged demonstrations in educational exhibitions and created a sales system in our unit and on the Internet. The website *Konkkaronkka* (http://www.*Konkkaronkka*.fi) maintained by the students was also opened. Since then, there have been customers, especially from day care centers, and various educators have shown their interest in our product. However, we have to admit that the board game has not proved to be "a gold mine".

In order to find out what people in the field thought about our product, we decided to conduct a new study. Since we were busy with lectures and other assignments, we invited a student to join our team and help us with data collecting and applications (Marjanen *et al.*, 2011). We could not start with the study before we had received the local authorities' permission to collect data from the staff of the kindergartens. The decision to collect the data by videoing a group of preschoolers meant extra work, since we had to request the consent of the parents of each child for observing or videoing their child during the playing sessions. This was time-consuming but rewarding, since all the parents gave us their written consent. All of the children were happy to be videoed.

The study was twofold. We interviewed three teachers from two kinder-gartens. They had used the board game *Konkkaronkka* as an instrument in teaching socio-emotional skills to preschoolers for some months. We also videoed 39 children playing the game in groups of three or four players, in order to find out what kind of peer group learning took place during the playing sessions. All in all there were 19 playing sessions. We recorded the theme interviews and applied content analysis to the transcripts. The playing sessions were more problematic. We studied the contents of the interaction through video recordings. We also made an attempt to draw sociograms of the interaction during each session. We thought that a graphic representation of the links between the players would help us identify the structure of interpersonal relations in each session. Construction of the sociograms proved very challenging. The theoretical background of the study and the analysis of the material were based on Verba's article on socio-cognitive interaction in young children (Verba, 1994). Verba, who discusses various forms of cooperation among children in her study, pays special attention to the role of a peer group in a child's development.

In the analysis of the data we focused on the modes of activity, sharing and management. The results indicated that the mode of activity was typical of board game sessions where a player was asked to respond to an open-ended question. The player could respond by completing, modifying or repeating a peer's response. The mode of activity also turned up in tasks where the player could respond by moving, as in the session, where the player was asked to move and make a noise like an owl. The player who responded first could produce some kind of a sound, whereas another player demonstrated the movements of the wings by moving his arms. Soon two of the players were "flying" around the room. Such responses may be regarded as an indication of the players' commit-ment to the joint activity. In other words, the players had a need to be part of the session. The mode of management was best seen in the players' commit-ment to the rules of the game. The players were eager to make initiatives in their responses, for example, by passing the dice to the next player, reminding the player of his or her turn, or by helping a player to count the steps on the board. Quite often the players helped each other on request. The mode of sharing was focused on the common aim, i.e. the construction of the picture puzzle in the middle of the board. There was no mutual competition during the sessions. The interviews of the teachers suggested that the discussions stimulated by the questions the players had to answer and the tasks they had to perform in the course of the game contributed to the players' interaction skills. Transfer of the skills, such as sharing, turn taking and being patient could occasionally be seen during daily activities. The teachers considered the game a usable tool in teaching socio-emotional skills to preschoolers.

Videoing helped us analyze the sessions, since we could replay the sessions several times. But we only had one stationary camera, which did not cover the situations completely. In order to have more reliable results, the material should be gathered by two or three cameras. We also noticed that the teacher's role varied a lot during the sessions. Occasionally the teachers did not allow the players to negotiate the problems they had encountered. The teachers should be instructed not to interfere too quickly in the game.

The development of the board game *Konkkaronkka* is still going on with international versions of the game. A group of computer people also asked us to join their team in order to develop a digital version of the game. However, after having made a closer acquaintance with our board game, they concluded that as such the game is not applicable. We think that interpersonal interaction is at its best in the traditional board game sessions. So we have also declined the invitation.

A Board Game as an Integral Part of Curriculum and R&D Activities

The board game *Konkkaronkka* has been developed through tripartite cooperation between working life, our unit and its students. This is in line with the competence-based learning strategy of Laurea University of Applied Sciences. According to the strategy all projects must be linked with practical problems of working life.

In addition to the objectives connected directly to the projects the student researchers also have their learning objectives that are indicated in the curriculum. For example, during or after a course in research methods the students have some practical exercises related to a project. The exercises usually involve data gathering, data analysis and reporting. The methods are both qualitative and quantitative. The study credits the student obtains consist of both the theoretical course and work in a project. After the course the students should master the methods so well that they can apply them in their bachelor's thesis, and later in the development tasks in their workplaces. During the process they learn the basics of research ethics and have training in team work. Through the contacts with kindergartens and other institutions the students also make acquaintance with the representatives of the working life. Such contacts helped some of the students who worked with the *Konkkaronkka* game to find a job soon after their graduation.

Tripartite cooperation also poses challenges for the teachers and the unit. The teachers must organize the timetable so that the students can attend the obligatory lectures and courses while they are working with the projects. This is not always an easy task, since the students come from various fields of study. Hence, patience and flexibility are needed.

Our unit provided us with a frame within which we could operate with the board game, but it could not finance the production. Hence, extra funding was needed. We were lucky when we obtained a 5,000 euro grant from the Finnish Funding Agency for Technology and Innovation, which covered, for example, the design of the product. It also helped us make the product known in educational exhibitions. A little imagination and good contacts are needed to fund the projects.

Conclusion

It took a couple of years before the *Konkkaronkka* game was refined from an idea into its final form. The game cannot be considered a lucrative business. However, we regard the development process as a success story. The game is a response to the needs of working life. It has proved a useful tool in teaching the preschoolers communication skills. In addition, the students of our unit have learnt a lot during the long process which has been integrated in the curriculum of our unit.

Of course, there are also elements that are less successful. At times it has been difficult to find students who would have been motivated to join the teams. This seems to be a permanent problem. For example, we have promising prototypes, a memory board game for the elderly and a game for the handicapped, but there are no students who would be ready to join the teams to develop them into products. The process proceeds slowly, so one needs patience and has to believe in the power of the pedagogical board games. Occasionally it has been difficult to find common time for the meetings. The students have been busy with their studies. It has not been easy to recruit teachers, either, since they have their own interests and specialties. This is a weak spot of the development process, since the students need teachers whom they can consult when they need guidance. Careful planning of the projects may help us overcome such difficulties in the future. Our unit encourages us to join development projects, since they are in line with the strategy of Laurea University of Applied Sciences.

We have not been eager to join the teams who develop digital versions of the games. We still stick to traditional games in which the players can learn new skills while simultaneously having fun. We still believe in the power of pedagogical board games.

Note

1. The name of the game, *Konkkaronkka*, is an old-fashioned Finnish word referring to a crowd or a (whole) group of people. The word is informal like the English word 'caboodle', meaning 'crowd, pack' (Webster's 1989, s.v. caboodle).

References

Ahonen, T. (1995). Kehitykselliset koordinaatiohäiriöt. [Developmental coordination disorders.] In H. Lyytinen, *et al.* (eds.) *Oppimisvaikeudet. Neuropsykologinen näkökulma.* [*Learning difficulties. Neuropsychological perspective.*] Helsinki: WSOY, pp. 247–263.

Amaro, S., Viggiano, A., Di Costanzo, A., Madeo, I., Viggiano, A., Baccari, M.E., Marchitelli, E., Raia, M., Viggiano, E., Deepak, S., Monda, M. & De Luca, B. (2006). Kalèdo, a new educational board-game, gives nutritional rudiments and encourages healthy eating in children: a pilot cluster randomized trial. *European Journal of Pediatrics*, 165/9, 630–635.

Caillois, R. (2001). *Man, Play and Games*. Translated from the French by Mayer Barash. Urbana, IL and Chicago, IL: University of Illinois Press.

Dondi, C. & Moretti, M. (2007). A methodological proposal for learning games selection and quality assessment. *British Journal of Educational Technology*, 38/3, 502–512.

Heinikoski, T. & Muhonen, A. (2009). *Konkkaronkka-peli sosiaalis-emotionaalisen kehityksen tukena*. [*Konkkaronkka-game as support of socio-emotional development*.] Bachelor's thesis. Degree Programme in Social Services. Laurea University of Applied Sciences. Hyvinkää: Laurea Hyvinkää.

Kelly, H., Howell, K., Glinert, E., Holding, L., Swain, C., Burrowbridge, A. & Roper, M. (2007). How to Build Serious Games. *Communications of the ACM*. 50/7, 44–49.

Marjanen, P., Mönkkönen, I. & Vanhala, M. (2011). Peer Group Learning During the Board Game Sessions. *Proceedings of ECGBL 2011: The Fifth European Conference on Games Based Learning*, The National and Kapodistrian University of Athens, Greece, 20–21 October 2011, 388–394.

McMillan, D.W. & Chavis, D. (1986). Sense of community: a definition and theory. *Journal of Community Psychology* 14/1, 6–23.

Ogershok, P. and Cottrell, S. (2004). The pediatric board game. *Medical Teacher* 26 (6), 514–517.

Verba, M. (1994). The beginning of collaboration in peer interaction. *Human Development* 37/3, 125–139.

Vygotsky, L. (1978). *Mind in Society. The Development of Higher Psychological Processes*. Cambridge, MA: Harvard University Press.

Webster's (1989). *Encyclopedic Unabridged Dictionary of the English Language*. New York, NY Avenel, New Jersey, NJ: Gramercy Books.

7

ADVENTURE INITIATIVE GAMES
Playing towards Social Competence

JULE HILDMANN, CENTRUM FÜR ERLEBNISPÄDAGOGIK
VOLKERSBERG, GERMANY; UNIVERSITY OF EDINBURGH, UK

Introduction

Adventure initiative games (AIGs) are games dedicated to nurturing social and personal skills in their participants. They are frequently embedded in the *Experiential Education Approach*. This chapter will give an insight into essential features of initiative games and how to systematically design a new one, including security issues and other noteworthy aspects. A practical example is presented as well as the summary of an empirical study that investigated the effect of initiative games in school with teenage students.

Experiential Education

Experiential education is a holistic approach in pedagogics, which has established itself in various social contexts, from drug and violence prevention for youngsters to professional team trainings and therapeutic sessions (Silberman, 2007; Heckmair & Michl, 2004; Gass, 1993; Kolb, 1984 and others). Its main objective is to help participants discover and/or enhance personality growth, namely social and personal skills such as creative thinking, problem solving, or effective team behaviour.

Experiential education differentiates itself from other educational concepts through a number of underlying principles, which have also been demonstrated to be the keystone to this approach's success (compare Rehm, 1999):

- *Learning with Head, Heart and Hand*: a combination of cognitive, emotional and practical or multi-sensory learning techniques is employed to convey learning content, which enforces their neuro-cognitive anchoring and more sustainable memory (see Figure 7.1).
- *Challenge by Choice:* each participant is allowed to decide which challenge s/he wants to take on and to what extent.

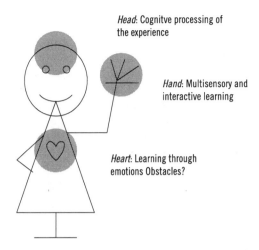

Head: Cognitve processing of the experience

Hand: Multisensory and interactive learning

Heart: Learning through emotions Obstacles?

Figure 7.1 Experiential learning with head, heart and hand

- *Self-responsibility & self-regulation*: Participants are given as much responsibility for themselves, the course of the activities and group decisions as possible.

Although frequently associated with outdoor sports such as climbing, hiking or rafting, the principles and basics of experiential education can also be implemented in activities with little or no requirements towards technical gadgetry or physical aptness, e.g. trust activities and the vast field of AIGs.

Adventure Initiative Games – Let the Games Begin

There is a broad scope of initiative games, varying in parameters such as indoor/outdoor use, recommended group size, prime learning goals, amount of equipment, space or logistics required, and so on.

With this diversity, they can also be implemented in various contexts, covering all age groups from elementary kids up, and ranging in content from individual-based personality growth courses through classical team-building events to therapeutic, spiritual, conservational and other topic-related sessions.

In variation to the phrase *adventure initiative games*, several others are found in the standard literature, such as *cooperative adventure games, initiative problems* or plain *initiatives* (Rohnke, 1989; Rohnke & Butler, 1995; Sonntag, 2002; Reiners, 2003; Gilsdorf & Kistner, 2003). Trainers tend to use the term *exercise* or the term *challenge* rather than *games* when presenting them to participants, since playing games is often regarded not only as a children's activity but – in adults – as childish, and is therefore often met with resentment in professional training (Hildmann, 2008).

The early literature on AIGs generates from a group of practitioners around Karl Rohnke and Project Adventure in the USA (Rohnke, 1989; Rohnke & Butler, 1995; and others). These early initiatives have a strong inclination towards New Games, a way of playing according to the make-peace-not-war philosophy of the 1960s and 1970s, aiming to engage large groups into simple and fun activities without the need of competition. All win or all . . . well, laugh, because 'failure' usually leads to some form of humorous chaos.

Modern initiatives on the other hand have much higher expectations of themselves in regard to educational goals and efficiency as training tools.

Educational Goals

AIGs can be considered learning games, since their objective – in accordance with the Experiential Education Approach – is to facilitate team development and personality growth. Among others the following are goals commonly addressed (e.g. Rohnke, 1989; Rohnke & Butler, 1995; Gilsdorf & Kistner, 2003):

- Developing team spirit;
- Effective communication and cooperation;
- Individual roles and their contribution to a shared project;
- Creative problem solving;
- Trust and responsibility within the group;
- Achieving a team goal despite interference factors.

Which of these goals can reasonably be pursued depends on a variety of parameters: number and age of group members, their usual working or social context, shared background, possible handicaps or psycho-social interference factors such as open or hidden conflicts. In addition, duration and other components of the programme, skills and abilities of the facilitator(s), and even weather conditions, can have a distinctive positive or negative effect on the progress and outcome of a programme (CEP, 2013).

Structure

The general structure of AIGs is quite simple and reoccurs in most examples. Generally, a group of participants is presented with some kind of problem or challenge that needs to be mastered. This can take place in an outdoor or indoor setting and usually requires effective group interaction and creative thinking. Quite frequently, the order of events is as follows:

1. A situation and setting is created by the facilitator by telling a frame story and/or arranging a real situation (blocking a path, tying a rope across a pond, etc.).
2. The group is given the safety instructions and rules necessary for the challenge.

3. The players engage with the game and attempt to solve the challenge. During this phase, the facilitator only intervenes to reinforce the rules or ensure safety for the players.
4. When the activity is ended, the trainer will resume his/her leading function and engage reviewing activities, methods to support the transfer of the learning increase, or create a link to the next activity, as appropriate.

Several variations are possible, such as:

- The group is asked to verbally work out a strategy before they are allowed to start the actual activity.
- Some or all members of the group are 'handicapped' (see below).
- Verbal communication is prohibited.
- The game entails several rounds or phases of increasing difficulty.
- And others, depending on group parameters as well as creativity of the facilitator.

Quite frequently, chains of initiative games are created, with several challenges linked together in an action-reflection pattern (see *Project Adventure*, USA – as described above).

Theoretically, initiative games can also be constructed for single persons (obviously then not-cooperative), for example for therapeutic purposes (Gass, 1993; Hildmann, 2008). But they are very rarely used in that way, since the vast majority of experiential education programmes are designed for groups to harness the momentum of social learning, for example in Figure 7.2.

Embedding the Game into a Story

The technical task that is the core of an initiative game is often embedded in an adventurous narrative frame such as getting lost in a desert storm or finding oneself in a tropical jungle after a plane crash. The purpose of this is to enhance the game aspect of the activity and aid the participants to unleash creativity for the problem-solving process (CEP, 2013). It also helps being at ease, because often a certain amount of playful silliness is required to complete the task within the story compounds (Rohnke, 1989).

Furthermore, the visual language employed in narrative frames can be helpful in extracting learning outcomes from the games. Even stronger metaphors are created around AIGs and used for processing the experience and to open up new perspectives through multi-faceted interpretations (for more information see Hildmann & Moseley, 2012).

Designing New AIGs

There is truly a large choice of well-proven AIGs and standard literature on them (at least in German language: Gilsdorf and Kistner, 2001 & 2003; Reiners,

Figure 7.2 One player acts, the other directs

2003; Sonntag, 2002; König & König, 2002). Still, sometimes we have a specific group, goal, location or other starting point at hand, and it appears reasonable to design a completely new game or to alter a known one. Both can be achieved fairly simply with the following steps (and some practice in this will make it easier and swifter every time).

Before going into detail on some of the issues, here is a brief step-by-step list of topics to think through:

1. Starting point (What are my known determinants? E.g. group factors, location, specific material, objective)
2. What is my training goal? (cooperation, trust activity, conservation, etc.)
3. What are my boundaries? (time frame, location, resources, etc.)
4. Now brainstorm with the parameters defined so far. Do you already know an AIG that merely needs some altering? If not, keep on brainstorming until you have a rough idea that 'feels' good.
5. Maybe at this point or at a later stage you can come up with a frame narrative that makes the game more engaging.
6. Define the goal (i.e. end) of the game. When exactly is it finished, won, failed?
7. Try to estimate the ideal measure of difficulty for your particular group. (E.g. shall some or all players have handicaps?)
8. Clearly define (preferably even write down) the rules of the game. Think of appropriate consequences to administer when a rule is broken.
9. Check mentally and on site for safety hazards. If necessary, take steps to avoid or minimize risks of injuries.
10. Take notes on what and how to introduce the AIG to your players, including:

   - The narrative and context;
   - The actual challenge and goal;
   - Rules and consequences;
   - Resources allowed or given;
   - Safety measures.

To give this list a little more substance, some of these steps will now be given a closer look.

Working with Handicaps

A feature frequently applied to initiative games is the use of handicaps. This means that single persons or the entire group is deprived of a certain straightforward means of communication or action. The objective of using handicaps is to a) direct the group's line of thinking or b) increase the degree of difficulty presented by the game. Following is a list of examples, but there is no restriction to the creativity of the game designers.

- One or all players are blind (folded) during part of or the entire game (see Figure 7.3). This calls for exact verbal descriptions, responsibility for the blind persons and heightened sensitivity in general.

Figure 7.3 Many AIGs use handicaps such as being blindfolded

- Speaking is prohibited throughout the activity. However, non-verbal interaction is encouraged to entice experimentation with alternative ways of communication.
- The group has to start acting immediately without a planning phase. Thereby, stress and the risk of mistakes or unfortunate strategies is increased.
- Hands or legs of players are bound together (e.g. left foot of person A with right foot of person B), which draws attention away from the original task and also forces them physically to cooperate.
- All group members have to take part in the activity in one way or another. This way, no one can be singled out or can evade participation.
- Time pressure can be introduced by a fixed termination time or through the game master (e.g. urging on, yelling, letting a clock tick away loudly). This increases stress immensely, forcing the group to (inter)act more efficiently in order to succeed.
- Each person or subgroup is given only parts of the full picture or necessary information. Thereby, communication among the sub-groups is a crucial aspect.
- Some object relevant to the frame story has to be carried along throughout the activity. This hindrance can require increased cooperation and also be used as a metaphor in a consecutive reviewing phase.

- The area of movement or action is restricted, or distinct areas are allotted for certain phases of the game.
- The players have to stay in permanent physical contact to a) each other or b) certain pieces of material, which creates again a need for closer interaction and cooperation or simply a hindrance that needs to be overcome through strategic thinking and acting.
- And others. Be creative.

Dealing with the Violation of Rules

An aspect not to be neglected in the planning and presentation of an AIG is to consider what should happen if one of the game's rules is violated – either purposefully or accidentally. This issue is of importance since unintentional mishaps such as touching a sacred zone can occur at any time. After all, if there was zero risk of crossing a line, the game would be boring and far from being a suitable challenge for the group. A rule that does not provoke a consequence when broken is not a rule worth establishing. Therefore we have to define appropriate consequences for such accidents or voluntary trespasses. Here are a few suggestions to trigger ideas for the game designer:

- In a planning phase, the group is to decide itself a) when exactly a rule is considered broken (e.g. at every contact or every other) and b) which consequence should follow.
- For each mistake, one participant receives a handicap. To avoid punishing the less talented or agile, this should not be the same player who happened to break the rule.
- The group loses one piece of material per trespass. Additionally: When the group finds that it needs extra material, the players can bargain for them with the facilitator. What they offer in exchange (a time limit, handicap or whatever – the players are encouraged to be creative) has to be accepted by the entire group as well as the trainer.
- One extra object has to be carried around.
- The allowed time frame is shortened by 1 minute each time.
- The group has to go back part of the already covered distance.
- The entire game starts over.
- A certain number of mistakes is allowed before consequences start.

If a programme or event is comprised of a series of initiative games, it is best to alter the choice of consequence to keep the process active and intriguing.

Whichever consequence is chosen, it has to be explicitly named – or bargained over – at the start of the activity to avoid the sense of injustice when participants experience unexpected and seemingly arbitrary 'punishments' from the trainer. Such situations could result in an antagonism between facilitator and participants and distract from the original objectives. This would strongly contradict the facilitator's purpose and role.

The Facilitator's Role

What is our purpose as facilitator of AIGs? Ignoring the basic outdoor trainer's liking to be portrayed as smart, adventurous and cool, we have to realize that our job is to act purely as human catalysts, helping the players and groups to reach *their* objectives as closely as possible. And just as broadly as the goals may vary, as diverse is the repertoire of actions and interventions that the facilitator can employ in order to support the players' learning process. Following are three of these functions for illustration.

Safety Manager

Even with adult groups, the facilitator holds the main responsibility for the players' physical as well as psycho-social safety. He or she needs to have a watchful eye on the activity, and must spot dangers early and eliminate or divert them as appropriate.

Especially in natural surroundings, we cannot guarantee 100 per cent safety. And we would not want to do that, since a certain amount of real-life risk is considered an essential momentum for the learning process in experiential education.

However, to prevent injuries, we are in need of a simple but effective safety management plan, and my *SimpleSecurity* model, shown in Table 7.1, allows

Table 7.1 *The SimpleSecurity model*

Up:	• *Can anything or anybody fall down (e.g. from a newly created construction)?*
	• *Is the weather risky (hypothermia, heatstroke, dehydration, etc.)?*
Down:	• *What is the ground/floor like (slippery, uneven, covered with dips or roots, etc.)?*
	• *Are objects lying around that could cause accidents (chairs, backpacks, etc.)?*
Inside:	• *Is any material used that holds special risks (scissors, knives, flammable materials, etc.)?*
	• *Could any material or piece of equipment be strained to its limits (ropes, chairs, boards, etc.)?*
Out:	• *Are the players physically apt for the planned game (weather-proof jackets, ability to lift someone up, etc.)?*
	• *Are the players psycho-socially apt for the planned game (age, cognitive ability to detect and avoid dangers, etc.)?*

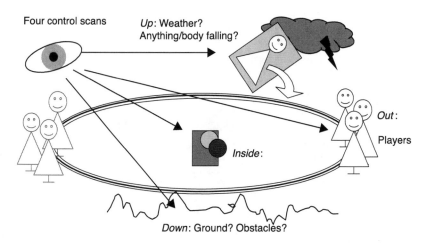

Figure 7.4 Four control scans to prevent accidents

just that: with four simple scans we can approximate a high degree of safety for our participants (see Figure 7.4).

This is just one patch in a compound safety net. Others include medical checks conducted at the beginning of programmes, emergency strategies and first aid skills.

Nevertheless, we encourage the players to exercise self-responsibility. Two ways to do this explicitly are a) to ask for a safety scheme or manager set up by the group, and b) introduce guardian angels, e.g. in activities with blind-folded players, who silently intervene to prevent accidents.

The Game Master

The way we introduce an AIG has great influence on how well the players engage in the game. Good preparation, some experience and a knack for acting can jump-start a frame story and ignite the social and problem-solving process in the players.

Once the game is running and the rules are clarified, the facilitators try to make themselves 'invisible' by situating themselves where they can observe and hear the participants clearly but preferably are noticed little in return. Also, they should abstain from chatting with players in order to not distract the attention of the group. After all, the game is directed towards the group interaction, while the facilitators' function merely is to *facilitate* the process. Therefore, they should reduce their (inter)actions to those that seem to serve this purpose. This includes *not* giving hints on how to solve the task. The problem-solving process is an essential part of social learning!

Reviewing

When the game is finished and the quest accomplished – or not! – there are several ways to proceed. One is to engage a reviewing phase (see Figure 7.5), which strives to filter out the essential learning insights of the game and refine them for future applicability.

Unfortunately, the standard reviewing session of many trainers consists merely of a verbal discussion with little focus and structure, which turns out tedious and of minimum effectiveness: a sharp contrast to the fun and excitement of the previous game. However, there are a few tricks for reviewing an activity in a smooth continuation of the action to harness the energetic flow of the game and bolster the learning outcomes.

- Don't get lost in details of what has just happened. Remember, the purpose is to process the experience for future use. Therefore, work with an explicit or implicit three-step-structure:

  1. *What?* Briefly look at what happened. Direct the attention by giving a clear focus (see below).
  2. *So what?* Summarize, prioritize and define the group's essential lessons learned.
  3. *Now what?* Turn to the future. Based on steps one and two, what altered behaviour, strategy or else does the group want to attempt in the future? If necessary, create means of support to implement this change (e.g. a stop sign raised when discussion rules are ignored again).

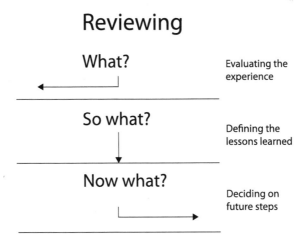

Figure 7.5 A classical three-step-structure for a reviewing session

- Although an AIG usually provides a plethora of noteworthy aspects to focus on, choose one or two at the most and address these with one concise question or input. This improves effectiveness and efficiency.
- The duration of a reviewing session should be of reasonable length in comparison to the game. This is especially important for purely verbal reviewing methods.
- Get the players into physical action also during the reviewing phase. Action and interaction is a lot more engaging than pure sit-and-discuss sessions.
- Re-use or include the constructions or materials used in the game. This way, the transition is more fluid and the players' experiences and emotions are already linked to them.
- Many games or parts of games hold great potential for metaphorical interpretations. By offering a double meaning to the physical activity the players have just exposed, these *interactive metaphors* can have a strong learning impact with little need for words.
- Even the greatest reviewing technique will turn boring when used too often. To avoid this, alternate your methods, content focus and social constellations (single persons, partners, small groups, plenary) during a multi-game session.

This way, you can lift some of the treasures unearthed by the AIG in regard to social and personal growth.

Roger Greenaway has to be mentioned alongside this subject, since he has become an expert in active reviewing, and his homepage (www.reviewing.co.uk) provides (free of charge) a generous selection of practical methods and ideas.

A Practical Example

To put some life to the previous theoretical elaborations, an example of an AIG is presented here that incorporates quite a few of the mentioned features. However, it should be regarded merely as an illustration of one possible implementation and not a description of how it is run in general!

Goals and Preparations

Let us have the players be a team of technicians in an international IT company. Their objectives are a) to improve the efficiency of their communication and interaction and b) to strengthen their team spirit. Within a one-day course, the trainer selects the game *Pedestrian Crossing* because it appears suitable in regard to the topics hidden in it, its level of difficulty and chosen narrative.

In order to play it, the trainer seeks out an obstacle at approximately chest height – in this case a hedge row – that is easily accessible from several sides.

The surrounding ground is checked and found even, free of obstacles (such as chairs or other shrubs) and not slippery. Also the trainer has come up with at least one way to solve the challenge with the material available in the surrounding.

Presenting the Task

Since the group has already done some activities today, there is no need for a general introduction and start-up session, and the facilitator can address the players immediately within the narrative frame:

Welcome, ladies and gentlemen, to our city council's building department! It's great that we could employ your renowned company, *Big'n'Large Constructions*, for this prestige project. If you look here, you can see the new motorway [hedge] about which the inhabitants of this district have complained so much. Living quarters on the one side, shopping centres on the other. And no bridge or subway in sight! So yes, there was a planning mistake and we want you to change that by building a fancy new pedestrian crossing!

Here are the details of your contract [rules]:

- It is entirely up to you to choose and supply the building material.
- Neither people nor material may get into direct contact with the 'road' [hedge].
- At least one test passenger must cross your final construction in order to prove its stability.
- The traffic noise is so loud that verbal communication among your team will unfortunately be impossible while someone is on the bridge.
- Also, since the bridge needs to be safe on dark nights as well, the test person will be blind, i.e. blind-folded for the crossing.
- Before your 'dummy' tests the bridge for the first time, you have to ask this department (i.e. me!) to approve your structure.
- For any enquiries during your work I am at your disposal.

During the game (see Figure 7.6), the facilitator needs to keep a close eye on safety, since even adults can get carried away in an AIG and lose their common sense of dangers. Obviously, the team's safety management plan is checked critically, and if necessary altered.

Once the team has successfully passed the bridge's test by safely crossing a person over, they are congratulated by the trainer, their 'beautifully designed' bridge is admired and predicted to increase the city's architectural fame far

Figure 7.6 Constructing a foot bridge over a busy motorway

across the national borders and the cheque is promised to be sent the following week. If any of the other players wish to test the bridge, they are welcome to do so (all safety rules still applying!).

And finally, the players are ushered away within the narrative and re-welcomed as their real life-identities.

Reviewing

The group is introduced to a metaphor that is physically linked to their structure by labelling various parts with large coloured notecards:

- "What is the most dangerous or imminent obstacle your team has to face at work?" (sticking the card "Obstacle" to the hedge)
- "Which personal abilities, institutional structures, or other aids could you activate to help you overcome this obstacle?" ("Aids" → bridge)
- "Who are your secret or known guardian angles in this struggle?" ("Guardian angels"/"Human supporters" → place where team members stood during the test)

Each notecard has a different colour and after this intro, the group is split into pairs who discuss the presented questions and collect answers for each. These are written onto notecards of the respective colour and laid or stuck to their master card and discussed in the plenary. The need for further processing activities might arise from here.

It Works! – Empirical Evidence

The study on AIGs in a school context was conducted in a secondary school in the city of Bremen, Germany, as a PhD project of the Ludwig Maximilians University (CMU), of Munich, Germany (Hildmann, 2010). The main research question was to what extent AIGs could be effectively introduced into an everyday classroom setting and could promote social and personal skills while delivering regular curriculum contents (see, for example, Figure 7.7). A qualitative experiment was designed using a mixed-method set-up with questionnaires, interviews and other methods. Additionally, ten single case studies were conducted, aiming at a more in-depth look at the strengths and weaknesses of this approach.

The evaluation of the data clearly indicated that employing AIGs in regular school lessons has a positive effect on a range of social and personal skills in the students as a group and as individuals:

- Students became more active and involved in the lessons.
- The social climate among the students improved.
- Communication grew more open and positive.
- Attention span and motivation grew.
- Cooperative interaction increased.

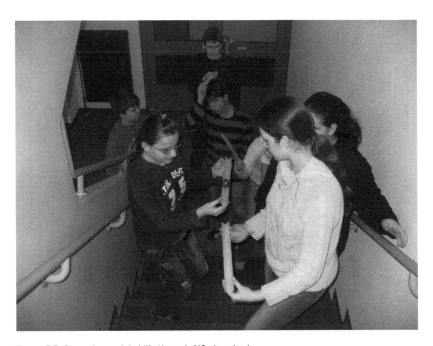

Figure 7.7 Promoting social skills through AIGs in school

- Group communication became more effective and orderly.
- Quiet students contributed more to the class action and shared their ideas.
- Endurance and frustration tolerance improved in most students.

This covered short term as well as medium term (six months follow-up) improvement.

From the teachers' point of view, initiative games can be connected to curriculum contents with little or no demand to material, locality or time budget. Also, all teachers agreed that the approach should be implemented more broadly in schools. Yet, to achieve this, some practical and institutional conditions would have to be met as well as suitable training courses administered.

For more details on the study and the full test results see Hildmann (2010).

Conclusion

Adventure initiative games are a good and healthy method of training or education and there is a plethora of well-tried initiative games to choose from for various settings and age groups. With the simple steps presented in this chapter, new initiative games can even be designed from scratch or customised for specific groups, topics or contexts.

If implemented and facilitated skillfully, they hold great potential for educational objectives in the area of personality growth and social competence and AIGs are often made use of in experiential education programmes.

Obviously, AIGs can also be played simply as social games and for good fun. However, in order to reap their full educational potential, a lot more goes into an AIG than just adventurous narratives and group challenges. The facilitator needs to have a broad scope of methods and intervention forms at their command to choose appropriate games, know when and how to intervene, counsel crises constructively and develop efficient reviewing activities to continuously support the learning process of the players. So in order to use AIGs as a serious training tool, facilitators are advised to take courses in soft skills and other issues constituting the Experiential Education Approach.

References

CEP Centre for Experiential Education and Pedagogics Volkersberg (eds) (2013). *Simple Things – Adventure Initiative Games with Everyday Means*. Bad Brückenau, Germany: CEP Press (unpublished reader).

Gass, M. (1993). *Adventure Therapy: Therapeutical Applications of Adventure Programming*, Dubuque, IO: Kendall & Hunt.

Gilsdorf, R. & Kistner, G. (2001). *Kooperative Abenteuerspiele 2*. Seelze-Velber, Germany: Kallmeyer.

Gilsdorf, R. & Kistner, G. (2003). *Kooperative Abenteuerspiele 1. Praxishilfe für Schule, Jugendarbeit und Erwachsenenbildung*, Seelze-Velber, Germany: Kallmeyer.

Heckmair, B. & Michl, W. (2004). *Erleben und Lernen. Einführung in die Erlebnispädagogik.* Munich, Germany: Reinhardt.

Hildmann, J. (2008). SimpleThings. Erlebnispädagogik mit Alltagsgegenständen. *Erleben & lernen*, 3/4, 45–47.

Hildmann, J. (2010). *Probleme sind verkleidete Möglichkeiten. Kompetenzförderung durch Erlebnispädagogik im Unterricht.* [*Problems are Chances in Disguise. Promotion of Competences through Experiential Education in the Classroom.*] Dissertational Thesis at the Ludwigs-Maximilians-University Munich, Germany. Available: http://edoc.ub.uni-muenchen.de/12312/1/Hildmann_Jule.pdf (accessed 12 January 2013).

Hildmann, J. & Moseley, A. (2012). Metaphern und Rahmengeschichten – mit Bildersprache Brücken bauen [Metaphors and Narrative Frames – Building Bridges through Images]. In Ferstl, A., Scholz, M. & Thiesen, C. (eds) *Einsam und gemeinsam – sich und Menschen begegnen.* Augsburg, Germany: Ziel, pp. 216–225.

Kolb, D.A. (1984). *Experiential Learning: Experience as the Source of Learning and Development.* Englewood Cliffs, NJ: Prentice Hall.

König, S. & König, A. (2002). *Outdoor-Teamtrainings. Von der Gruppe zum Hochleistungsteam.* Augsburg, Germany: Ziel.

Rehm, M. (1999). Evaluationen erlebnispädagogischer Programme im englischsprachigen Raum. Eine Übersicht über 65 Studien. In: Paffrath, F.H., Salzmann, A. and Scholz, M. (eds.) *Wissenschaftliche Forschung in der Erlebnispädagogik. Tagung Hochschulforum Erlebnispädagogik*, 14 November 1998, Ziel, Augsburg, 153–172.

Reiners, A. (2003). *Praktische Erlebnispädagogik. Neue Sammlung motivierender Interaktionsspiele.* Augsburg, Germany: Ziel.

Rohnke, K. (1989). *Cowstails and Cobras II: A Guide to Games, Initiatives, Ropes Courses, & Adventure Curriculum*, Dubuque, IO: Kendall & Hunt.

Rohnke, K. & Butler, S. (1995). *Quicksilver. Adventure Games, Initiative Problems, Trust Activities and a Guide to Effective Leadership*, Dubuque, IO: Kendall & Hunt.

Silberman, M. (ed.) (2007). *The Handbook of Experiential Learning.* San Francisco, CA: Pfeiffer.

Sonntag, C. (2002). *Abenteuer Spiel – Handbuch zur Anleitung kooperativer Abenteuerspiele.* Augsburg, Germany: Ziel.

8

AN ARTIST'S APPROACH TO BOARD GAMES

SAM INGLESON, UNIVERSITY OF SALFORD, UK

This case study focuses on the development of board games within an arts educational context and looks at how methods of generating creative content and reflective practice within the board game mechanics can be adapted to other subject areas. I will discuss three board games: *Proposal*, a game that encourages players to evidence their creative processes; *Student Life*, a game aimed at new students from all subject areas as an induction to the university; and *Studio Practice*, a board game designed to be played by first-year undergraduate art students that reflects aspects of studio culture at university and encourages idea generation and peer group working. These games have been created over a number of years and ideas from the first game informed the subsequent games.

Introduction

Proposal was conceived and created during my Masters study in Contemporary Fine Art and reflects some of my own learning and an awareness of the challenges and barriers faced by peers in translating their creative habits to satisfy vocational and professional criteria as distinct from educational assessments. I wanted to design and develop a board game that would visually evidence an individual's (my own) learning. I was concentrating on curriculum design but from the students' point of view. Having re-entered education after being a practicing artist I struggled with the concept of needing to visually evidence and reflect on the processes relevant to the creation of artwork. The act of evidencing for assessment purposes – how, for example, I take inspiration from objects found in junk shops, and then develop stories from these objects – seemed to run counter to the idea of creating through a process-led approach. However, in order to respond to the learning outcomes of the course modules, and pass them, this was required. So the origins of my interest in board game design was informed by an existing appreciation of the aesthetic look of board games combined with an understanding that game mechanics could help to highlight and contextualise my understanding of my own creative processes.

What I have found to be important is the presence of such a contestation, a diversity of contextual norms that provide multiple or optional scenarios and, therefore, choices that empower participants. From these origins it has become clear that the performative dimension of games has the potential to empower players and can create unpredictability and devious behaviour. The game situation is an ideal platform for opening up relationships that are immediately both challenging and positive. My more recent experiences have been primarily concerned with this aspect of relinquishing authority in the educator/learner relationship and developing peer interaction to better encourage open mutual exchange.

I have a large collection of vintage board games, bought mainly for their visual appeal, and it was these that I used as inspiration when I was looking for creative ways to evidence my learning. At this stage, game mechanics and playability were not considerations. I was not planning on having people play the 'game'; I was merely using the format as a visual map to house a large amount of information about my working methods. Whilst working within the established visual expectations of a board games appearance, I could introduce various concepts and themes running through my arts practice. These themes included perceptions of scale, multiples, appropriation of found objects and a love of 1950s and 1960s packaging. However, once I started to develop the areas on the board I realized that in order for tutors assessing the work to understand my processes they would have to play the game. It was at this stage I began to consider the game within a wider context of its audience and players. Whilst this was a game about me (because of its context within the structure of my Masters Programme) I realised I could use this format to model a creative approach to idea generation and reflection that may be relevant to other artists. My approach to game design was as an artist and not as an educator looking to use games to enhance teaching and learning.

Proposal Board Game

The aim of the game *Proposal* was for each player to collect various artist research cards, and from these to develop a proposal for an artwork, with the best idea being selected by the players democratically in order to select the winner. The game is played in two stages. In the first stage players are each given an Artists' Brief – for example, 'write a proposal for a new Public Art Piece taking inspiration from the cards collected.' This involves players moving around the board collecting specific artist's research in the form of playing cards. Cards featuring objects I have bought and that have personal significance can be collected at the secondhand shop (see Figure 8.1). Cards housed in the library and the gallery respectively featured quotes and theories that were an influence on my arts practice. In this way I am still present via representation in the 'live' game. Players can move into different zones (e.g. the artists' studio

Figure 8.1 Examples of cards and objects found on the board

or the pub) to collect other cards or call fellow players together for discussion or time-outs that occur in real time during the game.

Stage 1 allows the player to randomly generate source material on a topic – in this case "The influences of artist Sam Ingleson". However if you keep the board layout and game structure and replace the content with alternate source material then you have a system of collecting a random set of primary resources that can be used within the game to generate peer discussions and player engagement with the cards (primary research) as they generate ideas and content in response to the stimulus.

Stage 2 requires the players to reflect on gathered material and use this to respond to their artists' brief. Each player reviews the cards collected and their own notes taken during the game to propose an idea for a new artwork. All players must then discuss the merits of each proposal and, as a curatorial panel, come to a group consensus as to the 'best' proposal. This should be based on the quality of the proposal as well as evidence that the collected research had fed into the final proposal. This is a fairly arbitrary process, although one that echoes the tastes and judgements of any arts judging panel. Through peer assessment the player with the best proposal is deemed the winner. This process can be extended into a third stage that moves away from the board game format and involves a physical studio-based realisation of artworks. This is the stage where the game becomes more focused as a teaching tool and moves away from the recognised board game format. The game becomes part of a blended reality and extends beyond 'play time'.

Through the act of devising the rules and functionality of the game, my focus moved away from the manipulation of the board game structure, to an interest in the social interaction between players. What happens once a game has been invented and is open to players' interpretation of the rules? How are the changes captured and how do rules become a shared knowledge within communities? I wanted a way to focus the interaction between players during the playing of *Proposal* and decided to invite a group of strangers (to each other and myself) to play the game in front of an invited audience. By inviting an audience, the playing of the game would become performative and each player's actions would be imbued with a sense of theatre. The players were selected through an application process after an advert was placed on an arts jobs website. The advert asked for participants with an interest in board games who would be willing to take part in a performance. Six players were selected via email, from forty applicants. They were sent the rules the week before, but had not seen the board, met myself or each other prior to commencement of the game. I had no idea whether the players would turn up to play the game; five out of the six selected players attended and took part in the performance (see Figure 8.2).

Figure 8.2 Playing proposal

During the performance of *Proposal* the participants played for three hours and their actions were filmed. Over the course of the evening an audience of approximately 50 people observed the game being played, with some audience members witnessing the complete performance. The game was played in the 1830s Warehouse, a listed building that forms part of the Museum of Science and Industry (MOSI) in Manchester, England. The audience ascended a glass lift to an open plan darkened space, where the board game was set out on a table illuminated by stage lighting. The players were seated around the table, each wearing numbered bibs, their identities remaining anonymous to the audience. A camera was fitted above the board to film the actions taking place on the board and this footage was relayed live back to a TV screen in the same room. Members of the audience were able to walk around the players and study their actions. Audience members did not receive any instruction on how they should behave in the space, but none of them interfered with the playing of the game or conversed directly with the players. The players ignored the audience and communicated only with each other.

In order for the audience to follow the progress of the game, players had to log their creative thoughts each time they collected a new piece of research or visual imagery. These thoughts were written on individual player blackboards placed around the edges of the gaming table, meaning that the players had to leave the private space of the board to write on the blackboards. Written reflections ranged from appreciation of imagery to identifying parallels with their own arts practice. As all of the players were artists or poets they accepted and probably found this instruction easier to carry out than players without formal arts training may have done. This immediate creative response was shared publicly via the blackboards, referencing traditional pedagogy; however the players could have equally posted comments via a social media network such as Twitter. The players then utilized these reflections in Stage 2 of the game to influence their written proposals.

The game can support and even generate complex relationships focused on content with an almost immediate impact. The players had to contend with a number of different factors: understanding and responding to the rules of a new game; playing a game with strangers; taking part in a performance as opposed to playing the game within a private setting; and giving input and commitment to a game where fellow players and audience could pry on their creative thought processes. Each player received £30 in expenses for playing the game and this may have been one factor in the level of commitment they all showed to progressing with the game. Being part of a performance may have been more of a challenge to some of the players than others, although all knew it would be played live before accepting the offer.

As an observer, it was interesting seeing how each player interpreted the rules and how they came to a communal consensus on how they would interpret rules that they did not fully understand. I imagined that they would skip sections, or make up their own rules, but they generally stuck to the constraints. As with other board games I am sure that with the assimilation of the rules and familiarity with the game, this would develop with a number of plays. At this point the players would be more likely to adopt their own communities version of the established rules.

In terms of playing approach, all five players submitted a proposal; two collaborated producing a less serious or less considered list of responses to the artists' brief while the other three players produced something more like a conventional proposal for an artwork. One player whose influences and approach was most similar to my own produced a genuinely interesting proposal that could have been worked up to an artwork. Because of a similar background history in community engagement through the arts, it is difficult to know if her proposal was genuinely the 'best' or if simply it more closely aligned to something I may have suggested. All the players were using my imagery and frames of reference to build ideas from so there were bound to be some ideas that felt like my own.

There are three didactic outcomes arising from the creation of this game. First, it evidenced my own arts processes, which was pertinent to my Masters enquiry and was the original aim of making the game. The second outcome was the creation of ideas and fresh enquiry by the players, through their own critical interaction with the board content. Finally, the process of playing the game requires reflection at various stages and culminates in a written proposal that can be taken away and worked up away from the game. It is this legacy of idea stimulation and adoption away from the board that I want to pick up on in the final part of this chapter.

Board Games and Teaching

Since the initial board game was created I have gone back into teaching within the HE sector and have become interested in how board games can be used as a learning device. I am particularly interested in the peripheral conversations that take place while playing a board game. Playing a new game means that all the players have to learn the rules and explore the board together. This is a way of bringing new students together to meet and ask general questions related to the board content (in the next example, university study) and get to know each other. Looking back over *Proposal* the key elements that I believe were worth taking forward into a new game were:

- *Starting with a brief* – giving each player an individual brief that involves not only collecting cards on the board but then instructing the player to put forward a new narrative based on the information found on the cards and their own creativity.

- *The zones* – themed areas of the board where specific content can be housed (The Library & The Second Hand Shop).
- *Discussion areas* – areas on the board that require players to enter and bring other players in to talk through ideas (The Pub).
- *Players deciding between themselves who is the winner* – all players responded creatively to their briefs and read out their responses to each other. Having discussed the merits of each proposal a winner was decided democratically, thus representing a version of self-assessment and a model of peer-to-peer assessment within a teaching context.

Student Life Board Game

Having identified the key areas I wanted to use, I wanted initially to create a game that would be a fairly inclusive representation of what it was like to be a new student at university, moving around areas of the campus collecting cards that would highlight different teaching styles and learning experiences. The Student Life Staff Team had been keen on having a game that could be used during Freshers' week (the induction week for new students) to orient students around the campus, so this became my focus.

I devised a game whereby players needed to find accommodation, sort out their finances, make friends and successfully complete a module of study over a 14–week semester. Colleagues were enthusiastic with the idea of having a bespoke board game and came up with ideas as to what information should be covered. As conversations developed, colleagues became more specific as to what should be represented and each area began to be divided into subsections. The idea that players (new students) could pick up information that they could take away with them as they moved around the board was particularly appealing. Cards that players collected featured useful information about where to get advice on study skills, for example. Having staff collaborate was helpful; however, getting the balance between imparting information and designing a game that students wanted to play was becoming hard due to the amount of information I had to fit in to the game.

The aim of the *Student Life* board game is to successfully complete a semester of study, collecting teaching experiences and undertaking activities along the way in order to pass your module. Players have briefs that guide them through the board in the form of *Learning Module Handbooks*. A facilitator from the Student Life Department oversees the game; the facilitator stays with the game during play and acts as adjudicator. The facilitator takes in to consideration each player's combination of module marks, research and extra-curricula activities and decides which player is the winner.

In the previous game, *Proposal* players were required to roll a dice and move a number of squares in order to land in an area where you could collect cards and perform further actions. This meant that some of the game was taken up by the act of moving towards an area of the board rather than engaging with the cards and discussions. I created a spinner that randomly selected areas of the board to move to, in order to speed up movement across the board. I wanted students to understand the time scale of a semester, so I created a Semester Timetable Indicator that set out the semester into 12 weeks with each round being one week of study. The indicator also mapped specific activity such as assessment hand-in dates. This, combined with the spinner and instructions on individual cards, enabled players to visit all sections of the board over the course of the game. As opposed to restrictive rules, the navigation is designed to highlight permissions or options for the player to lead or take control on decisions, solutions or interactive conversations.

The board comprises of areas that house different cards and visual props. Areas include *Accommodation, Student Life, Clubs & Societies, Research, Student Union Bar* and *Learning Environment* cards. All the cards feature either a positive or negative experience and score a number of points. Players could swap and discard cards with lower scores in order to achieve the highest score for the module assessment and win the game. As well as visiting the bar during the game in order to be social, the bar provides an area for players to swap cards in order to get the best and highest scoring match for their *Learning Module Handbooks*. Players need to check that they have enough money to carry on with the game and most visit the cash machine. The cards in this area feature a QR code that the players access to find out their bank balance. If they have no money they need to miss a turn in the game and get a part-time job. Within the mechanics of the game, the cards' purpose is to impart information, enable the players to gain points and work towards collecting a set of cards as indicated by the initial brief.

The game introduced a facilitator role, a member of staff able to guide students and answer questions or expand on issues raised by the cards. The facilitator also takes into consideration each player's combination of module marks, research and extra-curricular activities collected and, in discussion with all players, adjudicates on identifying a winner. Facilitating the game enables the member of staff to introduce university terminology and regulations while getting to know the students in an informal situation. Students are equally able to ask questions and clarify their understanding of university procedures or locations as well as having someone to help with smooth playing of the game.

Playtesting the Game

Staff from the Student Life Team playtested the game in prototype version and through this playing it emerged that the game was trying to replicate the student experience in too much detail. It was felt that for the target audience of students dropping by during Freshers' week, the game should be completed in a short time scale. The game was shortened to a six-week period of study (six rounds) with less emphasis on the collection of the Learning Environment cards. The focus of the game was pulled back to what is important to know in the first few weeks of study. While tutors want students to identify good teaching experiences and recognize that teaching and learning can happen in a number of different ways other than 'Lectures', it was enough to introduce these concepts on a much smaller scale. Therefore, *Learning Module Handbooks* were revised to collect three cards each. An additional area of the board tutorials where the player could talk with the facilitator about cards collected was scrapped from this version of the game (but would be picked back up in the later game *Studio Culture*). This was because the game had to work for students across different programmes of study, therefore the teaching content had to be generic: so, for example, a teaching card would refer to 'A good lecture' rather than a real-life scenario from a specific subject. It was felt that the facilitator's role should be left in to advise during play and lead discussions among the players at the end of the game.

The latest version of *Student Life* is much shorter and has been tested by a number of existing students who enjoyed playing it, and it will be used during Freshers' week from 2013. From a game designer's point of view, however, it feels too generic with the focus on collecting information and experiences rather then generating new material through discussion and interaction. This experience made me realise that I prefer to make games that are designed for a smaller target audience so that the game can be tailored to generate more focused responses from players. The university Student Life directorate through the collaboration had adopted the role of commissioner or client and as such designed itself as an intermediary and controlling role in both the design and execution of this game. My current thoughts are focused on the relationship I have as a designer and educator with the actual client, the participants. I need to consider to what extent I can design board games to develop a dialogue between the players and myself through interaction with the board, as well as between players during the game.

Studio Culture

I decided that in order to design a game that would function as a useful tool for my own teaching, I would have to design it around the specific needs of my own students, Undergraduate Visual Art Students in their first year of study. The students are provided with a shared studio space, given a number of studio briefs to work toward over a 12-week period and access to workshops and tutorials; however, a large part of each week is taken up with independent making and enquiry. As staff contact time in the studio is limited, I wanted to create a game that would offer semi-structured support and inspiration that would complement the more traditional teaching that currently takes place.

I had the two previous games from which I could adapt elements for the new *Studio Culture* game. I incorporated Accommodation and Student Union Bar from the *Student Life* game as both impact on student engagement in the studio; however, the main focus would be on the players discussing and adding their own experiences to the board as demonstrated in the original *Proposal* game. While *Proposal* was all about one person's creative approaches and influences, this game needed to be flexible and wide ranging enough to have content that would be useful and motivating for students with many different interests within the visual arts. The students were also still fairly new to university life, its structures and terminology, so I wanted to incorporate some elements of the *Student Life* game, as long as they didn't interfere with the main focus and game mechanics. The aim of the *Studio Culture* game is for players to create ideas for generating artwork (that could be worked up in the real studio after playing the board game) through learning how to work in a studio, carry out research, record and reflect on ideas and share ideas through group debate.

The previous game, *Student Life*, had been too prescriptive with a specific end point factored in due to the time restraints of players. This game did not need a winner or a point in the game where play was officially over, although a winner could be awarded via peer review if players wished. In the previous game I had introduced the facilitator to help direct discussions and expand on information. This was a factor I was still interested in developing as it provides a focus for a tutor to join in with the game and add to discussions and scaffold the experience. However, the facilitator does not need to be a tutor; the role would be equally well suited to a fellow student who enjoys taking part in discussions around art.

Building and Sharing Content

I wanted players not only to discuss and get inspiration from cards on the board but to also be able to generate their own content, creating their own cards to be added to the packs. This content could be created while playing the game or added to the board at a later date. The board looks similar in layout to the previous games in that the board is split into areas; however, the largest area, the studio, takes priority and is where the majority of play takes place. The studio area on the board has three walls and a large table, reflecting the real studio. On the walls are miniature drawings and artifacts. A player entering the studio has two choices: they can select an *Idea* card or a *Work in Progress* card.

The *Idea* card will suggest an activity that they can undertake to generate experiments within their practice, for example: "Using one of your own images, generate multiple copies of this image. Organise the copies into different layouts and consider the size of the reproductions". The player can try out this idea away from the game and, if pleased with the results of this experimentation, can contribute a card depicting the new image to the physical game as a *Work In Progress* card and to the *Studio Culture* game blog.

Work In Progress cards depict current students' visual ideas and experiments, and selecting one of these cards is an opportunity to discuss the idea or the method of production with fellow players. While this is a good way of seeing what fellow students are doing it also directly supports 'Group Crits' whereby students are required to be able to critically engage with and comment upon other students' work. Many students struggle with this and tutors often dominate these sessions due to lack of student input. By making this part of the board game I hope to build the students' confidence within the realm of the game and then transfer this learning to the actual studio. The facilitator may join in these discussions but the players must lead the debate.

The *Studio Culture* blog (http://www.tumblr.com/blog/studioculturegame) functions as a way of recording the history of the game as it is being played. In *Proposal*, players were required to write down thoughts on blackboards after picking up a card. This open, reflective process has been transferred to tumblr in order to reach a larger audience and develop a game play archive. During the game players post their thoughts and ideas to the *Studio Culture* blog and later they can post images and reflections that have come about as a result of playing the game. This provides a potential resource for all students across all three levels of the Visual Arts Programme. The blog can potentially attract a wider audience of viewers who have never played the game but are interested in the observations and reflections generated from the playing of the board game. This emphasis on reflective writing addresses the lack of confidence that students currently feel about producing statements about their work at the end of a module. Writing reflectively during game play gives students the opportunity to practice this skill in a situation where they are not being assessed. The writings also function to record the ideas and learning from each game played to create an archive.

Players move across the board using a Spinner; navigation is limited to this and directions issued on cards. Players can visit the Library that houses key texts, significant artists and events of cultural relevance to their level of study. These cards widen a player's knowledge and may pose an idea that has significance to the player's own practice (see Figure 8.3). Library cards can be discussed with fellow players or can form the basis of mini-tutorials with the game facilitator. While the main focus of play is around the studio there are other areas on the board, the pub, the housing area and the local cultural centre that players can visit. Cards can be collected with a mixture of positive and negative scenarios. Blank cards are provided for players to add content to build up a bank of real student experiences.

The game is still in development as a prototype and will require more ongoing support once it is finalised. The blog will need monitoring, new

"To photograph is to appropri...
the thing photographed"
Susan Sontag

When playing a game there is a collective history
of the game (unless it is a new or prototype
game) therefore rules are known
but adopted subconsciously
Games playing is a form of cultural behaviour
and people learn most of their behaviour from
other people not from books.

David Parlett - Thoughts on Rules

Figure 8.3 Examples of library research cards containing quotes

miniature art work will need to be placed in the board game mock studio and a supply of blank cards for students' experiences will need to be kept up to date. This should not require a great deal of time and I will be playing the game with the students as part of my teaching anyway. The game is interactive and as the players (students) adopt the game within their physical studio space it is hoped that they will take control of the game and manipulate or re-engineer the rules in line with the development of their independent learning. It is my intention that the game is blended with other learning and experiences and can be revisited over an extended play period as a focus of reflection and learning. The board game's permanent home in the Level 4 studio will remind students to re-engage with it and create new artworks for the board and blog. Over time it should generate content and ideas about what to learn and how to learn from all constitute parties.

Conclusion

I previously held the enthusiastic opinion that you could make a board game about anything, which in theory you can. However, through trial and error I have realised that this does not necessarily result in an interesting or playable game.

Reflecting on my own experience of board game design has led me to understand that I am interested in a specific type of board game, one that demands the player to contribute ideas during play. The focus is not on strategy or winning but in developing content for the game in play and for subsequent games. The games form an area for generating and sharing ideas both visually and through discussion.

This approach to game design offers opportunities for other educators to design games around their own subject specialism to facilitate group discussions and enable students to reflect on prior knowledge. If this is something you wish to put into practice, I would advise you to identify a specific group of students (either by year group or by topic) to play the game with, rather than designing for a wider generic audience. In this way you can personalise the design of the board, factoring in classrooms or popular social spaces. Factor in questions or tasks that require players to generate their own cards as part of a larger learning experience (either during game play or prior to the game in a more traditional classroom environment). These cards can then be reused in future games to prompt discussions.

In regards to the actual design of the game, make it look like a 'proper' board game so that students treat the exercise with respect. Invest in some blank cards rather than relying on sticky notes or scraps of paper. Consider what you will use as counters to move around the board; these could be found objects that relate to your subject area. Consider the areas of the board you wish the players to move to, and how these can be personalised. You can incorporate technology into the board game by using QR codes for instance to reveal 'secret answers' or a set-up blog related to the game. However as demonstrated in the earliest game blackboards work just as well for sharing information within the room.

The last piece of advice I would offer is to get started with the game as soon as you think you have an idea. If you think about the game mechanics and strategy too much in the early stages the idea becomes bigger and bigger within your head and becomes too unwieldy to design or play. The game will develop much quicker once you start to prototype and playtest with others. The best way of designing a game would be to do it in collaboration with students. If possible work with students in the year above the group you are targeting and design around their experiences of the topic. In this way those students refresh their own knowledge and help shape their peers' learning via the production of the game.

9

SIMULATION GAME: TAKING THE HORSES TO WATER

IVAR MÄNNAMAA, VILJANDI ACADEMY OF CULTURE,
TARTU UNIVERSITY, ESTONIA

In spring 2010 I was asked to design a simulation game on acculturation. The client was looking for a study-aid for upper-secondary school pupils to enhance their comprehension of inter-cultural integration. The game was intended to be used in regular classroom settings without extensive use of computers or other types of information and communications technology (ICT). In this chapter you will be introduced to the product we ended up with, understand some major steps in the design and discover how we facilitate the game. As the material part of the game is simple, you will be able to prepare a set yourself and test it within your own teaching context.

Context

To introduce the game it is important to outline the context. First, Estonia, although a traditionally mono-cultural country until the Soviet occupation during the Second World War, has a minority population of 30 per cent Russian-speakers today. The integration of different cultural groups has not been as successful as expected due to several reasons – including, but not limited to, different language groups and interpretations of history. The conflict escalated until the Bronze Night in April 2007, with massive riots in Tallinn, including thousands of violent protesters and tens of injured policemen. We had just started to design our game when the German chancellor Angela Merkel announced that the attempt to create a multicultural society had "utterly failed" in Germany. The Utøya massacre took place soon after that. These and other more recent cultural conflicts provide evidence that cultural integration, whether an achievable goal or not, is a topic which should play a significant part in the education of modern society.

Although it is difficult to speak about 'standard' classroom sessions it might be said, that in general, multiculturalism is not a thoroughly covered topic within the official curriculum in Estonia. The national curriculum for higher secondary schools includes classes on civic education, with a syllabus mostly focusing on legislative aspects connected to national structures and principles of governance of the state. Similar to other countries the teachers seem to be overwhelmed with covering the academic curriculum and there is not much time, nor many teaching aids, to introduce cultural topics. Thus I had quite good reason to believe that in spite of the sensitive topic an educational game on cultural integration was a necessary thing to do.

General Design

The design process started with listing the very basic expectations of the client. The crucial role of such clarification of design specifications has been stressed by various authors (Klabbers, 2006; Wenzler, 2009). In brief the requirements we agreed with the client were as follows:

- *General topic:* Acculturation strategies, focusing on integration of ethnic groups with special attention to inclusion of minorities.
- *Purpose of the game:* To raise awareness about cross-cultural issues, and improve knowledge of acculturation processes.
- *Intended audience:* Pupils of age group 14–18.
- *Time:* Maximum 90 minutes, including debriefing.
- *Number of participants:* 18–30 (expected number of students in an average Estonian classroom).
- *Context of use:* As part of the secondary school syllabus of civic education.
- *Technical:* Playable in a regular classroom setting and without major computer support; repeated gameplay possibility.
- *Other:* User-friendly: strong, cheap, quiet, compact, and attractive.

Most of the requirements were actually discussed with the client only after signing the contract. Although design specifications should ideally be agreed before signing any contracts it is useful to remind readers that this process takes some time; therefore it makes sense to devote time to this aspect within the game design timetable. To illustrate this point I shall bring up some of the problematic issues we faced as designers while discussing the feasibility.

First, the number of players appeared to be a much more complicated issue than expected. A group of 30 is very different from the perspective of game design to a group of, say, 18. It is not an easy task to arrange a game for 30 players in a way which achieves and maintains the overall and active participation of all participants. Though the full inclusion of all participants is not always obligatory, it is generally required for a game designed to be used in a regular classroom. Therefore, it became clear that the game should be played in teams: although a teamwork setting allows some participants to stay more passive than others it promotes in-group discussions which provide extra value to the game as an educational tool.

Second, the expected duration of the game was 90 minutes, as a regular school unit in Estonia is 45 minutes. Two consecutive units was the maximum amount the school curriculum could allow for a teacher to conduct the game. At first sight the time might seem sufficient, but it takes around 15 minutes to introduce the game (briefing) and 30 minutes to the post-game discussion (debriefing). Therefore, the game-play itself must fit within a maximum of 45 minutes. Also, one should be aware of any breaks between school units: depending on the game the breaks may or may not be acceptable. It is also important to keep in mind the time required to set up the classroom for game play and vice versa, as the process should not take too much time: a teacher willing to implement the game has no extra time to prepare the venue and clear it up after, as a colleague often steps into the same space a few minutes later.

Third, during recent years the main attention of designers of educational games has been focused on digital games, while traditional table-top simulation games have been somehow neglected. While discussing the issue with the client we ended up with a solution which eliminates all kind of ICT support. There were several reasons for this: mostly from teachers who claimed that a crashing computer is the last thing they want to see in their classroom; and the feeling that students are spending too much time with laptops and smartphones already. Besides that, from the designer's perspective it is obvious that while transforming a regular board game to a digital one is a relatively simple task, reversing the process is often quite impossible. Development of a digital game inherently requires the designer to create tasks which are based on quick processing of univalent data by certain algorithms. While trying to transfer these processes to a non-digital version we immediately face the problem of data ambivalence and unpredictable algorithms. The decision was therefore taken to begin by perfecting gameplay in a traditional game, which could then be converted to digital in the future if required.

Fourth, we arranged a focus group of teachers representing the potential end-users. What they said to us was not surprising, but it set some quite severe limitations on the game format. They announced that a user-friendly educational game should be small – a teacher does not want to see a game which takes much more space than a shoebox. Also, the game-kit should be strong, meaning play-resistant: nobody wants a game which breaks apart in two or three sessions. Game-play should be relatively quiet, i.e. not cause too much noise which could disturb the lesson in a neighbouring classroom. And a user-friendly game should be cheap and attractive-looking. If not, a teacher will not be willing to spend the limited resources they have to purchase it over and above other materials.

By then I had recognized that a single person, however enthusiastic he or she is, would not be able to fulfil the design and development task. I personally did not know enough about the content area, i.e. acculturation theories and systems analysis. Thus a team of four was established for the game design, covering knowledge areas of sociology, mathematics, psychology and education. What I did not know then, is the simple paradox: it is painful to design an efficient game in a team but it is quite impossible to do it alone. If you are going to design in a team then be prepared for endless discussions on the models and types of games to be used as backbones (we started with traditional case-based role-plays and ended up with ideas around ball games and aggregation tasks). On the other hand, if you decide to design a game alone, then there is a danger that you will miss key design aspects and will end up with a product understandable to yourself only.

Prerequisites of Learning

Educational simulation games can provide high levels of motivation and enable students to gain an understanding of constructs which are difficult to handle with traditional methods of teaching (Hofstede *et al.*, 2010; Garris *et al.*, 2002). Cultural integration is a topic fitting to this schema: the construct is quite complex and students should be motivated to participate in the topic. Moreover, although students and teachers do not agree on all issues, they usually share a conviction that teaching methods should be efficient and interesting. While designing our game (which we called *Fountains*) I tried to follow four teaching and learning prerequisites: a game should involve voluntariness, excitement, meaning and development.

Voluntariness is identified as a *sine qua non* play-element by Huizinga in *Homo Ludens* (2001). Still, the requirement that playing the game should be voluntary for each participant is not easy to fulfil in a regular classroom. My assumption is that this is an important if not the crucial reason why educational games often fail: one should probably not expect that all 30 students are willing to play at the same time. If we look closely at the original cat-and-mouse game then it is quite clear that the cat feels voluntariness, excitement, development and, at a larger scale, the meaning. The mouse, probably, has the sense of all the latter three but not the feeling of voluntary participation. This is sufficient reason for us not to describe the process as a game for the mouse. One possible solution to this problem is to arrange classroom-based games in teams: this allows for the inclusion of students who are not willing to take the active role at the very beginning of the game session.

Excitement, according to Caillois (2001), arises from the combination of four potential sources: competition, chance, pretending or vertigo. As our choice was to design a simulation game based on a real – rather than ideal – situation, we decided to go for a game which is based on a tendency to compete. Another option would have been to design a game which encourages all of the playing parties to cooperate with each other, a dilemma which is described well by many authors, e.g. Axelrod (1997) or Johnson and Johnson (1989). Although the latter would also include a situation described as 'group of players against a game' (Salen & Zimmerman, 2003: 250), it was assumed that in real life the ethnic groups typically tend towards competition rather than collaboration as the resources they are looking for are limited.

Meaningfulness has been said to be an essential characteristic of a simulation game which intends to be educational, compared to a game with merely entertainment purposes (Pavlas *et al.*, 2009; Salen & Zimmerman, 2003) Meaning-making refers to the quality of being model-based: an educational game should be based on a more or less validated model of either a real or expected situation. For our needs, the most appropriate model of an acculturation process was that arising from the four-fold acculturation theories, which claim that ethnic groups can favour the dominant culture, their own minority culture, both or neither (Rudmin, 2003). The model of acculturation suggested by John Berry differentiates four acculturation strategies by using two orthogonal dimensions: cultural maintenance and contact-participation (see e.g., Berry, 2007). Our aim was to focus the game on twofold intentions of ethnic groups – the willingness to preserve one's own comprehensive culture and at the same time provide the other groups with access to limited resources, and so Berry's model was the most appropriate for our purpose.

Scale of development refers to the qualities of a game which enhance learning among the participants. Although the discourse of simulation games is largely based on the constructivist approach and problem-based learning in particular (Kiili, 2005; Lainema, 2009), there is still little evidence of how learning takes place in game sessions. For our game we set three preconditions for effective acquiring of knowledge: allowing players to practice and improve their performance in the game; ensuring knowledge could be articulated and shared with other players; and ensuring transferability to real-life situations. Further, in order to design a game that enables understanding of the constructs of cultural integration, we formulated four basic principles of acculturation theories:

1. It is important both to stand by one's beliefs and to find common ground with other parties.
2. Access to resources may improve even if the borderlines between groups remain intact.
3. In case of integration it is important to consider two oppositional processes – the agents' rationality and pragmatic considerations on the one hand and the fears and emotions on the other.
4. The topic of integration is accompanied by various controversies, for instance, between the wish to retain one's original qualities and to gain access to resources.

In the design process we tried to keep in mind that these principles should be testable, articulated and connected to real life by the participants.

Design Elements

We began by searching for case study approaches to use within our game, but soon realised it would be impossible to find cases which have a similar meaning for different students (a story carrying weight with an urban group might hold nothing for a rural group, for example). As contextuality of the experience was one of our key requisites, we therefore looked for a metaphor to use in the game design.

The model we used includes two basic structural components described by the majority of acculturation theories: the cultural sub-groups and the common resources, enabling sustainable development. As our intention was to keep the game materials as simple as possible, we ended up with only two game elements: horses representing the cultural groups and fountains representing the resources (Figure 9.1).

Although our initial idea was to design a colourful and fancy board for the game, we ended up with a solution where no designed board exists. The reason behind this was pragmatic: a board which could be visible to up to 30 players

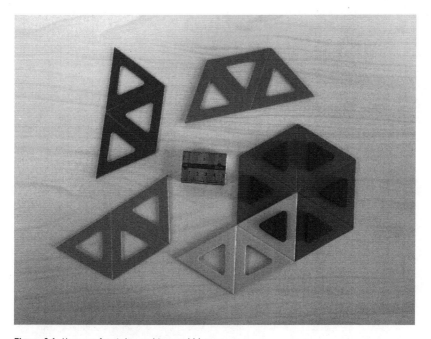

Figure 9.1 Hexagon fountains and trapezoid horses

would be so big that storage and transportation of it would be inconvenient. Therefore, we decided to restrict our design to one which would work on a regular metallic whiteboard: these are available in most classrooms, make the game visible to all pupils, and don't require an extra-large space in the centre of the room. Finally we ended up with only two types of pieces in the game.

Game Pieces

The fountains are hexagon-shaped, 16 cm by diagonal, each side 8 cm. A fountain has a magnet on its back-side and six relief-triangles on the front side, with a height of ~7 mm. They are all of the same colour. Usually 14 fountains are enough but I provide 16, just to be prepared for unexpectedly eager players (sometimes, although the plainland is filled with 12 fountains already, the players want to play a couple more rounds).

Horses are trapezoids, exactly half the size of the hexagon (see Figure 9.2). A horse has three triangle-shaped spaces in it. There are six different colours: red, orange, yellow, green, blue and violet – 18 of each (altogether 6 x 18 = 108 pieces). Usually this is sufficient but based on practice, 4–6 extra neutral (e.g. white) coloured horses which could be used to represent extra pieces of any colour would be useful.

Figure 9.2 Horses positioned to their drinking spots at six fountains

Game Cycle

The macro-cycle of a game as described by Klabbers (2006) includes four basic stages. First, the briefing that includes the introduction and formation of teams, explanation of rules and some time for questions and explanations: depending on the number of participants, this takes 5–15 minutes in the case of *Fountains*. Second, playing the game takes about 50 minutes. The third and fourth stages – reviewing game narratives and conceptualization – take at least 40 minutes and is known as debriefing. Thus, for *Fountains* at least an hour and a half should be reserved for the whole game.

To begin the teacher divides the participants into six groups, each group representing one tribe and forming a team. The easiest way to do this is with the horse game-pieces: each student picks a horse from a pre-set pile and the students with the same colours will form a team. When the teams have gathered around their tables the teacher introduces the game rules (Table 9.1).

Table 9.1 Fountains *game rules*

Rules	Commentary
There are six tribes meeting on the Plainlands with all of them trying to make it to their home. In order to survive they need water fountains for their horses. Each tribe has horses of different colour and at the beginning of the game each tribe has three horses. Your team has to position the horses at the fountains in a way that earns your team the maximum number of points. The game will be over when the number of fountains has doubled (to 12): the team who has the biggest number of points after the last round is the winner.	Explain that in the game the Plainland is represented by the whiteboard. While positioning the horses to the fountains the participants have to follow a strategy which enables them to open new fountains: if the number of fountains does not increase during the game, everybody will lose their points.
As you arrive, there are six fountains in Plainlands. Up to six horses can drink at each fountain and you may take your horse to any vacant drinking spot. You may place the horse at the fountain in several ways, for instance, one horse can occupy up to three drinking spots. Thus you may "close" the fountain with only two horses. Once the fountain is closed, other players cannot bring their horses to it.	Show the players the fountains. Place six fountains on the board. Demonstrate how one horse may occupy either one, two or three drinking spots at one fountain.

The game is played in rounds. In each round you get two more horses to be placed at the fountains. In order to provide water for your horse place it on a vacant spot. If you wish to change the position of the horses in the course of the game, you may do so but only within the boundaries of the same fountain. Once the horse is taken to a fountain, it cannot be transferred to another fountain.

Explain that the position of a horse at one fountain may be changed during the game but removing a horse from one fountain to another is not allowed.

The success of the tribes is reflected by the number of your horses and the way that you have managed to take them to the fountains. You get five points for each fountain where you have four or more horses. You get four points for each fountain with three of your horses, and three points for fountains with two of your horses. One horse at a fountain earns no points for you.

Refer to the table on the whiteboard reflecting the score. Inform the participants that after every two or three rounds the interim results will be calculated.

If several horses are contending for the same vacant drinking spot, there will be a competition. In case you want to initiate a competition for the vacancy, place one of your horses upside down (the colourless side upward) onto the horse you want to contend against. The competition initiator is the tribe whose horse was the last to be placed at the fountain.

Explain that on some occasions it happens that there are no vacant drinking spots left at the board. Demonstrate how to put a horse onto another one in case of competition.

The competition will be decided by a dice roll with both competing teams casting the dice. If the sum of two dice rolls is 9, 10, 11 or 12, the competition initiator may put his horse at the fountain. The losing horse must leave the board. If the sum is 2, 3, 4 or 5, the competition initiator will lose his horse. If the sum is 6, 7 or 8, both competing horses must leave the board.

Tell the players that the dice must be rolled so that also the opposing team members could see the result.

When any of the fountains has six horses drinking there, the teams will receive a bonus: depending on their decision they will either get three extra horses or one additional fountain. The decision will be made together; however, if there is no consensus, the player with the highest number of horses at the given fountain gets to make the decision. The same player will also decide on the colour of horses that are allowed to a new fountain in the next round, or the colour of horses that are allowed to join.

Demonstrate how you will mark on the whiteboard which teams may bring their horses to the bonus fountain in the next round.

Debriefing

In order to ensure efficient transfer of knowledge from the game to real life, the game session should always be followed by a debriefing. This phase is widely acknowledged as the most important part of a simulation game (Crookall, 1992; Peters & Vissers, 2004). Put briefly, it enables the participants to share their emotions and, if needed, step out of their roles as players; it provides a chance to go through the main events of the game and review important details or decisions. And importantly it is where lessons learnt during the game are conceptualized and connected with the real-life context.

In the case of *Fountains* it is important to demonstrate during the debriefing that the dynamics of the relations between groups is connected to their decisions – all participants make decisions in various stages of the process which come to determine the success of mutual adaptation. To enhance the learning process of the participants it is recommended in the *Fountains* game to conduct the debriefing in two phases: inter-game and post-game.

Inter-game Debriefing

For the inter-game debriefing, taking place after every third or fourth round, the participants will be asked to formulate a general principle or ground rule which could help to achieve the success in the game. Quite often the list of responses includes statements like: "Don't be greedy", "Avoid occupying more resources than you need", "Be friendly", "Don't start competition till you haven't been deceived", or "Try to find partners and find a joint strategy." The principles are written on the sheets of paper, exposed to all participants and discussed briefly, if needed. This technique allows the learning process to be followed: usually the principles written down by the participants demonstrate their deepening understanding of the concept. During the post-game debriefing the facilitator will return to the principles suggested during the game and this provides a good starting point to formalize and transfer the knowledge by asking the participants about the importance of similar principles in real life.

Post-game Debriefing

After participants have had the opportunity to share their feelings and discuss problematic situations in the game, the facilitator can ask them to think about the strategies which lead to the highest score: "Why was the score of some teams higher than that of others?" or "What were their decisions based on?" – resisting the temptation to tell the 'right' answers to the participants. Usually it appears that the teams who ended up with the highest scores were the ones who focused on cooperation rather than competition: instead of fighting for limited resources they try to make coalitions for mutual interest.

In the test-sessions the topic of the game – acculturation – was not announced to the participants beforehand. During the debriefing we asked the participants about the possible parallels they could draw between the game and real life. Most commonly the first responses refer to companies competing on the business market, activities of political parties at the pre-election period or cases from families – where parents, children and grandparents are trying to impose themselves. This was not surprising as *Fountains* is a highly metaphorical game: the game materials provide no direct clues to ethnic groups of sub-cultures. Still, as soon as the attention of participants was drawn to the game-board, covered with horses of different colours gathering around fountains, they quickly came up with responses referring to the behaviour of ethnic groups in multi-national regions or countries.

In the game every team receives two more horses to be placed on the board each round: a process mirroring the natural increase of population in the real world. The fountains serve as metaphors of social resources, e.g. educational system, labour market, medical care, etc. Drinking spots simulate the limited access to those resources. If the horses of different teams are competing for the same vacant drinking spot, the competition will be solved by dice roll. Given the rules, the odds to win the two-die roll are only slightly better than one out of four (28 per cent); the probability that both players lose is around 45 per cent. In other words, the initiation of conflict may be considered, but in most cases it ends with both parties on the losing side. This mirrors real-life situations, where conflict often jeopardizes opportunities on both sides.

The patterns of horses on the board metaphorically allows us to demonstrate that the cultural adaptation is influenced by processes of similar logic. On the one hand the agents' rationality and pragmatic calculations influencing the decision-making process highlight the importance of maximising individual scores, and on the other hand the agents' fear and sense of security focus primarily on the factors related to identity. Although mathematically it makes no sense to set more than two horses of the same colour to one fountain, the teams typically end up with five or even six horses at a fountain. Thus it should be emphasized that cultural integration is an essentially controversial process in which rationality and emotions are bound to compete. As it is difficult to end up with a rational solution in the game, we can infer that cultural integration is equally irrational in real life. In various environmental conditions either fear of being deceived or willingness to collaborate dominates, and thus the expression of these two principles within the game can be analyzed in the discussion (Männamaa *et al.*, 2011).

Sample questions to follow the debriefing could be broadly characterized by two categories: drawing parallels with real life (transfer) and articulation of acquired knowledge (generalisation). Transfer of knowledge could be facilitated by questions like, 'What does the image created on the board by the end of the game tell us? Which processes and phenomena in real life does it remind you of?' or 'What do the horses and fountains in the game stand for? How can we improve everyone's access to resources in our daily life?' Articulation of acquired knowledge might be supported by questions like, 'Why is it important to reach a consensus with other parties? Why is it so difficult? What can we do to improve the situation in real life?' As the background of the participants of different groups varies hugely, the content and style of questions asked during the debriefing depends a lot upon the group and intentions of the facilitator. As a general rule it still makes sense for the facilitator to prepare a set of possible questions beforehand.

What happens quite often in the game is that the players who have their turn first will occupy all the drinking spots and the last team or two have no other choice than to start competing. This kind of result is pretty symptomatic and can lead to interesting generalizations during the debriefing. First, it pinpoints the fact that it is not always easy to identify the initiator of the competition. The team in the game, or an ethnic group in real life, is sometimes just put into a position where there is no other option than competition left for them. Second, the rules governing the competition are set in a way that on almost three occasions out of four the initiators of the competition will lose their horse. Even so, this doesn't seem to reduce the temptation to compete: even a small chance to defeat a co-player outweighs the much bigger risk of losing one's own resources. As the rules of competition in *Fountains* are working against the interest of both competitors, the facilitator has a pile of 'killed' horses on the table by the end of the game. This pile has turned out to be a powerful metaphor during the debriefing. If such a huge amount of resources have been lost during the game, then is it possible that similar waste is happening during acculturation in the real world? If that is true, then what kind of decisions could be made in order to change the situation?

What about Efficiency?

While designing and/or implementing a simulation game, it is important to know about the efficiency of the game. Does it support the intended learning objectives, is it fun for the participants, and last but not least, does it make the work of the teacher more efficient? To answer these questions we set three research questions. First, as designers we were interested in whether the short-term impact of the game corresponds to the expected learning outcomes. Second, we wanted to know how much the model we introduce via *Fountains* responds to the complex reality it is supposed to represent. And third, what is the face value: does the game 'look like' it will work?

To assess the learning outcomes we developed a five-item questionnaire, containing five statements which correspond to the basic principles of acculturation theories. Participants were asked to answer whether they agree or disagree with the given statements. A rating scale from 1–10 was used (strongly disagree–strongly agree as extremes). Some statements were presented on reverted scales, i.e., for three questions the answer supporting cultural integration was on the agree-end of the scale, for two questions it was on the disagree-end. Statements were phrased in a way that they were not directly connected to the narrative of the game, nor were they specifically discussed during the debriefing:

1. To promote the development of our own culture common grounds should be found with other groups.
2. Supporting the interests of minority groups will decrease the chances for development of native inhabitants.
3. Immigrant groups should have access to decision-making processes on a national level.
4. Inter-cultural cooperation is hindered more by rational reasons than by emotions.
5. In order to achieve success the common interests should be superior to the individual needs.

The sample consisted of year 11 pupils (age ~18 years) from the same school (n = 44). The sample included two groups: one group participated in the *Fountains* game (test-group, n = 21); the other group attended the same lessons but did not take part in the game (control group, n = 23). Both groups had attended the same civic education classes previously and had a similar ethnic-cultural background. Members of the test-group filled in the questionnaire immediately after the game. In order to evaluate differences between two groups the t-test was implemented, which shows a difference in relation to students' attitudes towards statements on acculturation (t = 2.354, df = 38.061, p = 0,023). Though no inter-group difference was found for statement number four, the students attending the test group tended to support the statements favouring the integration of cultures. The learning outcomes from playing the game corresponded, therefore, to those intended.

Next, we were interested in whether the strategies chosen by participants in the game were isomorphic to those chosen by ethnic groups in the real world. As we did not have a suitable way to assess such similarities by quantitative means, we asked a group of international experts to observe the game and decide upon the educational value of the tool. Experts on cultural integration agreed that the game could be a valuable resource for teachers within civic education classes. Although *Fountains* is primarily meant as a model for inter-cultural integration, the experts who attended the session mentioned other potential topics: for example, social processes dealing with the topic of collaboration in smaller groups (e.g., family, organization); cooperation and competition in the business sector, etc. Experts on simulation gaming pointed out the high functionality of the technical design and mentioned some similarities of the game-scheme with tragedy of commons (Hardin, 1968) and diners' dilemma (Glance & Huberman, 1994).

Face validity of the game was evaluated by the end-users. The game was introduced to upper-secondary school teachers by eight-hour training sessions: the first half of the session was devoted to the topic of cultural integration and migration policies; the second half included game play and debriefing. The game was introduced to 62 teachers of civic education, 56 of them were interested in obtaining the game for their schools and expressed willingness to run the game in their classes. Their feedback on the usability of the game was encouraging and referred to the face-value of the game as an educational tool.

Final Remarks and Limitations

The first sessions of an educational game you facilitate, however brilliant you are, will probably end up with a failure of some proportion. You don't notice all the details, you misinterpret some rules, you run out of time or have no chance to debrief the game. Teachers often do not have this time for practicing. They try a game once or maybe twice and then get disappointed either in the game or in their own skills of facilitation. This may be one of the reasons why educational games are not in wider use. I occasionally lecture at a university and for me this provided a good opportunity to test the game on students. Maybe it is not the best pedagogical practice but I hope that the students can learn from my failures as much as I do. I therefore firmly recommend any designers to test any game, even the simplest one, in a smaller circle of friendly participants before going to the real classroom with real students.

As a rule an educational game cannot be considered a standalone learning tool; the experience arising from the game should be integrated to the further learning process. A teacher could and should use the game experience as an illustration within the surrounding lessons. It is not the game that 'works' on students: the efficiency of a game depends largely on the skills of the facilitator, quality of debriefing and ability of the participants to connect the game experience with their general body of knowledge. As Hofstede *et al.* (2010: 837) write: "A well-designed game can be jeopardized by inadequate facilitation. Conversely, good facilitation can make the most of modest games."

This makes it almost impossible to explicitly assess the potential long-term effects of a single education game as an artefact. Any teacher looking for new training methods is interested in evidence based-proofs on their efficiency. Therefore, if you are inspired to use *Fountains* yourself in your own learning context, then please try to assess its impact and, if possible, let me know the results, whatever form they are.

Acknowledgements

The development of the simulation game *Fountains* was funded by the Integration and Migration Foundation of Estonia. I thank the co-authors of the game, professor Raivo Vetik (Tallinn University, TU) and assistant professor

Innar Liiv (Tallinn University of Technology, TUT), who contributed a lot to the design process. Excellent artwork and technical design was done by Lis Pikkorainen from Tartu Art School.

References

Axelrod, R.M (1997). *The Complexity of Cooperation: Agent-Based Models of Competition and Collaboration*. Princeton, NJ: Princeton University Press.

Berry, J.W. (2007). Acculturation. In J. Grusec & P. Hastings (eds), *Handbook of Socialization Theory and Research*. New York, NY: Guilford, pp. 343–558.

Caillois, R. (2001) *Man, Play, and Games*. Chamapaign, IL: University of Illinois Press.

Crookall, D. (1992). Debriefing. *Simulation & Gaming*, 23, 141–142.

Garris, R., Ahlers, R. & Driskell, J.E. (2002). Games, motivation, and learning: a research and practice model. *Simulation Gaming*, 33, 441.

Glance, N.S. & Huberman, B.A. (1994). The dynamics of social dilemmas. *Scientific American*, 270/3, 76–81.

Hardin, G. (1968). The tragedy of the commons. *Science*, 162/3, 859, 1, 243–1, 248.

Hofstede, G.J., Caluwé, L. & Peters, V. (2010). Why simulation games work – in search of the active substance: a synthesis. *Simulation & Gaming*, 41, 824–843.

Huizinga, J. (2001). *Homo Ludens: A Study of the Play-Element in Culture*. London, Routledge.

Johnson, D.W. & Johnson, R.T. (1989). *Cooperation and Competition: Theory and Research*. Edina, MN: Interaction.

Kiili, K. (2005). *On Educational Game Design: Building Blocks of Flow Experience*. Tampere University of Technology, Publication 571.

Klabbers, J.H.G. (2006). Guest editorial: artifact assessment vs. theory testing. *Simulation & Gaming*, 37/2, 148–154.

Lainema, T. (2009). Perspective making: constructivism as a meaning-making structure for simulation gaming. *Simulation & Gaming*, 40/1, 48–67.

Männamaa, I., Vetik, R. & Liiv, I. (2011). *Mudeldusmäng Allikad. Juhend* [Simulation Game Fountains. Facilitator's manual], University of Tartu, Estonia.

Pavlas, D., Bedwell, W., Wooten S.R., Heyne, K. & Salas, E. (2009). Investigating the attributes in serious games that contribute to learning. *Proceedings of the Human Factors and Ergonomics Society 53rd annual meeting 2009*, 1999–2003.

Peters, V.A. & Vissers, G.A. (2004). A simple classification model for debriefing simulation games. *Simulation Gaming* 35, 70–84.

Rudmin, Floyd W. (2003). Critical history of the acculturation psychology of assimilation, separation, integration, and marginalization. *Review of General Psychology*, 7/1, 3–37.

Salen, K. & Zimmerman, E. (2003). *Rules of Play: Game Design Fundamentals*. Cambridge: MIT Press.

Wenzler, I. (2009). The ten commandments for translating simulation results into real-life performance. *Simulation & Gaming*, 40/1, 98–109.

10

Larps in High Schools

J. TUOMAS HARVIAINEN, UNIVERSITY OF TAMPERE,
FINLAND, AND RITVA SAVONSAARI, LUMO SENIOR
HIGH SCHOOL, FINLAND

An easily overlooked option for game-based education in classrooms is live-action role-playing, commonly known as *larping*. In larps, participants play characters, fictional personas created for that game. They do so physically, in a way that much resembles improvisational theatre, but is not exactly the same. The setting can be anything, ranging from history and fantasy to modern-day realism, and thus tailored to fit each subject at hand. For example, imagine six people in a room, pretending for an hour that they really are a rock band about to fall apart, who have to sort out their problems, all the while tacitly learning linguistic skills. In this chapter, we discuss examples from applying larps to the teaching of verbal skills in second language acquisition, and provide some instructions on how to use existing larps for education and how to design one's own.

Larps as Educational Tools

Larps have several attractive qualities to them as educational tools, qualities that come in addition to the advantages and challenges of game-based learning (see e.g. Lainema, 2009; Whitton, 2009; Bedwell *et al.*, 2012 on games as learning tools and how their use ties into existing paradigms of educational theory, especially as constructivism). They significantly increase student-talking time (STT) in class, reducing teacher-talking time (TTT) and make sure that what TTT that remains is used in a focused, efficient manner. They likewise focus the STT, so that it is not spent on idle chatter but on the task at hand. They can, if the organizers seek super-realism and large scale, be expensive. A typical classroom larp, however, costs next to nothing to organize and run, if one does not count the effort put to its design and/or implementation by the teacher. The first person audience nature of larps allows the creation of new perspectives through characters, and enables the changing of discourse settings – a cafeteria hosts very different elements than does a medieval castle. The context change is very significant, especially for language learning, as through the choice of setting a teacher has much control over the type of vocabulary used during play. With a little more thought, it can also be applied to other subjects; for example, mathematics could be taught within a spaceship needing a new course before it plummets into a black hole, or natural sciences with a game about field researchers tracking a mythical creature. These go way beyond the 'Jack has three apples, Michael two' level, because the characters are played by the students, not just presented as hypotheses.

Even though the occasional educational larp has been seen since the 1970s (rumor has it that larp-like games were, for example, used to teach languages and mathematics in some Soviet schools) a significant amount of research on, and experimentation with, them is quite recent. The most important of these comes from a Danish boarding school, Østerskov Efterskole, which teaches its entire curriculum by way of role-playing, most of it live action. According to its former principal, Malik Hyltoft (2010), four factors make educational larps functional.

The first of them is *distraction*: Larp is a step away from mundane life, and provides freedom through costumes and roles, and focuses attention on events taking place within the game-space. The second one is *motivation*. Instead of studying for an exam or because the teacher requested it, participants get to study for a purpose they enjoy – a nice game. Additionally, motivation can be built within the game, by giving characters interesting goals, by pre-scripting intriguing events into the scenario and also by emphasizing the setting in a captivating manner. For example, playing nobles in the court of the French king during the start of the revolution has large numbers of story and character hooks that students can easily appreciate.

The third element is the *activity level* – in a good educational larp, students take the leading role in their own learning processes, with the teacher optimally acting solely as a facilitator, who may (depending on the game type) guide the larp or let it run by itself, whatever fits it best. Hyltoft especially recommends making characters experts – for instance, in a laboratory crisis, everyone should play top-level researchers, rescue team members, and so forth. This drives the players to learn, so as to close the gap between their own knowledge and that of the character, because it makes them play better and also, in many, fits their desire for competition and triumph against the odds. The fourth key element is *power*. With the teacher present only as an observer, the player-students will feel a sense of holding control over their own actions, further fueled by the expert status of their characters, and this too guides them to seek to excel, through personal performance and by co-operation with others.

We have, as one more essential advantage, observed *commitment*: whether due to immersion, flow or some other hard-to-define phenomenon, the game experience drives its participants to try to succeed. They do not freeze during play and say "I don't know", "I don't have the words". They attempt to at least say something useful, as they know the momentum of the play keeps going, that time is limited, and that their characters' goals will be crushed if they don't fight for them. Therefore, new courage to actually speak and act despite one's perceived limitations is often found through immersive play.

Educational larp bears a strong resemblance to drama-based methods in education, including bibliodrama, psychodrama and improvisational theater done in schools (see Blatner, 2007, for various uses of drama techniques in education, and how they connect). Larps, however, differ from drama in education through the presence of individual characters, which are played as persons, not as dramatic roles constrained by a script or guided by a teacher or director. In a role-playing game, players have the option not to play their characters to their full extent (for example, picking only some traits from the description to embody, and ignoring others), but it is quite likely that the character will nevertheless seem quite whole, a person. Thus, if necessary, some key words that the player does not understand can be ignored without much damage, even if it changes the character concept. This fact grants the participants additional freedom of interpretation; a freedom they can, if guided right, use to learn. Each player is either given an opportunity to write their character or given one by the teacher. Both approaches have their advantages: for a short game with clear goals, it is often easier to simply distribute pre-written material that includes the characters, as that is in a classroom situation faster and allows the teacher to define much of the game's dynamics beforehand.

For some subjects, however, the opposite is optimal. Finnish educational larp designer and teacher Jori Pitkänen, for example, has experimented with teaching history through not just the playing of larps, but also through the shared design of them. The larp was used as the culmination point of the course, and the students were encouraged to do research that went into the design of their characters and the enhancement of the setting. They were motivated to study harder by the promise of improving their own game experience. Sadly, Pitkänen's work (2008) is not yet available in English. Fortunately, other examples exist (see e.g. Bruun, 2011).

The defining factor of larp as an educational tool is its undeniable physicality. All players play their characters with their own bodies, own thoughts and own words, even as they try to act as their characters. This creates many opportunities for learning, but also carries its own problems. For example, it usually takes a lot of larp experience to be able to play against the physical appearance of another player – it is quite hard for many to remember after a while that a 17-year-old girl's character is actually a 40-year-old mother. Extra information on name tags helps, but it is by no means foolproof. Done well, however, such changes in age, posture and especially sociability may do wonders to student groups. We have witnessed several occasions, in both schools and corporate training larps, where a normally shy person, given a highly social character has, for example, suddenly exhibited strong leadership or oratory skills. During the final course feedback session, as well as immediately after the larp, students have also repeatedly mentioned these game experiences as their favourites, over any other activities offered during the course.

The frame of the game serves to protect its players, which enables the participants to act differently from their normal selves. An information barrier created by the social contract of play changes the meaning of activities within the playing area (see Harviainen, 2012, on the nature of the barrier). This is commonly called the "magic circle of play" in game studies, following the appropriation of a concept of Johan Huizinga (1939) by design scholars Katie Salen and Eric Zimmerman (2004). Within the magic circle, normal rules need not apply: a weak person can play a strong character, a nice person a bully, and so forth. Even changes in intelligence can be simulated to some degree. As noted by game philosopher Ari-Pekka Lappi (2010), this also goes for morality: within the magic circle of boxing, for example, it is completely right to hit another person, and not okay to not try to hit him, whereas the opposite is the proper expectation in our mundane life. Similarly, it is possible to examine quite serious themes within the magic circle of a larp, providing the players with a simulated first-hand experience of what it is to perform morally ambivalent or even evil actions. Several larps have, for example, been used to show how and why people can be attracted to totalitarian ideals, a result very useful for teaching certain facets of ethics, philosophy and history.

While key to the success of educational larps, the social contract is nevertheless vulnerable. If the subject matter of the game cuts too close to home, the game may break. For example, Laurie Schick (2008) describes a game designed to teach that school bullying is bad, which while a very valuable tool, in some circumstances has led to players re-experiencing the bullying they themselves have suffered. While that too can be a learning experience, we feel that in a school environment, the blending of character and player experiences (often called "bleed" in game studies) has to be for the most part avoided. Therefore, we recommend that highly emotional games only be organized for students by a teacher who knows the dynamics of that class or group well. In some cases, however, bleed can also drive a player to succeed against the odds: we have, for example, witnessed a student with a weak command of English striving to have her character acquire something she herself would have wanted to possess in real life, a horse.

This is by no means a recommendation for staying away from emotional content. On the contrary, some of the most impressive educational larps have used this very approach, in both schools and elsewhere. One of our two case examples here, *Prelude*, also deals with that theme, teaching its players not only communication skills but also the ability to read emotional reactions and reasons behind the discourse that takes place. Additionally, if a larp provokes no emotional response from the player, it is not sufficiently engrossing. One of the key advantages of using an already existing larp for educational purposes is that it is already known to work. In this, larps are no different from other games used for educational purposes (see Whitton, 2009).

An excellent, if brief, introduction to the basics of deploying larps for educational purposes can be found in the book *Playing the learning game* (Andresen, 2012). As that book, however, deals much more with historical and political awareness education than with school curricula, it is necessary to present the core concepts here, too, in an expanded and more school-contextualized form.

Preparing the Larp

Most of us do not have the luxury of teaching in a school already devoted to game-based learning, like østerskov. Therefore, we have to adapt the games to fit our curricula, not vice versa. Therefore, if one uses a pre-written larp (which can be downloaded from various repositories, such as http://jeepen. org) in a school environment, it is good to start with three things: familiarity with the game material, familiarity with the primary subject being taught and familiarity with the student group in question. The familiarity does not have to be very deep, but a good, educational larp deployment is built out of the combination of these factors.

It is important to think of the primary learning goal, and then, keeping it in mind, to read the game material thoroughly, a few times, and actually see if the larp has the potential to achieve the set learning goal. It is also good to think about some permutations of the larp. Players tend to engage in what David Myers (2010 p. 21) calls 'functional bad play' – they will not follow the set goal directly, and are likely to explore around the game's limits, which is basically good, yet problematic for game-based education, as it lacks the necessary focus. Owing to this, quite linear games tend to be better for learning purposes than very open games.

Both of the example larps discussed in this chapter have endings that are somewhat set in stone. This allows for iterative play, which enhances learning. By discussing, for example, the dividing of an inheritance while knowing that it must be decided when the larp ends provokes many players to hone their argumentation in a "round by round" manner. Such iteration anchors the learned skills better, through practice and instant feedback on any improvement. Because of this, analyzing and anticipating the permutations is important. By doing so, the teacher ascertains that even when the game won't go exactly as planned (it never will), learning, and the improved anchoring of what was learned before and gets used during play, will take place.

Something that may seem to create problems is game scale – most mini-larps are written for groups far smaller than a full class. We therefore recommend splitting the students into smaller groups fitting the game's scale, preferably ones that slightly disrupt the normal dynamics of the class, so as to get people to interact outside of their normal friendship groups. It is then possible to either deploy several runs of the game at once, or to have one group per turn play elsewhere while the rest continue with normal studies. With some experience, a teacher can even supervise several runs of the game (as was done with some runs of both of our example larps here), switching rooms at appropriate times or hosting several in a single room. While this seemingly presents the problem of leaving the play without observation, its advantage is that the power and freedom aspects of play may get emphasized when the students see the teacher leave, leading to better, more educational, play. The game, when set in motion, tends to stay active even when the teacher is absent. In the case of very emotional scenarios, such as the aforementioned bullying, we do nevertheless recommend constant teacher oversight.

Marketing, Briefing and Debriefing

As noted by Whitton (2009), not everyone likes games, and saying 'let's play a game' will not entice those students who do not like games. Reasons for this are many, and very much include the social insecurity of kids of high school age. Therefore, we have found it best to use tailored marketing: for many classes, "let's do this thing, with roles" has, in our opinion, worked better than "let's play a game" or "now, we'll larp" would have. That being said, for others, being clear about playing a game was more effective, so try to choose the wording that will most likely get students to anticipate a positive experience.

When you've sold the concept, it is time to distribute at least some of the game material and to brief the players about the setting and the roles. When briefing them, it is important also to clearly convey the playing style, theme and genre of the larp (such as "it may not be played as a comedy" or "you know, in murder mysteries . . .") and to emphasize that the idea is to stay in character as much as possible. This invokes the right attitude in the minds of the students, leading not only to the right sort of play, but also tuning their styles of playing to a frequency closer to each others'.

A second important discussion, the debriefing, must take place after play ends, preferably as soon as possible. It both allows the players to settle back from the game and to remember that it was just a game, and also serves a learning goal. Through guided reflection, the teacher has the essential capacity to foster learning that the students will build upon. In many cases, things learned under alternate circumstances – games very much included – become simply situated learning that is not used as the basis of reflective extrapolation (see Kim, 1993). In other words, skills learned in a certain setting often remain tied to that setting, with the learners thinking that they can't be applied elsewhere. With proper control, however, the new content can be anchored in the minds of the participants, granting them the ability to access the newly gained knowledge later in various contexts (Lave & Wenger, 1991). The anchored, new content will also foster a desire for further learning.

Assessment

While learning to learn is one of the most important goals of education, teachers still have to assess the students, if they work within an educational system that measures performance with grades. Evaluating exactly what is learned during gameplay is very hard, so we recommend their use for mainly three reasons: motivation, exercise and anchoring. If marketed properly, a school larp increases the activity level and motivation of its participants, before the game actually takes place, during play, and again when debriefing. Players eager for a good game will work harder. The same reasons that make such games good teaching tools may, however, make them difficult to assess, especially since players may not value the same things as the curriculum does (Harviainen et al., 2012).

To solve the conflict, we recommend the use of reflective writing as a form of assessment and grading, supplemented by the teacher observations during play (with regards to the subject at hand, naturally). While mostly suitable for university level studies, deployed in a classroom setting, reflective essays allow the teacher to get an inkling of what exactly was learned, and how. If a student does not answer, that too can be gauged as a result, put into context with the observed play event. We do not, however, recommend traditional testing after a game, as that would bring a goal-oriented (test-score) focus to the process, interrupting individual learning curves.

We think it best to assess these games on a case-by-case basis, especially if they are a part of the normal curriculum and thus graded mostly by traditional means by the end of the course. The games, however, may have points of their own regarding their assessment, which are elaborated in the case examples.

Case Example: *Prelude*

Prelude is a short game designed by school psychologist Lauri Lukka. It deals with a band that is about to break up. What sort of a band is up to the players. They are close to glory, having published one album and working on the so-hard second hit. The warm-up act is already playing. Unfortunately, Destiny has it that the band will – inevitably – break up before it goes on stage. The 'why' is up to the players.

Prelude was initially written to demonstrate the underlying emotions behind intragroup communication. Every band member gets a random relation to every other, and those are asymmetrical. For example, the drummer may find the lead singer a big inspiration, but the singer thinks that the drummer is an incompetent douchebag. When run with proper instructions and debriefing, the larp shows its players the underlying presumptions behind communication, while also teaching practical linguistic skills in a highly enjoyable setting.

Deployed so far five times by Ritva Savonsaari as a part of her teaching in Lumo high school, *Prelude* proved to enhance its participants' active foreign language use significantly. Runs of the game by others in various parts of the world (ranging from Belarus to Norway) produced similar results. The setting, for which the participants get to choose the place of the concert, the band's history, and the type of music the band plays, is surprisingly adaptive. The idea of a musical group breaking apart by causes such as artistic differences, personal ambitions, drug use, and so forth, are issues of public knowledge and can easily be stated to form a part of current-day celebrity storytelling. This allows even not very musically oriented – or discourse-oriented – players to have a lot to say during play, as everyone tries to create various reasons for the inevitable break-up.

School rules permitting, the effect can be accentuated strongly by suitable props, such as having the 'backstage' (i.e. room where the game takes place) already filled with empty bottles – or by having fake 'shots' the musicians can drink (let's face it – high school age kids tend to have a fascination with self-destructive musicians, and a clever teacher takes advantage of that – up to and including the chance to use the game to later discuss proper behavior and the risks of intoxicant use). As an example of a larp that requires minimal investment of time and preparation, yet offers educational potential on not only second language acquisition, but also music history and theory and even health education, *Prelude* is excellent.

Case Example: *The Family Andersson*

Our perennial favorite, *The Family Andersson*, is a Swedish-made larp about five siblings dividing a family inheritance under time pressure. It has been deployed eight times at Lumo, and numerous others elsewhere. Due to the limited number of characters, roles are divided so that each character is played by one to three people, who switch places and take turns. The inheritance has to be divided by the end of the game. Some runs have included also a lawyer present, which tends to harmonize the debate somewhat, but under the basic rules, he only arrives at the end. The siblings represent different values in life, such as conservative versus liberal, committed versus single, middle class versus self-expression. One of them is bound in a wheelchair and another is going through gender reassignment. Like *Prelude*, and many other mini-larps, *Family Andersson* is mostly a discussion played seated around a table, but its power arises from the contrasts and conflicts between the characters and the nuances each player brings to their personalities and behavior.

In addition to argumentation skills, vocabulary, grammar (especially modal verbs) and self-expression under pressure, the scenario teaches also empathy, value judgements and the ability to walk for a moment in the shoes of someone very different from one's own experiences and ideals. During it, students find in themselves the ability to speak even when they don't have the perfect words, but know they might nevertheless get their points across. When provoked, they can also instinctively recall idioms they have heard but forgotten, as culturally correct situational responses. Above all, they have loads of fun while learning and bonding as a group. The teacher can furthermore work as a facilitator, by for example, writing on the board some key words he or she sees the players are looking for but not using.

While awesome, *The Family Andersson* and *Prelude* are not without challenges. For example, if the students are given their characters in advance, not everyone necessarily shows up. In turn, some who were absent during preparation may. This makes the dynamics unpredictable and may lead to an imbalance between player involvement. In our experience, however, even the newcomers who received less briefing were able to partake in playing quite well. Occasionally the setting does not have time to sufficiently develop, but a solid (re-)briefing just before play (time permitting) lessens this problem. When lacking words, some students, unable to cope with the linguistic pressure due to their more limited vocabularies, may resort to native-language use and thus disrupt the magic circle of play. Sometimes this, instead of breaking the illusion, actually inspires other students to help that person, leading to enhanced peer teaching.

Most of all, however, the true challenge is time. A teaching lesson is quite short, and having time for briefing, the play and then a proper debriefing is extremely challenging. People also tend to be very reluctant to alter their schedules to accommodate playing. We believe it to be worth all the trouble – watching high school students with self-esteem issues debate, shine and accomplish their goals in a friendly environment, while learning, is a rare treat. Excepting the one student who completely refused to play, using this scenario has been a definite success, as it has been easily observable that even those who stay silent during the game are very much engaged in active observation. While other parts of the spoken English curriculum focus on theoretical phrasing and formal contexts, a game environment such as *The Family Andersson* facilitates practical, goal-oriented skill use that is much harder to efficiently teach in a normal classroom setting. Both have their uses.

Designing Your Own Educational Larps

The first and foremost thing to keep in mind when designing a larp for educational purposes is that while educational purposes and entertainment may be at odds (see Henriksen, 2008), they are neither opposites nor enemies. On the contrary, it is a question of balance: too much entertainment and freedom, and the educational ability of the larp is lost. Too strong an educational push, and game engrossment suffers so much that no learning takes place, because the players are too busy complaining. Too little of either, and there's no real point in running the larp. Luckily, creating a suitable balance is not at all hard, and a clever teacher adjusts the game template slightly after every run, improving it each time (see Harviainen, 2009, on how to make larps easily repeatable).

The second issue is the educational content itself: what is supposed to be learned by playing the larp, and what might be learned in addition to that? Østerskov Efterskole, for example, uses very different types of role-playing scenarios for different subjects. A larp teaching mathematics, for example, probably needs to be more precisely designed than one for linguistics, as its focus is narrower. At a later stage (both during design and after a few runs), it is therefore also important to look back at the game, and analyse what exactly is being learned through it. The results may turn out highly surprising, even when the primary learning goal is met. The freedom of play can cause stealth learning of many more things than expected. This is important also because one does not want the students to learn the wrong things, or stuff that remains too tied to the game and thus unusable outside its context.

To facilitate suitable types and goals of learning, it is best to seek a somewhat linear, yet not completely pre-scripted ('railroaded'), story. In this, elements such as *Fates* will be of immense help to you. They are things that players know will have to take place during the game, yet there is freedom to explore at other times. For example, the only rule set in stone regarding the story in *Prelude* is that the band must break up. The participants get to choose how. Fates and other similar tools also enable the necessary iteration for enhanced learning, while keeping the play enjoyable and engaging. The works of Norwegian larp designer and theorist Eirik Fatland (2005, 2006) provides a reader with many clues on how to use these techniques.

Emotional content requires extra attention as well during design: how close to the reality of the players' lives does one want the larp to go? When teaching sciences, this is rarely an issue, but a larp close to psychodrama or dealing with interpersonal, emotionally charged issues may cause significant bleed, some of which can be unwanted. Therefore, some failsafe systems are in order, the most important of those something akin to a safe word, i.e. a way for the players to interrupt the game, should the content prove problematic, without any social stigma. The teacher has an important role in this, both as a designer and as the person controlling the game.

Finally, a point also worth addressing is team structure. Players learn differently when they act as groups or as individuals. Groups enable wider skill sets and new task divisions, but they also restrict player options, sometimes including the choice of personally optimal learning strategies (see Kayes *et al.*, 2005). As the designer is able to facilitate group cohesion and interaction to a great extent through writing character personalities and motivations, it is quite easy to optimize the basic dynamics to match the primary learning task. That is actually one of the greatest advantages: students learning by larp are learning *together*, not just in the same room.

Summary

In this chapter, we introduce the principles of using live-action role-playing games (larps) to not only teach subject matter knowledge, but also to foster the desire for further learning in students. Larps motivate their players to learn, by providing freedom of action, a sense of personal control and group commitment, and an alternate setting that creates a suitable context for their subjects of study. With proper briefing and debriefing, also games written mostly for the sake of entertainment, such as both *Prelude* and *The Family Andersson*, can be used to teach active foreign language skills. In addition, the chapter contains instructions on how to design larps suitable for one's own curriculum, and how to assess and grade what the students learn by playing the game.

Ludography

Family Andersson, The (2008). Designed by Åke Nolemo & Johan Röklander. Available at http://chambergames.files.wordpress.com/2009/05/family_andersson_web.pdf and as a part of Andresen, 2012 (accessed 10 April 2013).

Prelude (2011). Designed by Lauri Lukka. Available from http://laurilukka.wordpress.com/ (accessed 10 April 2013).

References

Andresen, Martin E. A. (ed.) (2012). *Playing the Learning Game: A Practical Introduction to Educational Roleplaying, Based on Experiences from The Larpwriter Challenge.* Oslo: Fantasiforbundet and Education Center POST.

Bedwell, W., Pavlas, D., Heyne, K., Lazzara, E. & Salas, E. (2012). Toward a taxonomy linking game attributes to learning: an empirical study. *Simulation & Gaming*, Online First, published on May 14, 2012, doi:10.1177/1046878112439444.

Blatner, A. (ed.) (2007). *Interactive and Improvisational Drama: Varieties of Applied Theatre and Performance.* New York, NY: iUniverse.

Bruun, J. (2011). Pre-larp workshops as learning situations. In T.D. Henriksen, C. Bierlich, K. Friis Hansen & V. Kølle (eds) *Think Larp: Academic Writings from KP2011.* Copenhagen, Denmark: Rollespilsakademiet, pp. 194–215.

Fatland, E. (2005). Incentives as tools of larp dramaturgy. In P. Bøckman, & R. Hutchison (eds), *Dissecting Larp. Collected Papers for Knutepunkt 2005.* Oslo, Norway: Knutepunkt, 147–180.

Fatland, E. (2006). Interaction codes: understanding and establishing patterns in player improvisation. In T. Fritzon & T. Wrigstad (eds) *Role, Play, Art: Collected Experiences of Role-playing.* Stockholm, Sweden: Foreningen Knutepunkt, 17–34.

Harviainen, J. T. (2009). Notes on designing repeatable larps. In M. Holter, E. Fatland & E. Tømte (eds) *Larp, the Universe, and Everything.* Oslo, Norway: Knutepunkt, 97–110.

Harviainen, J. T. (2012). *Systemic Perspectives on Information in Physically Performed Role-play.* Doctoral dissertation, University of Tampere.

Harviainen, J. T., Lainema, T. & Saarinen, E. (2012). Player-reported impediments to game-based learning. *Proceedings of 2012 Digra Nordic*. University of Tampere, Tampere, Finland: June 2012. Available: http://www.digra.org/dl/db/12168.02279.pdf (accessed 16 April 2013).

Henriksen, T. D. (2008). Extending experiences of learning games – or why learning games should be neither fun, educational or realistic. In O. Leino, H. Wirman & A. Fernandez (eds) *Extending Experiences: Structure, Analysis and Design of Computer Game Player Experience*. Rovaniemi, Finland: University of Lapland, 140–162.

Huizinga, J. (1939). *Homo ludens: Versuch einer Bestimmung des Spielelements der Kultur.* [Homo ludens: A study of the play element in culture]. Amsterdam, the Netherlands: Pantheon akademische Verlagsanstalt.

Hyltoft, M. (2010). Four reasons why edu-larp works. In K. Dombrowski (ed.) *LARP: Einblicke. Aufsatzsammlung zum MittelPunkt 2010*. Braunschweig, Germany: Zauberfeder pp. 43–57.

Kayes, A.B., Kayes, D.C. & Kolb, D.A. (2005). Experiential learning in teams. *Simulation & Gaming*, 36/3, 330–354.

Kim, D.H. (1993). The link between individual and organizational learning. *Sloan Management Review* 35/1, 37–50.

Lainema, T. (2009). Perspective making: constructivism as a meaning-making structure for simulation gaming. *Simulation & Gaming*, 40/1, 48–67.

Lappi, A.-P. (2010). Contra-moral of play: from ethics of game towards ethics of playing. In E. Larsson (ed.) *Playing Reality*. Stockholm, Sweden: Interacting Arts, pp. 193–203.

Lave, J. & Wenger, E. (1991). *Situated Learning: Legitimate Peripheral Participation*. New York, NY: Cambridge University Press.

Myers, D. (2010). *Play Redux: The Form of Computer Games*. Ann Arbor, MI: University of Michigan Press.

Pitkänen, Jori (2008). *Pedagoginen liveroolipelaaminen historian opetusmetodina* [Pedagogic live action role playing as a method of teaching history]. Master's thesis, University of Helsinki.

Salen, K., & Zimmerman, E. (2004). *Rules of Play: Game Design Fundamentals*. Cambridge, MA: MIT Press.

Schick, L. (2008). Breaking frame in a role-play simulation: a language socialization perspective. *Simulation & Gaming*, 39/2, 184–197.

Whitton, N. (2009). *Learning with Digital Games. A Practical Guide to Engaging Students in Higher Education*. New York, NY: Routledge.

11

WAR OF WORLDS – AN INTERACTIVE BOARD GAME ABOUT LIFE BEYOND EARTH

BARBARA OTTOLINI AND CAS KRAMER,
UNIVERSITY OF LEICESTER, UK

Introduction

Is there any life out there? The question of whether life exists beyond Earth has fascinated mankind for many decades. Indeed, with its mysterious aura, space has engaged the imagination of innumerable generations, inspiring both fear and wonder. The latent curiosity of man for extraterrestrial life and the interest in space explorations has never dimmed; from the first moon landing in 1969 to the supersonic space jump in 2012, millions of people have held their breath in front of the radio, television or now computer screen. A new mission to Mars is under way and we continue to scour the skies for habitable biospheres. Clearly this fascination can be used to inspire budding scientists.

The *War of Worlds* is an interactive board game aimed at students in secondary education. The game is structured to explore the crossover between astrobiology and genetics and was developed for and first used during Space School UK in July 2011. Space School UK is a highly successful residential summer school organised by the Department of Physics and Astronomy at the University of Leicester (2012) and is aimed primarily at young individuals (13–18-year-olds) who have a strong interest in science and space-related subjects.

Playing the *War of Worlds* actively encourages students to utilise all of their knowledge and understanding across the different science disciplines. In fact, it stretches students to think outside the box and use their imagination to the full. If one had the power to create a life form on another planet, which traits ('genes') of known extremophiles (organisms that thrive under extreme and often very hostile conditions on Earth, such as microbes living in deep ocean hot springs) would you choose to create such a life form? Would those chosen genes convey traits useful in the extreme conditions on a planet like Venus or Mars? The *War of Worlds* is a competitive and fun, yet very educational game, a hybrid game utilising the positives of both a board game and a trading card game.

Ideation Process

We set ourselves a challenging high bar, creating an interactive activity at the crossover between astrobiology and genetics for an audience of very space-orientated young individuals.

The images evoked linking the words 'genetics' and 'space' may vary greatly among different people. However, a common theme in all of those images could very likely be summarised by the two questions: "Is there life in space?" and "If so, what would it look like?" If we erase for a moment the stereotypic image of the Green Man coming from Mars, either bringing peace or destruction according to the movie director's or writer's vision of the moment, we will realise that imagining a possible new life form on another planet is not possible without taking into account the particular environmental characteristics of its new life cradle. Nevertheless, in order to imagine and to present the unknown we need to set our basis in the empiric sphere. The only yardstick of life we know is the enormous species diversity present on Earth.

We therefore decided to aim to create an interactive activity that could help students reflect on how life evolved on our planet creating the diversity of organisms we now know, organisms that can be so different from each other which may appear almost alien at a first glimpse. First, one of the key concepts that we wanted to convey is 'adaptation', the process that describes how species face a succession of environmental challenges developing adaptive plasticity in response to the imposed conditions.

Second, another crucial point we wanted to get across to the students is the difference between our planet with its current climate and atmosphere, and an Earth four billions of years younger. Without realising, we tend to think that evolution of life started in a sort of Garden of Eden, with calm, warm waters and rolling hills, protected by the ozone layer surrounding the Earth as we know it today. On the contrary, life had a completely different beginning on an Earth highly exposed to UV radiation, with dramatic changes in temperature, and with quite a different atmospheric composition. The highly accredited iron-sulphur world theory (Wächtershäuser, 1988; Martin & Russell, 2007) places the origin of life in volcanic hydrothermal flows at very high pressure and temperature. Pioneer organisms evolved under these extreme conditions and slowly aided environmental changes, allowing new species to develop. As millions of years passed by, the Earth's temperature gradually decreased, an ozone layer was formed and water covered the majority of the planet's surface. This environmental diversification opened the way to the evolution of (and conversely to the extinction of) a huge variety of species, that ultimately created the biosphere as we know it today. Interestingly, if we look in the right places we will realise that pioneer organisms belonging to the Archaea (a domain of single-celled micro-organisms evolutionary distinct from bacteria; Carey, 2005; Javaux, 2006) are still present on our planet, successfully colonising the most hostile environments on Earth. From this, another key point of our budding game activity arose. If ancestors of Archaea were able to survive and evolve under such extreme conditions on a primordial Earth, life would theoretically be possible on other planets under similarly extreme conditions. Moreover, existing Archaea on Earth are fantastic examples of the power of adaptation and evolution and represent a significant starting point to imagine how unknown life forms may look on other planets. For example, volcanic hot springs may seem a harsh and almost 'alien' environment, yet many species of Archaea are able to thrive right in the middle of them.

Another topic that we wanted to emphasise is one often ignored by the most famous sci-fi movies. In these movies highly technologic alien beings are ready to invade Earth and/or are perfectly adapted to parasite humans, ready to hatch from a human chest. However, the difficulties caused by environmental changes for a terrestrial species trying to expand into a different niche are challenging enough. For an alien species trying to establish itself on a new planet these difficulties are likely to be insurmountable.

Finally, a key variable we wanted to introduce into the interactive activity was 'luck'. Evolution on Earth is not a granted process. In the fight for survival, species with similar adaptation may thrive or die out as result of the combination of series of non-predictable events. In analogy of Death playing chess (Bergman, 1957), we decided that in our game Life would play with dice.

Game Considerations

While a game concept had developed in our heads, we had to make decisions about the finer game details. First, we decided to create the *War of Worlds* as a hybrid between a board game and a trading card game; we utilised all of the advantages of a board game (like social interaction and team work) and we incorporated a number of the exciting features of a trading card game (like traits with different values and battle). While the board game industry is a well-established one, the trading card game industry is still relatively new. In the past twenty years trading card games have constituted a highly successful game formula within entertainment (Wikipedia 2012b; Toy reviews and news, 2012). These games are very popular with young people, being funny, social and at the same time extremely challenging. "*Magic the Gathering*" is still played by 12 million people worldwide (Wizards of the Coast, 1993; Wikipedia, 2012a), and similarly, "*Pokemon*" and "*Yu-Ghi-Oh!*" are very popular with school-aged children (Wizards of the Coast, 1998; Konami, 1999).

Second, we decided to utilise 20-sided (D20) dice in the battle between the different players instead of the conventional six-sided (D6) dice. In this way, we could incorporate a much greater influence of luck into the game. Moreover, the use of multi-faced dice, like D20 or D12, added a 'geeky', novelty aspect to the game, well liked by children.

A final game consideration was the choice of setting for the *War of Worlds*. Obviously, it would be difficult to imagine a successful life form evolving in the outer space, as life as we know it is based on the concept of aggregation (individual entities clumping together, forming and acting as one unit) and on the use of components to create energy. This would clearly be lost in the immensity of the cosmic void. Hence, planets (being aggregates of matter with heterogeneous composition) would better fit these criteria. Instead of creating a fictitious planet for our game, we decided to convey scientifically proven facts about existing planets to students. Among the planets in our solar system there is no doubt that Mars and Venus are both the better described and the ones that collectively carry the most imagination. Moreover, these two planets have profoundly different characteristics and yet show some analogies with Earth (see Table 11.1). We concentrated in our information gathering on characteristics that presented analogies with the extreme environments still present on Earth. If Archaea had been able to adapt and survive under these circumstances here on Earth, our hypothetic extraterrestrial life forms may do the same on Mars and Venus.

Game Description

War of Worlds is played with two groups of six teams. Each team represents an alien species that will commence a battle for survival with (some of) the other species. The game is especially versatile with respect to the number of players, from a minimum of 12 players (each team consists of one person) up to 36–48 players (each team consists of 3–4 people). To incentivise discussion it is recommended that each team has at least two people. Depending on the group size it is possible to adjust the game dynamics to meet the needs of different classrooms.

Table 11.1 *A list of information presented in simple and clear language about the planets, Earth, Mars and Venus. Students will receive the information about Earth and one of the other planets only*

	Earth	Mars	Venus
Position	Third planet of the Solar System	Second planet of the Solar System	Fourth planet of the Solar System
Volume	1.083×10^{12} km^3	85% of Earth	11% of Earth
Mass	1 M ° = 5.9722 × 10^{24} kg	81% of Earth (0.81 M °)	15% of Earth (0.15 M °)
Satellites	Moon	Deimos and Phobos	None
Orbital period	365.26 days	224.70 days	686.97 days
		1 Venusian day = 116.75 Earth days	Rotational period and seasonal cycle similar to Earth
Sea level pressure	1 bar = 100 kPa	9,393 kPa	6 kPa
Average temperature	14 °C	462 °C	−55 °C

	Earth	Mars	Venus
Atmosphere composition	78% nitrogen (N_2), 21% oxygen (O_2) and trace amounts of water vapour (H_2O), carbon dioxide (CO_2) and other gaseous molecules	Extremely thick atmosphere that masks 72% of the solar light	Low density atmosphere composed of 95% carbon dioxide (CO_2), 3% nitrogen (N_2), 1.6% argon and traces of oxygen (O_2) and water (H_2O)
		96.5% carbon dioxide (CO_2), 3.5% nitrogen (N_2)	
		NOTE: Due to the thick atmosphere its N_2 concentration is still four times higher than on Earth!	
Ozone layer	Present in the upper atmosphere that blocks 98% of the UV rays	Recently discovered (Montmessin & Bertaux, 2011; European Space Agency, 2008; Surkov *et al.*, 1986)	No ozone layer: UV rays not shielded

Presence of water	78% of the planet surface	100, 000 times less than Earth (European Space Agency, 2008)	Water present on the surface either in vapour or solid state (polar caps). NOTE: Water cannot be present in liquid state because the pressure is too low and it would evaporate!
Magnetic field	From 25 to 65 µT	~ 10^5 times less intense than the terrestrial one	No magnetic field
Volcanic activity	Ongoing	Ongoing	Probably ongoing. Important activity in the past (Carr, 2006).
Rock composition	Nearly all oxides: silicates, alumina, iron oxides, lime, magnesia, potash and soda; chlorine, sulphur and fluorine are the only important exceptions	Granite-like materials and basaltic rock (of volcanic origin) (Surkov *et al.*, 1986)	Surface slightly alkaline (pH8.3) and containing high quantity of salts (*e.g.* $MgCl_2$, $MgSO_4$, NaCl)
			Red appearance, due to iron dioxide (rust) on its surface
Environment	Diverse and extreme: hot springs, salt lakes, marshlands, deep oceans, glaciers	Atmospheric layer from ~ 50–65 km above the surface has pressure, temperature and air composition similar to Earth. Sulphuric acid clouds and acid rain	Polar carbon dioxide (CO_2) ice caps
			Presence of caves (protection from UV radiation, solar flares and bombardment with high energy particles)
			Active gas sources producing methane

The following materials are needed to play *War of Worlds*:

- One game board (A1 size) with an image of the planet Venus seen from space. On the other side there is an image of the planet Earth (used in the final phase of the game).
- One game board (A1 size) with an image of the planet Mars seen from space. On the other side there is an image of the planet Earth (used in the final phase of the game).
- For each team a deck of 17 cards, representing traits (or 'genes') that can be chosen (for card descriptions see Table 11.2); each card containing the following information (see Figure 11.1):
  - a statement of the key characteristics of the trait
  - a funny cartoon of an alien life form, for an immediate understanding of the trait's function
  - a brief description on how organisms with a very similar characteristic actually exist on Earth
  - three adaptations scores, for Mars, Venus and Earth, each ranging from –5 to +5; the higher the score, the better the trait is for survival on that planet.
- For each team two laminated A4 sheets containing the vital statistics of either Venus or Mars and of Earth for comparison (see also Table 11.1).
- For each team a die with 20 faces (D20).
- For each team a battle log sheet, for either Venus or Mars (shown in Figure 11.3 under 'How to Play').

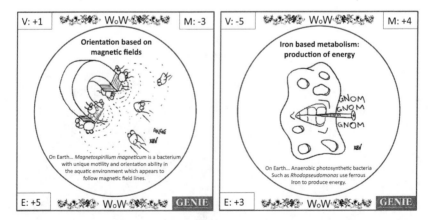

Figure 11.1 Two examples of the *War of Worlds'* trait cards

Figure 11.2 Demonstration of the use of CD windows

Table 11.2 *The 17 trait ('gene') cards used in* War of Worlds, *including full card descriptions and planet adaptation scores. See also Figure 11.1 for the card layout*

	Card description	Value on Venus	Value on Mars	Value on Earth
1	In space . . . Metabolism based on sulphate (SO_4) reduction: the reaction generates hydrogen sulphide (H_2S) and biochemical energy used for survival. On Earth . . . Sulphate-reducing bacteria live in seawater, sediments or salt marshes. The rotten eggs' odour is a marker of their presence in nature.	+5	−5	+2
2	In space . . . Photodissociation with UV photons: a chemical reaction in which a chemical compound is broken down by photons, with energy production. On Earth . . . Photosynthesis is possible primarily thanks to visible light photons, as 98% of UV rays are shielded by the ozone layer.	+3	+5	+1

(Continued overleaf)

Table 11.2 *Continued*

Card description	Value on Venus	Value on Mars	Value on Earth
3 In space . . . Carbon dioxide (CO_2) fixation, with methane (CH_4) and biochemical energy production, used for metabolic purposes. On Earth . . . Methanogen bacteria are common in wetlands, where they are responsible for marsh gas and are present in the guts of different animals, like ruminants and humans.	+3	+5	+1
4 In space . . . Survival at low temperature. On Earth . . . A species of bacteria called *Colwellia* 34H thrives at temperatures of about −50°C and evidences show that cells can survive at the boiling point of liquid nitrogen (−196°C).	−3	+4	+2
5 In space . . . Silicium-based exoskeleton, to increase body resistance. On Earth . . . Diatoms are unicellular algae encased within a unique cell wall made of silica (hydrated silicon dioxide) called frustule.	+5	−3	+3
6 In space . . . Survival at high temperatures. On Earth . . . Hyperthermophile bacteria are able to live at extremely high temperatures. *Methanopyrus kandleri* strain 116 thrives at temperatures of 80–122°C.	+5	−5	+2
7 In space . . . Photosynthesis with visible light photons, with energy production. On Earth . . . Photosynthesis is a chemical process that converts carbon dioxide into organic compounds, especially sugars, using the energy from sunlight. It is vital for all the aerobic life on Earth.	−2	+3	+5
8 In space . . . Ability to form underground colonies. On Earth . . . Extremophile bacteria are found in the "solid" rock of the Earth's crust, kilometres below the surface.	−1	+4	+3
9 In space . . . Iron-based metabolism. On Earth . . . Anaerobic photosynthetic bacteria such as *Rhodopseudomonas* use ferrous iron to produce energy.	−5	+4	+3

10 In space . . . Survival in extremely acidic   +5   +1   +1
    conditions.
    On Earth . . . *Picrophilus torridus* is able to
    grow in extreme environments with a pH
    of –0.06.

11 In space . . . Survival in environment extremely   –4   +4   +2
    enriched in salt.
    On Earth . . . Extreme halophile bacteria are able
    to survive in environments containing 30% of
    salts (the mean seawater salt concentration is
    around 3%).

12 In space . . . Ammonia oxidation through   +4   –4   +3
    nitrogen fixation.
    On Earth . . . Diazotroph bacteria fix atmospheric
    nitrogen gas into a more usable form such as
    ammonia, producing biochemical energy
    through the process.

13 In space . . . Low pressure survival.   –5   +5   –1
    On Earth . . . Bacteria taken from cliffs at Beer on
    the English South Coast survived 553 days outside
    of the international space station.

14 In space . . . High pressure survival.   +5   –3   +3
    On Earth . . . Particular strains of bacteria show
    physiological and metabolic activity at pressures
    of 68 to 1680 mega Pascal (MPa) in diamond
    anvil cells.

15 In space . . . Ability to float in the wind and   +5   –5   +1
    form aerial aggregates.
    On Earth . . . Bacteria and other particles of
    biological origin are able to collect water vapour
    to form cloud droplets.

16 In space . . . O_2 fixation and CO_2 production.   –5   –5   +5
    On Earth . . . Aerobic respiration requires oxygen
    in order to generate energy. It is a highly efficient
    mechanism, shared by different life species.

17 In space . . . Orientation based on magnetic   +1   –3   +5
    fields.
    On Earth . . . *Magnetospirillum magneticum* is a
    bacterium with unique motility and orientation in
    the aquatic environment which appears to follow
    magnetic field lines.

War of Worlds: How to Play

The *War of Worlds* game can be divided into four phases (each phase is described below in detail), which should be preceded by a brief introduction and should be followed by a final recap with overall game conclusions. We normally introduce the game with a short 10-minute PowerPoint presentation, aimed at describing the characteristics of the primordial Earth, introducing the domain of Archaea, unicellular microorganism often living under the most extreme conditions on Earth, and explaining the concepts underlying astrobiology. This introduction helps the students to create the right frame of mind and helps to awaken their creative thinking with respect to the existence and survival of possible life forms somewhere out there in space. For increased student involvement the classroom setting is also very important. We normally organise tables to form two distinct islands, on which the Venus and Mars game boards are placed. The players are then divided into two groups of six teams each. The six teams around Venus are told they now are 'Venusians' and likewise, the six teams around Mars are 'Martians'.

Phase One: Creating an Alien Species

Each team is provided with two laminated A4 sheets, one with the characteristics of either Venus or Mars (depending on what planet the team is 'located on'), and the other with the characteristics of Earth for comparison (for full planet information see also Table 11.1). Each team is also provided with a deck of 17 cards (for full card information see Table 11.2). The cards are identical for both Venusians and Martians. At this stage of the game all the cards are placed in paper CD envelopes with a circular window, only showing the cartoon and the card description, and not the planet adaptation scores (see also Figure 11.2). In the first phase of the game, the teams are asked to create an alien species selecting only five cards from the deck, representing five traits (five 'genes') that would assist their new life form to survive on their respective planet. The teams will of course need to take their planet's characteristics into account and also the fact that they will subsequently need to battle for survival with the other new species on the same planet (the other teams at the same table). Therefore, students are actively encouraged to discuss the advantages and disadvantages of all the cards with members of their own team, but not with members of other teams, who will be their enemies in the next phase of the game.

Once all the teams have chosen their five trait cards, we ask the students to take the cards out of the card sleeves. By doing so, they will discover on each card the presence of the three planet adaptations scores (see also Figure 11.2). Each team will add up the adaptation scores for their planet for their five chosen cards and will note the total on the battle log sheet (Figure 11.3). The final task for this phase will be to come up with a scientific name for their species, as well as a battle name.

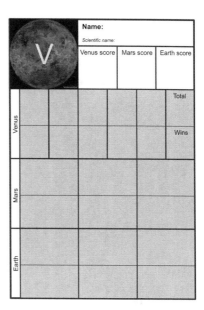

Figure 11.3 *War of Worlds'* battle log sheets

Phase Two: Battle for Survival

And now the real *War of Worlds* can begin! Each Martian team will have to fight against all other Martians, and the same will happen on Venus. Each team will be involved in five fights in total, to ascertain which species are the strongest of the planet. As it is fundamental for the students to realise how the combination of chance and unpredictable events can affect survival for a given species, the battles will involve D20 dice. When two teams are in battle, each of them will roll the die and get a chance score between 1 and 20 which will be added to the species' adaptation score (see Figure 11.4). The team with the highest total wins the fight, and in the case of a draw the fight is repeated. Once all the species on both planets have finished their five fights, on both Mars and Venus species can be ranked according to strength for survival.

Phase Three: Expansion to Another Planet

In the following phase, the three strongest Martian species will try to invade Venus, and the three strongest Venusian species will try to invade Mars. For this, the strongest teams will actually physically move planets (i.e. move to the other table with their cards and log sheets). Clearly, the invading species will have to recalculate their adaptation score, as the conditions of the planet they are trying to invade may be profoundly different from their mother planet. All invading species will notice a dramatic decrease in their adaptation power of

Figure 11.4 Students involved in a *War of Worlds'* battle

their five chosen traits. On each planet the three weakest teams will stay and defend their planet against the new invaders. Venusians will clash with Martians, using the same battle rules. It will be very obvious that even the weakest defending species have huge advantages against the invading species not adapted to the planet conditions.

Phase Four: Battle for the Blue Planet

For the final phase the game boards are turned over and students will discover a picture of Earth, which will be the setting for the last round of battles. Both the Martians and Venusians will now try to conquer the Blue Planet. Students may be surprised to find out that all of their cards will have a small positive adaptation score for Earth. Of course, our planet has a striking diversity of environments which allow the adaptation of many different species. The trait cards are in fact designed to give balanced Earth adaptation scores if teams were able to create well-adapted Venusian and Martian species. In this last round of battles chance (the rolling of the dice) will be crucial to determine the winners and the losers!

Finally, the winners of *War of Worlds* are announced! Every team is then asked to present their species name and to comment on their trait card selection. The students proudly present their choices and a lively discussion often emerges. In a final recap the main characteristics of the three planets can be reviewed. This final stage of the game can easily be expanded into more in-depth conversations about the extreme environmental conditions on different planets or about some of the bizarre Archaea on Earth, like halophiles and acidophiles.

Conclusions

The *War of Worlds* board game fully met our expectations and aspirations. We have trialed the game with students of different age groups and different educational backgrounds; 13–15-year-old students attending the Junior Space School UK 2012, 16–18-year-old students attending the Senior Space School UK 2011, and students (15–17 years old) attending an Interdisciplinary Science Summer School held at the University of Leicester in 2012. On all occasions all the key messages were delivered satisfactorily and all students showed a great commitment and enthusiasm for the *War of Worlds* game.

On one occasion, we also had the chance to observe the reaction to the game by a 17-year-old male diagnosed with Asperger syndrome. The idea of creating new extraterrestrial life forms greatly stimulated this young man's enthusiasm; he actively participated in all of the tasks proposed, taking a leading role within his team (and in fact his planet) and proactively offering help in the card choice to others. Moreover, he engaged with us in a very constructive discussion with useful suggestions to increase the difficulty and the number of variables of the game.

The reaction of all summer school facilitators and science teachers accompanying the students was extremely positive. They asked interesting questions and were as fascinated as the students about the microorganisms in the domain of Archaea. They also showed similar astonishment on learning how life is possible even under very extreme conditions and studied all the trait cards with great interest.

We believe that we have developed a highly versatile educational tool that has clearly shown great potential in engaging students in a scientific field merging physics, genetics and astrobiology. According to the science teachers who have witnessed the game, it also has great potential in secondary education to raise the students' interest in science and to make them abandon the (in our view) false concept that science is boring.

Acknowledgements

The authors would like to thank the financial support from Space School UK 2011. Thanks should also go to Angelica Vittori and Xavier Tait for their artistic input in creating the cartoons depicted on the trait cards.

References

Bergman, I. (1957). *The Seventh Seal*. Synopsis available at http://www.imdb.com/title/tt0050976/ (accessed 2 December 2012).

Carey, B. (2005). Available at http://www.livescience.com/133-wild-extreme-creatures.html (accessed 2 December 2012).

Carr, M.H. (2006). *The Surface of Mars*. New York, NY: Cambridge University Press.

Department of Physics and Astronomy, University of Leicester (2012). *Space School*. Available at http://spaceschool.co.uk/ (accessed 2 December 2012).

European Space Agency (2008). *Where Did Venus's Water Go?* Available at http://www.esa.int/SPECIALS/Venus_Express/SEM8MYSTGOF_0.html (accessed 2 December 2012).

Javaux, E.J. (2006). Extreme life on Earth – past, present and possibly beyond. *Research in Microbiology*, 157/1, 37–48.

Konami (1999). *Yu-Gi-Oh! Trading Card Game*. Available at http://www.yugioh-card.com/ (accessed 2 December 2012).

Martin, W. & Russell, M.J. (2007). On the origin of biochemistry at an alkaline hydrothermal vent. *Philos Trans R Soc Lond B Biol Sci.* 362/1486, 1887–925.

Montmessin, F. & Bertaux, J-L. (2011). A layer of ozone detected in the nightside upper atmosphere of Venus. *Icarus*, 216/1, 82–85.

Surkov, L.P., Yu, A. & Moskalyova, O. (1986). Rock composition at the Vega 2 landing site. *J. Geophys. Res.* 91.

Toy reviews and news (2012). *Trading Card and Role Playing Games*. Available at http://www.toy-tma.com/trading-card-role-playing-games/ (accessed 2 December 2012).

Wächtershäuser, G. (1988). Before enzymes and templates: theory of surface metabolism. *Microbiol Rev.*, 52/4, 452–84.

Wikipedia (2012a). *Magic: the Gathering*. Available at http://en.wikipedia.org/wiki/Magic:The_Gathering (accessed 2 December 2012).

Wikipedia (2012b). *Trading Card*. Available at http://en.wikipedia.org/wiki/Trading_card (accessed 2 December 2012).

Wizards of the Coast (1993). *Magic: The Gathering*. Available at http://www.wizards.com/Magic/Summoner/ (accessed 2 December 2012).

Wizards of the Coast (1998). *Pokemon Trading Card Game*. Available at http://www.pokemon.com/uk/pokemon-trading-card-game/ (accessed 2 December 2012).

12

CONTEXTS AND CONCEPTS
Crafty Ways to Consider Challenging Topics

CLAIRE HAMSHIRE, RACHEL FORSYTH, MANCHESTER METROPOLITAN UNIVERSITY, UK

Introduction

The games described in this chapter both had their beginnings in research projects: one exploring students' perceptions of their higher education experiences (*Staying the Course*), and the other investigating staff experiences of curriculum development (*Supporting Responsive Curricula*). Neither project was initially tasked with developing a game, but both research teams wanted to ensure that the data gathered during the projects could be utilised to facilitate future developments and share good practice identified as a result of the research.

In both situations, the project teams believed that sharing the findings of the projects widely would help to change behaviours and bring about service improvements but were unsure how to get most impact from the data. A conversation with the editors of this book sparked off some creative thinking about the possibility of using traditional board games to communicate the findings of the two projects and to encourage discussion and action planning about some challenging topics. These twin objectives were key to the process of designing and after a couple of planning meetings to discuss scope and applicability, two very different games for use in higher education (HE) began to take form.

In both cases, it was clear from the research findings that the intended audiences found it difficult to see the relevance of the outcomes to their own situations, or to feel comfortable in discussing what could at times be difficult issues. Using the medium of a board game therefore offered an opportunity to examine problematic issues within the 'magic circle' of game play (Charlier *et al.*, 2012).

In this chapter, we describe how we have used simple board game designs and linked discussion to get players thinking about different perspectives, working out how particular situations or processes would affect them and how they could make improvements to existing situations. We will also outline how the games evolved during the iterative process of testing and evaluation.

The Research

The initial research projects were entirely different: the first project, *Staying the Course*, was concerned with supporting students who might be considering withdrawal from their courses. The second, *Supporting Responsive Curricula*, looked at curriculum design processes in HE and how they could be made more responsive to the needs of students, employers and professional bodies.

Staying the Course Project

Staying the Course was a large scale mixed-methods, regional study undertaken at nine higher education institutions in the North-West of England, which investigated healthcare students' perceptions of their learning experiences and identified factors that contributed to attrition. The student sample for the study was drawn from a range of healthcare programmes across the North West of England, which were primarily nursing but also included a range of allied health professions.

Student feedback from interviews and an online survey suggested that they needed greater support during their initial transitions to university, as they described their initial experiences as 'information overload' and 'bewildering' (Hamshire *et al.*, 2012, 2013). For many students, this is one of the most significant and difficult learning transitions they will make (Yorke & Longden, 2007) and although staff made resources available and informed students about support services, significant numbers were unaware of university procedures and how and when to access services.

The literature on student attrition suggests that induction programmes should try to avoid information overload (Harvey *et al.*, 2006; Hamshire & Cullen, 2010) and facilitate the development of academic and peer relationships so that students feel welcomed to the university community and can become accustomed to university systems and procedures (Edward, 2003). As reported by Yorke and Longden (2007), simply making friends seems to be a crucial part of a positive transition to higher education. It seemed essential to try to provide information to new students in ways that did not contribute to the information overload and which signposted key sources of support without going into exhaustive detail about what that support might be.

Supporting Responsive Curricula Project

Supporting Responsive Curricula was a single-institution study which used a case study approach to review current practice and identify key drivers for change, and it faced similar issues in a very different context. The findings showed that staff needed to be fully engaged with the processes of curriculum change, but that they often felt overloaded and disempowered with regard to these processes. The project identified that staff should be more involved in the articulation and management of the accreditation processes, rather than viewing them as irrelevant and imposed externally. The interview data also highlighted that academic staff, in particular, found the processes bureaucratic and frustrating, while administrative staff thought that course teams did not always communicate their needs clearly, and students indicated that they had almost no involvement in curriculum redesign. These fairly strong positions made it more challenging to find ways to interest people in the processes and to get them to work together.

The lack of ownership of processes can make it easier to critique them, but may militate against constructive suggestions for improvement. In addition, Elton (2003) has described how it can be difficult to engage academic staff with the findings and recommendations of an externally funded project, even in situations where the individual may well be able to achieve change, such as over the teaching they do individually. This effect has been linked to theories of professional learning and it has been argued that innovation needs to be presented within the context of professional practice (Lave and Wenger, 1991) and not 'taught' separately through specially arranged dissemination events and reports. The combination of disengagement with curriculum review processes and with externally funded projects such as *Supporting Responsive Curricula* meant that it would be difficult to bring about real change using conventional activities such as dissemination events. Another approach was needed.

Why a Game?

Essentially the underlying philosophy of both authors was to design an active learning environment in which players could learn via discussion activities and testing their understanding – effectively a constructivist learning perspective. Board games commonly have the simple objectives of entertainment or social facilitation and while this was also incorporated into both games we were also guided by an awareness of what was appropriate within a given context and the logistics of game play within the HE environment.

More specifically, for *Staying the Course*, the team wanted to design something that would introduce students to common concerns and problems that they might encounter during their first year, and encourage them to think about possible approaches and solutions. The primary objective of the game was to facilitate students' inductions to higher education by providing an opportunity for both collaborative learning and peer support, with the game format used to provide a safe space in which students could interact and make mistakes, removing the pressure and adding a layer of fun to the learning experience. Guided by this philosophy the game was developed in close partnership with both students and the Students' Union staff to ensure that the game had real-world relevance.

In *Supporting Responsive Curricula*, the team wanted to focus on the actual process of getting curriculum material approved and accredited, to encourage staff and students to find out more about the accreditation process and also to discuss ways to make it more responsive to the needs of others. The use of a game would enable the team to highlight oddities, inconsistencies and important elements of the existing processes, while depersonalising them in a way which makes discussion more comfortable. If an incident occurs by chance in a game, like forgetting a key deadline or part of a consultation, or losing a laptop with all of the documentation on it, nobody is really responsible, which makes it easier to have discussions about how it may occur and how it could be avoided or at least mitigated.

Designing a Board Game

Although we both had plenty of experience of designing teaching sessions and of playing traditional board games, neither of us had ever combined these activities by using games in teaching. We certainly had no experience of designing any kind of structured game for any purpose and wanted to ensure that the games were seen as acceptable by their users and not as frivolous or an unnecessary distraction (Whitton, 2009). We sought advice initially from a game developer who had an interest in collaborative games-based learning and also reviewed research on game play (for example, Whitton 2009 and Prensky 2001).

During this discussion and planning we identified elements that we believed would be necessary to make our games effective, including:

- acceptability and real-world relevance
- goals
- fun
- competition/challenge
- opportunities for interaction and collaboration
- narrative
- simple rules.

The design of each game needed to capture and synthesise all of these elements without losing sight of the game's educational objectives.

Acceptability and Real-world Relevance

In order for the games to be perceived as acceptable and appropriate by our target group of players we believed that the purpose and the real-world relevance of the games had to be clearly articulated. We wanted players to recognise that the games were an appropriate context in which they could explore problems and concerns and be able to transfer any knowledge gained into real-world situations.

In both cases we felt that it was therefore worth thinking about a working title at this stage. The *Staying the Course* game retained the same name as the project as the team believed that the name made it clear that the purpose of the game was to facilitate students' journeys into higher education. The *Supporting Responsive Curricula* project called its game *Accreditation!*. Unfortunately, the title of 'Frustration!' was already taken. During testing, the title of 'Monotony' was also suggested; we were assured that this wasn't a reflection on the game, but rather on the processes it described.

Goals

For both of these games the goal was to be the first to complete the game. Conventionally, games need to have a clearly stated goal and there are few choices about what this might be in traditional board games: to be the first to get to the end, to gain the most points, or to be the last person still playing. The enduring attraction of successful traditional games such as Snakes and Ladders, draughts, chess or *Monopoly* shows that goals should be simple, even if game play is complex.

The choice of goal will have an impact on the game play: for instance, if the aim is to be the last person still playing, then you might want to include potential acts of sabotage, but that might conflict with underlying objectives about co-operative working. If players are collecting points for various actions, then there might be some benefit to them teaming up to support each other and disadvantage others.

Fun

The concept of fun was important to both authors. As previously stated, we were aware that the intended audiences found it difficult to see the relevance of the project outcomes to their own situations, or to discuss difficult issues. Therefore we incorporated humour into the scenarios used in the card sets, and both games included a 'Take a Chance' set of cards to introduce an element of luck into the games. These cards required players to pick up a card from a special pile with positive or negative events, which were not specific to the themes or the chronology of the game, such as losing your laptop on a train, illness or learning something new from a chance meeting. In both games it is possible for any of the cards to send you backwards instead of forwards. The game cards were also probably the most fun part of the games to design. In both cases, several iterations were necessary in order to make the instructions on the cards concise, jargon-free and credible (although exaggeration was frequently considered acceptable).

Competition/Challenge

In order to introduce competition it was important that there was at least some degree of difficulty embedded within the games. This was achieved by having a range of challenging questions within the card sets. Some cards included questions with obvious answers or merely instructions, whereas others required that the players already had some background knowledge of the game content. The goal of game completion also enabled the players to see easily how they were doing compared to others as they moved their playing pieces around the board. There were opportunities to help other players by using the 'Take a Chance' cards supportively, or to sabotage them if they were doing too well.

Opportunities for Interaction and Collaboration

In both of the games described here, the goal was to be the first to reach the last square on the board, but this turned out to be unimportant for most players. The process of playing, interacting and collaborating with the other players turned out to be the most important element of the experience, which entirely met our objectives of communicating research findings and encouraging creative discussion.

Narrative

Incorporating a story within the game to increase player engagement and enable them to identify with the 'characters' was essential. Both games followed a narrative linked to their underlying purpose. *Staying the Course* follows the course of an academic year and *Accreditation!* takes players through a cycle of course validation or review.

Simple Rules

Rules set boundaries for the players about their behaviours and actions during the game. Players may not like the rules, or they may not play by them, but at least everyone knows where they stand. The advantage of designing a traditional board game is that most of the rules you might want to use have already been tried and tested, and are familiar to the players. This makes it easy for players to settle down to play without much introduction or support.

In the case of both of these games, the rules were pretty simple:

1. You can play on your own or in teams.
2. Follow the instructions on the cards you pick up.
3. Move around the board in a clockwise direction unless instructed otherwise by a card.

Game Play

The way in which players progress through the game turned out to need quite a lot of thought and testing. As previously mentioned, the aim for both games was to reach the last square of the board first. The game play is thus concerned with the stages laid out on the board, the rules for moving along the board, keeping the movement regular and structured and making the play equitable. For both games, the design of the game play started with thinking about the layout of the board, followed by scoring systems which enabled movement forwards and backwards at a reasonably even pace and which enabled someone to get to the end in the intended time.

Staying the Course

The *Staying the Course* board follows the course of an academic year and the object of the game is to be the first player to complete a circuit of the board, which is laid out with coloured squares. Players have to move around the board itself by making decisions and answering the questions that are presented on cards, which they pick up depending on the colour of the squares they land on. The players roll a single die, move forward the indicated number of squares and then take a card of the same colour as the square they land on. The instructions on the cards then dictate if further places are moved – either forwards or backwards. The majority of the cards require action from the player who rolls the dice; occasionally the card dictates that all players have to do something for the game to proceed. Figure 12.1 is an image of the game board.

The starting point for the card questions was the thematic analysis of the students' narratives that had identified three broad themes:

- academic issues and uncertainties;
- personal difficulties;
- placement problems and issues.

The most frequently occurring issues from each of these three themes were developed into quiz questions and dilemmas that became three sets of cards for use within the game, using verbatim quotes from students wherever possible. A fourth set of cards – "Take a Chance" – was subsequently developed to incorporate unusual and unplanned circumstances that students had experienced and to add a random element of luck to the game play. These cards also provided checks and balances to players' progress around the board, preventing individuals from shooting ahead or saving them from being stuck in one place for too long.

A fifth set of cards giving information on Student Services was later developed to raise students' awareness of the campus-based advice and support services. These cards were linked to 'fast-forward' squares that are in the four corners of the game. Each of these four areas relate to one of the available student services:

- Library Services
- Students' Union Advice Centre
- Student Services
- Online Student Hub.

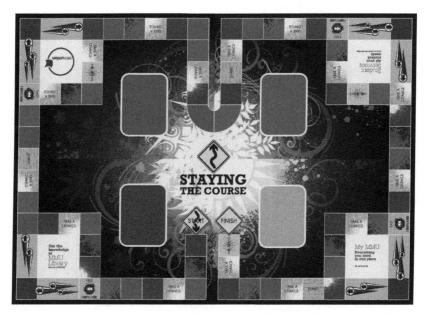

Figure 12.1 The *Staying the Course* game board

When students land on the fast-forward area they proceed to the relevant purple square, and then read the information on the corresponding purple card that is placed under the corner of the board to the rest of the players. All the players are therefore made aware of what help and advice is available to them during their time at university. These squares are named 'fast-forward' as they give players an advantage in the game by skipping over four squares, and we wanted to highlight to the students that if they engaged with these services it would facilitate their time while at university.

Accreditation!

The *Accreditation!* game also used a chronological structure and different sets of cards to determine movement around the board. However, for this game the players had to complete one section before moving on to the next; this reflects what happens in a real course approval process. Figure 12.2 shows the game board.

When a player (the active player) lands on a square, one of the other players picks up a card which corresponds to the colour of the section the active player is currently in; the card presents a dilemma and two possible courses of action. The other player reads these out, but does not tell the active player what the

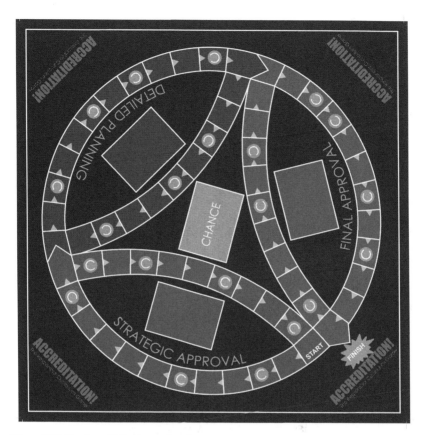

Figure 12.2 The *Accreditation!* game board

consequences of the actions might be. Figure 12.3 shows examples of two cards from different sections.

The active player is asked to choose between the two actions, and depending on their answer they could be told to move forwards or backwards, or to stay where they were. In addition, they might be awarded one or more 'quality stars' for their choice. In order to leave a section, they need to get to the last square of the section and be in possession of five quality stars. If they don't have enough quality stars, they will loop back around that section.

Although this was not intended when the game play was designed, going around in circles has turned out to make a useful discussion point, as real course teams frequently get stuck on particular aspects of the process when they need more information or support. Players quickly learn that there may be some compromise between speed and quality and this usually creates reflection about the processes.

You realise that your team will need to receive intensive VLE training for the programme to be effective. They aren't keen.

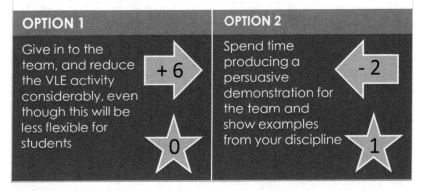

OPTION 1

Give in to the team, and reduce the VLE activity considerably, even though this will be less flexible for students

+ 6

0

OPTION 2

Spend time producing a persuasive demonstration for the team and show examples from your discipline

- 2

1

Figure 12.3 Sample cards from *Accreditation!*

In terms of the game play, after observing that most players stuck rigidly to the rules, even if chance conspired to leave them in a seemingly eternal loop, particularly on the first section, an additional rule was added to give them permission to be subversive: "You can cheat and skip out of a zone if things seem to be getting tedious and/or repetitive". This had a liberating effect on many people and definitely added to the interaction and discussion for teams: getting stuck at a particular stage of course approval is a fairly common real-life experience and players found it helpful to discuss why this might be and to think about ways they could leave that loop if they found themselves in the situation in real life (without cheating, of course).

The dilemmas on the section-based cards were initially based on experiences of real course teams and administrators. These were inevitably refined in order to make them concise and scorable, but they still seem to ring true for most players. The 'Take a Chance' cards do not contain dilemmas, and only have instructions. They tend to have high scores associated with them, so can make a big difference to a player's position on the board. This makes them risky and they help to sustain engagement and amusement for players.

Discussion Points

With both of these games, discussion occurs naturally without any particular need to stop the groups and highlight issues or situations. Because the dilemmas in both games are based on the outcomes of research, players are usually presented with a situation that they've encountered in real life very quickly, and this inevitably leads to discussion along the lines of "when this happened to me, I . . .". For future dilemmas, even if they are novel, players seem then to find it easier to say, "If this happened to me, I would . . .". Perhaps because playing the games is fun, groups usually socialise quickly, which helps to get them discussing what can be difficult issues.

In *Staying the Course*, we wanted the students to use the cards to stimulate discussion about potential problems and dilemmas that may occur during their first year and to talk about how they would manage difficulties. Therefore while the game is designed to be an interesting and engaging way of introducing students to many issues they might later encounter at university, it is the discussion around the game that is really important to learning. At the end of the game play session if students have any remaining concerns and questions they can access the companion website that includes FAQs, quizzes, videos and student case studies. This provides an ongoing source of support and information.

In *Accreditation!*, we want to get people thinking about the potential trade-offs which may arise between speed and quality, and to talk about ways to avoid getting into difficult situations with accreditation processes. In many cases, these situations arise because of a lack of understanding of the processes involved, so that essential steps or elements are missed out, or because teams don't realise how other colleagues may be able to help them, so it has proved particularly useful to play the game with groups who have different roles such as quality administrators, library staff, workshop technicians, information technology specialists and academic staff. The neutral situation of a game seems to provide an excellent opportunity for constructive discussion and to make it easy to contribute, whatever the hierarchy might be in the 'real world'. It also sparks previously unexpected connections across the roles, which can be beneficial when players are actually engaging in course accreditation activity later. Difficulties with process might also arise because the accreditation processes themselves are in need of review, and looking at particular examples presented in the dilemmas can be useful in provoking discussion about what needs to be done.

Piloting

The design process for *Staying the Course* was iterative, with each new board and set of cards tested by students and the Students' Union staff to test usability, playability and appropriateness of game questions. A further eight hour-long testing sessions were undertaken with 23 first- and second-year students and ten members of academic staff. During this process the game was refined to include greater information on university support services and collaborative cards that encouraged peer support.

Piloting was essential to get the game play right. In testing, we found that the original scoring systems in both games needed to be adjusted, either because it was possible for one person to romp around the board in 20 minutes while others were still stuck near the beginning, or because players were seemingly trapped in an endless loop in one stage of their journey through an academic year or a validation cycle. Trial and error was needed to refine the scoring systems so that movement was reasonably equitable between players and the game duration was generally around 45 minutes. We found that testing the games with colleagues in social situations was an effective way of getting genuine and helpful feedback.

Evaluation

Initial evaluations of the *Staying the Course* game were conducted by recording staff and student comments and suggestions during the testing sessions. Initial verbal feedback from students has been positive and the overall theme was that they particularly enjoyed the debate and discussion prompted by the dilemma questions:

> "This is great, I am a second year and I didn't know half this stuff!"
> (Psychology student)

Academic and support staff have also commented on how the game turns a process of information giving into a fun interaction.

> "I've really enjoyed playing this game; it raises awareness of all the main issues affecting students and is a fun way to inform students about support services."
> (Students' Union Advice Centre Manager)

A second stage evaluation when all question sets were finalized was conducted with 102 students attending a study day. These students were each asked to leave comments on sticky notes on their perceptions of the game and their playing experiences and the comments were overwhelmingly positive.

The *Accreditation!* game has been tried by around 90 academics and administrators at a series of seminars and conferences around the UK, after which players have been able to take away copies of the game for their own use, so we hope it has been effective in developing debate and discussion in other institutions as well. Evaluation has been very positive, although one must bear in mind that some of this may be in response to the novelty value of a game being played at a conference rather than the more usual slide presentation. Players are usually very lively and have been asked to lower the noise by colleagues in an adjoining room (this is counted as a positive element to the evaluation).

> "Really innovative approach to working through the issues of curriculum design – and engaging everyone involved. Excellent session."
>
> (Conference participant)

However, the favourite comment was definitely this one, from a table on which one player was able to relate to a particularly large number of the dilemmas posed in the game: "It's not a game, it's a biography!"

In *Accreditation!*, the piloting of the game led to the provision of additional examples which were turned into dilemmas, which was an unexpected bonus. It's definitely worth asking the piloters to suggest additional examples during evaluation.

The Future

Both games have been produced using internal printing facilities and the purchase of a few cheap playing pieces. It costs around £30 to produce a playing set for each game, including lamination of the board if that is required.

Initial evaluations of the *Staying the Course* game have been encouraging and both staff and student players have commented positively on their playing experiences. The majority of student comments have focused on their enjoyment of game-play and on their perceptions of having gained greater knowledge and understanding of student support services after play. Observations from academic and support staff included positive feedback on both the game design and content and several constructive comments on how the game could be further developed.

Development of the *Staying the Course* game has been iterative and continuously informed by game-play sessions with both staff and students. We are currently developing further versions of the game for use with other student groups, and two additional card sets have been developed: Finances and Futures. These card sets are coloured so that they are interchangeable with the Placement card set so the game can be adapted for the needs of a particular group.

Student attrition from higher education is an international concern and there is evidence that students leave for a range of personal, social and academic issues (Tinto & Goodsell, 1993). While there is no simple formula to ease students' transitions into higher education and the retention of a diverse student body, all interactions that promote social and academic integration should be encouraged. The findings from the initial evaluations indicate that *Staying the Course* can be used to promote social, academic and personal integrations and this suggests that it could be used to support student transitions to higher education. The board game gives players an opportunity to progress through an academic year. As such, by editing the cards and institutional logos on the board the game can be repurposed for any student group and age group. The board game is currently being developed as a 'giant' game to be used at induction events and study days.

Accreditation! is now used as a staff development tool and replaces what used to be a very boring lecture on accreditation. Feedback suggests that staff retain understanding and knowledge of the different parts of the process and the importance of working as a multi-disciplinary team to develop their course documentation.

Moseley (2010) has argued that simple gaming activities, played face-to-face, can be used to create context in a host of learning and teaching situations. The two games described here did this, but also had the advantages of flattening hierarchies, providing unexpected connections between players and sparking off a whole host of discussions and follow-ups. Being in a difficult situation as a playing piece gives anonymity to express opinions without them being linked directly to you. Because everyone in the game takes a turn, everyone has an equal voice, even if they would be too shy to offer an opinion in a normal group discussion.

Acknowledgements

The authors would like to acknowledge the Joint Information Systems Commitee (JISC) for providing support for the Supporting Responsive Curricula project, NHS North West for providing support for the *Staying the Course* project, Nicola Whitton for talking to us about game play and colleagues and students for participating enthusiastically in game playing sessions and making suggestions for improvements.

References

Charlier, N., Ott, M., Remmele, B. & Whitton, N. (2012). Not just for children: game-based learning for older adults. *Proceedings of The sixth European Conference on Games Based Learning 2012*, Cork. Academic Conferences.

Edward, N.S. (2003). First impressions last: an innovative approach to induction. *Active Learning in Higher Education* 4/3, 226–242.

Elton, L. (2003). Dissemination of innovations in higher education: a change theory approach. *Tertiary Education and Management* 9/3, 199–214.

Hamshire, C. & Cullen, R. (2010). Developing a spiralling induction programme: a blended approach. In K. Anagnostopoulou & D. Parmar (ed.), *Supporting the First Year Student Experience through the Use of Learning Technologies.* Middlesex: Higher Education Academy, pp. 34–36.

Hamshire, C., Willgoss, T.G. & Wibberley, C. (2012). 'The placement was probably the tipping point' – the narratives of recently discontinued students. *Nurse Education in Practice*, 12/4, 182–186.

Hamshire, C., Willgoss, T. G. & Wibberley, C. (2013). What are reasonable expectations? Healthcare student perceptions of their programmes in the North West of England. *Nurse Education Today*, 33/2, 173–179.

Harvey, L., Drew, S. & Smith, M. (2006). The first-year experience: a review of literature for the Higher Education Academy, York: Higher Education Research Academy.

Lave, J. and Wenger, E. (1991). *Situated Learning: Legitimate Peripheral Participation.* Cambridge: Cambridge University Press.

Moseley, A. (2010). Back two spaces, and roll again: the use of games-based activities to quickly set authentic contexts. *Proceedings of the Fourth European Conference on Games Based Learning.* Copenhagen: Academic Conferences Limited.

Prensky, M. (2001). *Digital Game-based Learning.* New York, NY: McGraw-Hill.

Tinto, V. & Goodsell, A. (1993). *A Longitudinal Study of Freshman Interest Groups at the University of Washington.* Washington, DC: Office of Education Research and Improvement.

Whitton, N. (2009). *Learning with Digital Games: A Practical Guide to Engage Students in Higher Education.* New York, NY: Routledge.

Yorke, M. and Longden, B. (2007). *The First-year Experience in Higher Education in the UK, Higher Education Academy.* Available at http://escalate.ac.uk/downloads/3365.pdf (accessed 12 December 2012).

13

Building Soma
The Development, Release and Postmortem of *Healing Blade*, a Novel Infectious Disease Card Battle Game

ARUN MATHEWS, MEDICAL CENTER HOSPITAL IN ODESSA, TEXAS, USA; TEXAS TECH UNIVERSITY, USA

Healing Blade is a tabletop card battle game that was released in March of 2010 as the sophomore effort of a disruptive education company called NerdcoreLearning. It was originally envisioned as a lighthearted way for health sciences students to practice antibiotic selection for different types of infections. The game, and the world it was set in, Soma, has now grown into a metaphorical representation of a complex ecosystem, replete with physiologic processes that tie in to our understanding of the human body and how it responds to infection.

This chapter is intended to take you through the very early days of the creative process, and will hopefully offer some coherent insights based on the lessons learned from the first iteration of the game. Before I launch into the specifics of the game, I will share how the entity known as NerdcoreLearning came into being. I do so in the hope that if two full-time physicians can strive to create a disruptive education company in their spare time, you, constant reader, can, too. Here is a brief synopsis of the process – mistakes included – for your review.

Introduction: Calendars to Clostridia

As with a great many left-of-field projects, the inception of NerdcoreLearning (or NCL as I'll refer to it from here on) came about in the form of a dare.

This dare came about after discovering a professional services marketplace called eLance (eLance.com). There are a number of professional services marketplaces in addition to eLance, such as Freelancer.com and Guru.com. My wife and I were drawn to eLance's clean user-interface and its integration with a financial platform that allows quick project management and payment of contractors.

At this point we had an epiphany. We lived and worked in a small town in south-eastern New Mexico. It became apparent to us that as long as you had a reasonable Internet connection and access to a decent mail service, it really didn't matter where on the planet you existed – services like eLance would provide the ability to, quite simply, get things done. Could full-time professionals with a baby on the way set about the task of designing, coordinating and marketing a simple product via the use of contractors alone? Therein lay the dare!

Medical mnemonics are simple memory short-cuts that allow students to quickly remember lists of abstract information by way of association. The following example details the steps of a biochemical pathway called glycolysis:

"Goodness Gracious, Father Franklin **Did Go By** Picking Pumpkins (to) **Prepare Pies**":

Glucose
Glucose–6-P
Fructose–6-P
Fructose–1,6-diP
Dihydroxyacetone-P
Glyceraldehyde-P
1,3-**Bi**phosphoglycerate
3-**P**hosphoglycerate
2-**P**hosphoglycerate (to)
Phosphoenolpyruvate [**PEP**]
Pyruvate

I had collected a small compendium of such medical mnemonics throughout medical school and released them as a published collection during my residency. We envisioned a simple concept for a medical mnemonics page-a-day calendar that we thought would be perfect for the debut product.

The traditional approach would have involved using contractors to help develop a proposal and possibly even a prototype of the calendar, with the ultimate goal of presenting it to an established publisher. But we opted to take the additional steps of designing cover art packaging, negotiating with print houses in South Korea, and commissioning a low-volume print run, essentially becoming the publisher.

This alternative method allowed us the flexibility of managing our lives in addition to remotely managing the other tasks at hand to complete this dare. Using eLance we were able to do the following things that we simply would not have been able to do otherwise:

1. Organize our mnemonics files into a database sorted by subspecialty.
2. Design a prototype for the calendar.
3. Design cover art and packaging for the calendar.
4. Create a corporate identity for the publishing house.
5. Build a website/webstore.

6. Research print houses both nationally and internationally that would do low-volume print runs.

This rapidly taught us a few simple concepts, including basic project management and how to appraise contractors quickly and negotiate accordingly. It was comforting to know that while we were managing our somewhat busy days (and nights!), contractors were hard at work in some other part of the globe, helping us to incrementally advance our project forward!

Hence, with very little fanfare, in 2009, the small, disruptive publishing company that is NCL was launched. All told, the calendar project design and the printing of the prototype cost us approximately $5,000. An additional $10,000 went into the first print run. What we learned: calendars are tricky nuts to crack. Value drops over time and inventory is a nightmare. We in fact needed to obtain a dedicated distributor that would take away the pain of managing inventory and order fulfillment. Last, and perhaps most important, we learned that while it was easy to fall in love with the design process of taking a product from 'napkin' to market, marketing and sales are in fact just as important, if not more so, to the lifeblood of the business as a whole.

This was hard-earned knowledge. We began to realize that this experience was in effect our masters of business administration. We would also be the first people to tell you that choosing a calendar for your initial project is perhaps a mistake. But the success of *Healing Blade*, our second project, is directly tied to the lessons from the ultimately failed calendar project. We were able to use our experience from the calendar project to build a better product. We were also able to re-engage with a number of the contractors we used in building and designing the Care Calendar when we moved forward with *Healing Blade*.

The inspiration for *Healing Blade* came from something that we like to refer to as "conceptual blending." As gamers ourselves, we love being able to dive deeply into worlds that other game designers have created. The particular software house that enthralled us was Bioware Interactive. Founded by three physicians, it has earned a dedicated following by creating consistently excellent mainstream role-playing games that feel extremely well thought out and fully immersive.

A particular favourite of the NCL team was a game called *Mass Effect*. A masterpiece of the genre, it skillfully blended storytelling, character development, and traditional role-playing game elements with action-based tactical engagements with enemy combatants. These engagements involved a combination of turn-based and strategic gameplay that allowed players to assess weaknesses and enemies they encountered and appropriately make strategic decisions to improve the probability of victory.

One morning after a night of involved gameplay I was making rounds in the medical intensive care unit with the nurse and a student. The question came up: "How does one choose the appropriate antibiotic for an infection when the infection has not been proven by way of cultures or Gram stain?"

This seemed, in essence, a sound question. In medicine, we prove the presence of infections by taking samples from where the infection is thought to exist (i.e. blood, urine or an infected wound site) and then literally placing it into a culture medium and incubating it, allowing the infective agent (usually bacteria, but sometimes a virus, fungus or parasite) to grow in large numbers to allow for identification by running tests on said cultures. Gram staining is named after the Danish scientist Hans Christian Gram, who demonstrated in 1884 that certain types of bacteria take up a certain chemical stain (Gram positive) while others did not (Gram negative). Gram staining allows for the rapid determination of certain families of bacteria, allowing for reasonable guesses as to which antibiotics should be used. Despite this, when a patient presents with an overwhelming and possibly life-threatening infection, antibiotics need to be administered as quickly as possible, while waiting for the results of the cultures, which can take a few hours to days to return from the microbiology lab. The cultures and Gram stain become 'confirmatory tests', which still leaves us with the decision – which antibiotic does one choose?

The discussion revealed that we were largely guessing which antibiotics to use for patients who were extremely sick. This proved to be a revelation to the students, which is always exciting to uncover, but we (the nurse and I) further elaborated. We agreed that there is a degree of guesswork associated with the initial management of extremely ill patients with significant infections. Yet educated guesswork based on various cues regarding the patient's clinical picture forms the basis of investigative medicine. This term is called 'clinical context' and is an important part of practicing medicine as a whole. Taking a complete history from the patient and performing a thorough physical exam allows clinicians to make 'educated guesses' about disease states which we then confirm with laboratory work, imaging and additional testing.

What occurred to me then and there was that there were numerous parallels between engaging with the dark forces of infection and the game I had been playing the evening before. In fact, it became very easy to draw parallels between sending scouting units out to identify weaknesses in the enemy ranks so I could make appropriate decisions when the battle ensued and taking a good history, performing a thorough physical exam, obtaining basic blood laboratory work, and making an educated guess about what type of infection a patient has. We are able to make very reasonable assessments in regard to which antibiotics (weapons) in our armamentarium to use against the forces we suspect are attacking an individual's body. If there ever was an aha! moment regarding the *Healing Blade* concept, that was it.

After two days of playing around with the idea, it occurred to me that simulating these engagements between antibiotics and microbes in a metaphorical manner would allow people to rehearse some of the decision-making that could ultimately be of benefit prior to stepping into a hospital, and applying them to real patients. While there are broad general rules which can be applied to making sound initial antibiotic choices, there are also several subtle nuances when it comes to antibiotic selection with processes such as healthcare-related pneumonia versus community-acquired pneumonia. With community-acquired pneumonia, certain standard organisms are of a higher prevalence in terms of infection. With healthcare-related pneumonia, other more resistant organisms need to be accounted for such as MRSA, Pseudomonas aeruginosa, and atypical organisms, in addition to the concept of antibiotic resistance coming into play.

This is the kind of information we hoped our game would allow players to learn and rehearse prior to entering a hospital. It was one of the founding precepts of *Healing Blade*. As we developed a very basic concept document, we also wanted to incorporate other features that students would learn while playing the game:

1. A respect and appreciation for antibiotics in general. These agents have truly revolutionized the field of medicine – a notion that is sometimes taken for granted. While impressive, they can have deleterious side effects and corrections that need to be accounted for.

2. An introduction to the concept of *antibiotics stewardship*, which is methodology for responsibly using antibiotics in the hospital. When unnecessarily potent antibiotics are used to treat a mild infection, the stage is set for antibiotic resistance. We wanted to teach this through our gameplay. When, in the game, the antibiotic card player inappropriately uses very powerful antibiotics, it essentially gives away that individual's hand, allowing the bacteria cardplayer to make strategic decisions and/or implement a resistance magic card.

3. The use of imagery to suggest features of the bacteria and the diseases themselves. For instance, Clostridium difficile is represented as a hulking monstrosity releasing spores from its back. The imagery of the spores alludes to the bacteria's primary mode of transmission, and the size suggests its virulence and potential for harm. We also tried to create parallels between fantasy lore and microbiology lore. An example of this is our handling of the bacterium Staphylococcus aureus. In fantasy literature, dragon mythology is as intricate as it is complex and expansive. We created a similar mythos with Staphylococcus aureus. Basic Staphylococcus aureus as depicted in our game is a very simple, small dragon whose skin is a yellowish hue. This is compatible with the commensal bacterium that occurs in our skin and is largely harmless. When resistance plasmids drive the virulence of Staphylococcus aureus, infected pathologies can occur. This brought to mind more powerful dragons, from the frightening methicillin-resistant Staphylococcus aureus to the terrifying multi-headed Golden Dragon that is vancomycin-resistant Staphylococcus aureus.

4. It was hoped that by playing multiple rounds of our game, students would begin to recognize patterns of attack that were successful in addition to appreciating the nuances of using certain antibiotics against certain types of bacteria. We hoped this rehearsal would better inform some of the clinical decisions that the students would make later in their medical careers.

With these four guiding principles in place we set to the task of hiring a team of artists and building the world that would be the backdrop for our game – the world of Soma.

A Final Consideration: Cool Versus Realistic

In the months after the release of the original version of the game, we were often asked, "Why are the bacterial creatures fantastical?" Such questions inevitably came from members of the scientific community who had grown to know and love these organisms as the various different iterations of single-celled organisms that they are. To us, slightly different spherical organisms with slightly different distinguishing features, including those resulting from Gram staining, while interesting to a certain subset of the population, did not capture the interest of our key demographic. Incidentally, creating a blank slate from which we could build any creature and implement various features of bacterial morphology, disease pathophysiology, and clinical features proved freeing and, at the same time, somewhat daunting.

Regardless, this was the direction in which we opted to proceed, and ultimately we were happy with the results. This approach also made the artists' task of conveying our ideas somewhat simple, as they weren't challenged with trying to draw multiple iterations of single-celled organisms.

A Methodology for Art Creation

Fundamentals in place, and an overarching directive to focus on things that were 'cool' over things that were realistic, heralded the next step of our journey which involved working with an art director and a small team of artists based in China.

Serendipity came into play here, as the perfect fit for our art director, Xiaolong Dai, happened to be a roommate of one of the original developers, Dr Francis Kong. Mr Dai was completing a degree in design in San Francisco, and had multiple contacts with artists in China. He proved to be very detail-oriented, and he was extremely diligent in regard to obtaining detailed descriptions of both the antibiotic agents (referred to as 'Apothecary Healers') and the various species of bacteria (referred to as 'Lords of Pestilence').

We then developed a short list of the various bacteria and antibiotics that would be included in the game based on a number of sources. The first was referencing the therapeutic and microbiologic tomes that we had come across in our medical education. The second was a needs assessment based on our clinical experience during rounds with medical and nursing students and internal medicine residents. My wife and I had both worked as chief residents in our internal medicine residency programs, and had some experience with the process of creating needs assessments in clinical education.

Inclusion criteria for the antibiotics included agents that we encountered and used on a day-to-day basis. And there were antibiotics that had certain special side effects and/or considerations for use that we wanted to include. We also wanted to create an even balance of broad-spectrum versus narrow-spectrum antibiotics for certain strategic elements of play that echoed the administration of said antibiotics in the real world.

For the bacteria, we made sure to include sufficient Gram-positive, Gram-negative, anaerobic, aerobic, and multi-drug-resistant bacteria to effectively mirror the more common infections that would be found in both university and community-based acute medical settings. And we added a number of rarer infections that are included in any standard microbiology or therapeutics text to reflect an adequate breadth of scope for board review purposes.

When the list was close to being finalized, we began the arduous and yet exhilarating task of breaking down each bacterium into a composite that included cues to its virulence, suggestions about what the fantasy equivalent of it might be, its weaknesses and its strengths. The following is an example of the development process for the antibiotic azithromycin:

Basic description:
A versatile front-line warrior whose name comes from the Latin root meaning "artist's brush." Despite her delicate beauty, she is one of the few fighters who can take down the malevolent VRE.

We would then take the limited description and use it to help build the imagery for the artists to work on. The artists would then create a rendering sketch and send it back to us for review and touch-ups. This would allow us enough time to continue to build the basic concept of the character (Figure 13.1). Once we were happy with the sketch, we would release the art for final development. Figure 13.2 shows the final image that we developed for ampicillin.

Next Steps

After the cards were developed, it occurred to us that we could further extend our metaphors for microbiology and therapeutics into a larger ecosystem that also took into account the surrounding environment. Since the human body was the backdrop in which all of these battles would occur, why not create additional allusions to physiologic processes within our world? Inspired by the various fantasy worlds that we had grown up with including Middle Earth and Narnia, we set about to increase the scope of our game substantially. Hence the

Figure 13.1 Character art for Ampicillin

concept and backdrop for our game was born – Soma – with its primary themes being *interconnectedness* and balance, or *homeostasis*.

Given this new direction, we hired a science writer to help us flesh out each character. Below is the extended backstory of the character Ampicillin:

> The penicillin tribes have a long and proud ancestry that dates back to the dawn of Soma. It was this family that struck an accord with the creatures of Pestilence, allowing for balance between the realms of creature and healer. It was with the rise of the dark entity named Vallejio that caused this delicate arrangement to be broken. Ampicillin played an important role in these early engagements and fights in conjunction with other healers that carry the 'beta-lactam' banner. Her main form of attack involves her broadsword that with the aid of its special amino ring, slices through the armour of certain types of pestilence.
>
> There was a time that Ampicillin, with her predictable attack patterns, was relegated to front-line or initial scouting missions. However, it was the famed 'Incident of Kaz'Jiek' where a small band of reconnaissance healers were ambushed by Vallejio and the horrific multi-headed Vancomycin-resistant Enterococcus, did it become apparent that Ampicillin had a clear role to play in the War for Soma. Of the thirteen or so healers in her party, she was the only Apothecary healer left standing that day, able to survive VRSA's attacks and even deal damage, before escaping to inform the leadership of this dread new foe.

Figure 13.2 The finalized card for Ampicillin

In the following description of the antibiotic Azithromycin (Figure 13.3), note how the various environments of Soma are starting to be developed as metaphors for human body systems and physiologic processes:

> Azithromycin, son of the great Erythromycin, is one of the most commonly called-upon Apothecaries. Like his mother, he inhibits the ability of the Pestilence armies to generate the basic structures of life, killing them from the inside out. Because of their similar attack styles, the two are effective against a similar range of Lords, although Azithromycin has a slightly better track record against those of the Gram Negative Legion, particularly *Haemophilus influenzae*. Furthermore, unlike his mother, Azithromycin is not susceptible to the acidic waters just above the Southern Dam, and can thus enter the aqueduct unprotected, simplifying his journey to the site of battle.
>
> Azithromycin is capable of launching an effective counterattack against a wide range of Lord species, including those that invade the aqueduct entrance at the back of Buccal Bay, the Occulos, and the Respiro Forest. He usually enters through Buccal Bay and is often transported to the site of infection by the Nodal Sentry. He is even sometimes sent in preemptively, when the Nodal Sentry is compromised in some way and the risk of a Pestilence attack is high.
>
> Like most Apothecaries, however, Azithromycin's protection comes at a cost. His presence can disrupt the flow of the aqueduct, causing it to discharge too quickly or even reverse directions. Furthermore, he has been known to put the Twin Heart Cities at risk, particularly if they are already impaired.

Gameplay and Basic Game Design Elements

Card Battle Versus Trading Card Game

Earlier considerations in the development of *Healing Blade* included the basics of how this experience would be delivered. Did we want to provide a complete game, or a piecemeal game that would allow the acquisition of new cards to affect gameplay? This boiled down to a choice between a card battle game and a trading-card game with card battle elements.

After a great deal of discussion, we decided that since we expected it to be a premium experience within a niche market, the mechanics of a piecemeal game would be potentially unfair to the early adopter. For this reason we opted to focus our efforts towards a complete game, acknowledging that we would eventually consider building expansion packs to further expand the gaming experience.

Figure 13.3 The card for Azithromycin

The original premise of the game is simple. One player chooses to play either the Apothecary Healers (antibiotics) or the Lords of Pestilence (bacteria), and the second player takes the opposite side. Each side is apportioned an even number of adenosine triphosphate (ATP) points, and battle commences. Battles occur on a play mat that includes a staging area and attack areas. Novice game players must use trial and error to determine which combinations of antibiotics can defeat combinations of bacteria. But with even a minimal appreciation of microbiology and therapeutics, one has the upper hand and can make strategic decisions that increase the probability of success. The entire current edition ruleset can be found at the end of this chapter.

Postmortem and Next Steps

We are often asked why we proceeded in the direction of a table-top card game when clearly much of our inspiration came from our experiences with video-gaming. There were two primary reasons: prior experience with developing a printed product and the substantial costs of developing a video game. Our experience with the calendar had created a small network of tried and tested relationships with individuals that we were interested in collaborating with again, decreasing some of the learning process and anxieties of new product development. Furthermore, the initial capital outlays associated with creating a digital version of the game seemed daunting, based on our initial assessments, so we opted to proceed for table-top, card-based play.

All told, the approximate cost for the *Healing Blade* project came to approximately $30,000, with much of the expenses going towards art and print runs. An initial print run with smaller, less established printer resulted in a poor-quality product, low-volume line that we ultimately ended up abandoning. This so-called 'lost run' allowed us to make a few more tweaks to the cards and gameplay, and also helped us realize the importance of working with printers that were specialized in the niche of table-top card games. It took a great deal of 'intestinal fortitude' to, despite this loss, proceed with a medium-volume, high-quality print run that we felt adequately captured the glory of our card art.

The game was released in March 2010 to mixed reviews. Many found the idea of a card battle game set in a fantasy world for antibiotics versus bacteria enthralling. We even received commendations on the art and concept of "learning in metaphor." Admittedly it was the strength of the gameplay that ultimately proved to be the greatest challenge. For starters, the first edition game rules seemed unbalanced in favor of the antibiotics despite the fact that we had tried to offset this by outnumbering the antibiotics almost two to one. There also proved to be a substantial learning curve which had to do with our insistence on using the actual scientific nomenclature. This proved especially difficult for non-clinicians, adding to an already steep learning curve.

Indeed, for non-clinicians gameplay often devolved into looking down the lists of susceptible bacteria on the antibiotics cards, and vice versa, to determine battle outcomes, which anyone could tell you is not a fun game mechanic. Despite appropriate focus group testing, it eventually became apparent that one of the spell cards – Reverse Transcriptase – proved to be the most powerful card, and players would simply wait until they had almost lost, and then play it to essentially switch places with the winner. Once this became a known tactic, gameplay simply became a race to obtain this card.

Fortunately, we decided at the very beginning of this project that it would be an iterative process. By their very nature bacteria develop resistance, forcing treatments to be revised accordingly. In addition to revising our therapeutics knowledge-base (i.e., which drug kills with bacterium), the next version of the game will include an updated rule set (see Appendix A) that addresses a number of these issues. Perhaps most exciting, however, is our recently announced partnership with Wulven Game Studios. Wulven will be responsible for transitioning the game to a digital format which will provide a streamlined, more dynamic gameplay experience that should address concerns such as having to reading through the lists as well as knowledge-base updates.

In Conclusion: On a (Dragon) Wing and a Dare . . .

The process of developing a game from scratch has been at once both exhilarating and terrifying. Our advice to novice game designers (which we consider ourselves still very much a part of) would be quite simple: know your audience. Conceptual blending is well and good, but if core gameplay elements contain fundamental flaws, the entire project is at risk. Second, assume that the first iteration will be flawed. Embrace this and work diligently to optimize and adapt. Conversely, if the core ideas surrounding the game are sound, that will provide the resilience to survive a few gameplay iterations. NCL is planning two additional games, the launch of the game for iOS and Android platforms, and a manual detailing the art and backstories of the various creatures and heroes of the game called *The Bacterionomicon*. It is hoped that the lessons outlined above will be helpful for those who wish to further meld gaming with educational experiences in compelling and meaningful ways.

Rules Edition 2.0

Healing Blade
Players: 2 / Ages: 12 & up / Playing Time: 50 minutes

OBJECT OF THE GAME:

Each player starts out with 13 life points. If you run out of life points, you lose the game.

OVERVIEW:

One player plays the Apothecaries (white-bordered cards) and the other plays the Lords of Pestilence (black-bordered cards). Using ATP (the green gems) to pay for the cards they play, the Lords of Pestilence player attacks the Apothecary player, and the Apothecary player plays defense. A player loses when they have zero life points.

PLAYING CARDS:

To play a card from your hand, you must pay its ATP cost and put the card onto the Sanctuary zone. The Lords of Pestilence player pays ATP to the Apothecary player. The Apothecary player pays by returning their ATP to the general supply.

- **Combatants** are played face-down and may be used later in battle. Players are expected to be honest about their ATP costs. Players can, however, look at their own face-down cards and move them around to prevent the opponent from knowing which card is which.
- **Spells** have an effect, then get discarded. Some spells set up a conditional effect that might happen later in the turn. The Apothecary player can prevent a spell by immediately playing Preventative Therapy in response to an undesired spell.
- **Items** are played face-up and stay in play for the rest of the game, unless destroyed by Broad-Spectrum Therapy or Outbreak. Some items change the rules. Others give the player a new once-a-turn ability.

SETUP:

Each player takes 4 ATP stones, keeping them in an ATP zone on their playmat. (The playmat is arranged symmetrically to allow right handed or left handed players the arrangement of their preference.) Each player shuffles their deck and draws six cards, keeping their hand hidden from their opponent.

HOW TO PLAY:

1) Lords of Pestilence (Pest) Turn:

If you are the Lords of Pestilence player, you play first. Gain 3 ATP from the general supply at the start of your turn. Then you may play cards or use once-a-turn item abilities. After playing cards, choose any number of combatant cards from the Sanctuary zone and move them onto the Battlefield to announce an attack. If you do not attack this turn, lose 1 life as a penalty.

2) Apothecary Turn:

If you are the Apothecary player, you usually receive ATP during the Pest player's turn. However, if you received zero ATP during the Pest player's turn, gain 2 ATP. You may play cards or use once-a-turn abilities. After playing cards, choose <u>no more than three</u> combatant cards from the Sanctuary zone and move them onto the Battlefield to announce an attack.

BATTLE!

3) Reveal/Play Tricks Step:

Both players reveal combatant cards in the Battlefield. This is the last chance to play any trick spells, or the item Resistance Plasmid. The Pest player announces spells first.

4) Resolution:

Players consult the cards (or Interactions Sheet) to determine the possible results of battle. If there is a discrepancy between cards, the Interactions Sheet is the final authority. A single Apothecary combatant may destroy several different Pest combatants in one battle. Pest combatants either survive and damage the opponent, or die and are discarded. Pest combatants that *can* be killed, *must* be killed; Apothecary combatants are not allowed to voluntarily let them live. Whenever there is more than one Apothecary combatant that could defeat a Pest combatant, the Apothecary player chooses which Apothecary combatant actually did the killing.

First sub step, the Apothecary player announces any <u>1st-line attacks</u>.

    a. vanquished Pest combatants are discarded
    b. the Pest player takes <u>2 damage</u> for each combatant lost
    c. the Apothecary player gets an ATP for each Pest combatant killed
    d. If an Apothecary combatant used two or more 1st-line attacks this battle, it is discarded. Otherwise, it remains in play.

Second sub step, the Apothecary player announces any <u>2nd-line attacks</u>.

    a. the vanquished Pest combatants are discarded
    b. Apothecary combatants that used 2nd-line attacks are discarded
    c. the Pest player takes <u>1 damage</u> for each combatant lost
    d. the Apothecary player gets an ATP for each Pestilence combatant killed

Third sub step, surviving Lords of Pestilence

    a. surviving Pest combatants do 1 damage to the Apothecary player
    b. the Pest player gets 1 ATP for each damage dealt

c. Apothecary combatants that did nothing, or *only* used 1st-line attacks, stay in play

d. if the item Recolonization is in play, the Pest player may choose to gain life instead of deal damage, but still gets 1 ATP for each damage that would have been dealt

BATTLE IS OVER.

5) Regroup:

All remaining combatants on the Battlefield go to the Sanctuary, *face-down.*

Then players must do one of the following:

1. draw cards to refill their hand to six (only if you have <6 cards)
2. draw one and then discard one (only if you have exactly 6 cards)
3. discard down to six (if you have >6 cards)

If there are no cards left to draw, you may continue to play without drawing cards.

You are now ready to start a new Lords of Pestilence turn.

OPTIONAL RULES:

For a more balanced game, exclude Reverse Transcriptase, Rest & Relaxation, Intrinsic Virulence, and Genetic Shift from player's decks. Resistance Plasmid is not allowed on C. difficile or F. necrophorum. Use Chlorhexidine only once, it never comes back to your hand.

ADDITIONAL CARD EXPLANATIONS:

Adverse Side Effects – Play this during the Reveal/Play Tricks Step. Immediately lose 1 life for each Apothecary combatant on the playmat (including the Sanctuary.) Later, during each sub step of Resolution, deal an extra 2 damage when you kill an enemy combatant.

Broad Spectrum Therapy – This may be played during either player's turn or during the Reveal/Play Tricks Step. The moment this card is played the destroyed item cannot be used. If played immediately as an opponent is trying to use an item's once-a-turn ability, the opponent does not get to use the ability, and must destroy the item instead.

Catch a Cold – This may be played during the Pest player's turn or during the Reveal/Play Tricks Step. It may be played immediately in response to a spell that would deal you damage, to prevent that damage. "Prevent all damage to you from your opponent that turn" lasts until the Regroup step.

Chlorhexidine – This may be played during either player's turn or during the Reveal/Play Tricks Step, however if an opponent immediately responds with a life-gaining spell or once-a-turn ability, or if the opponent played a life-gaining spell prior to Chlorhexidine, they gain life before taking damage.

Contaminated Hand – Play this during the Reveal/Play Tricks Step. You gain life before the first Resolution sub step.

Cross Resistance – You may play this during the Reveal/Play Tricks Step, after Apothecary combatants have been revealed. It only has an effect if Resistance Plasmid is already in play. Both combatants now share the Resistance Plasmid. If the original combatant or Resistance Plasmid is sent to the discard, the combatant that benefitted from Cross Resistance loses the extra resistance.

Decompose – Play this during the Reveal/Play Tricks Step. If the Apothecary combatant you choose does not end up in the discard after battle, nothing happens and the spell is wasted. If the card gains you life during the Resolution of Battle, you gain life *before* you take damage for that sub step.

Genetic Shift – When your combatants die, you must remove cards from your discard to prevent the damage *before* placing the recently killed combatants into the discard, and it is not optional. Genetic Shift also automatically prevents damage from Chlorhexidine and Shot in the Dark, but it cannot prevent the loss of life for not attacking. When Genetic Shift is in play, you can lose the game two ways: by not being able to remove a card from your discard, or by losing life for not attacking.

Epidemiological Forecast – This card can be played during the Apothecary player's turn or during the Reveal/Play Tricks Step.

Intrinsic Virulence – You may use this once-a-turn ability immediately after playing the card, but you may only use it during the Lords of Pestilence turn, you may not use it during battle.

Life Cycle – This may be played during the Pest player's turn or during the Reveal/Play Tricks Step.

Outbreak – This may be played during either player's turn or during the Reveal/Play Tricks Step to send opponent's items to their discard zone. The moment this card is played the destroyed item cannot be used. If played immediately as an opponent is trying to use an item's once-a-turn ability, the opponent does not get to use the ability, and must destroy the item instead.

Poverty & Filth – This may be played during either player's turn or during the Reveal/Play Tricks Step. If this is played immediately in response to a spell that would deal you damage, gain life before you take damage.

Preventative Therapy – Play this immediately in response to your opponent announcing a spell and paying you its ATP cost. Wait until bidding is finished to see if the opponent's spell works or gets canceled. You may not obstruct the playing of items or combatants, only spells.

Recolonization – "Countered by an opponent's fighter" simply means "killed." As long as this item remains in play, you may choose to gain life from successful attacks instead of dealing damage to your opponent. You may do this even if other combatants were killed, but you may not gain life from some and deal damage with others, you must choose "gain life" or "deal damage" for ALL successful attackers each battle. If the damage you take during the first or second sub step of battle puts you to zero life points, you lose the game before you get a chance to gain life.

Reinfection – This may be played during the Pest player's turn or during the Reveal/Play Tricks Step.

Resistance Plasmid – This is the only item you may play during the Reveal/Play Tricks Step.

Rest & Rehydration – When using this card's once-a-turn ability, it must be the very first thing you do during the Apothecary turn. Thus, after playing the card, you must wait until your next turn to start using the ability. If choosing the third option to kill enemy combatants, the Lords of Pestilence player checks their face-down combatants and, being an honest player, reveals and kills any of the following:

- B. cereus
- B. henselae
- C. jejuni
- C. perfringens
- V. cholerae

The Pest player takes 2 damage for each combatant killed this way.

Reverse Transcriptase – This card can only be played during the Pest player's turn.

Revitalize – You may use the once-a-turn ability immediately after playing the card, but you may only use the ability during the Apothecary turn.

Shot in the Dark – This may be played during either player's turn or during the Reveal/Play Tricks Step, however if an opponent immediately responds with a life-gaining spell or once-a-turn ability, or if the opponent played a life-gaining spell prior to Shot in the Dark, they gain life before taking damage.

The Healing Arts – Play this during the Reveal/Play Tricks Step. When searching for a card, you must search for a combatant, not a spell or item. You are not obligated to put a card into play, you may choose to shuffle without finding a card. The Healing Arts does allow you to add a fourth combatant to the Battlefield, it is the only way the Apothecary player can have four combatants in battle. You do not have to pay ATP costs for the card you put on the Battlefield.

Unconventional Therapy / Revitalize – You may use the once-a-turn ability immediately after playing the card, but you may only use the ability during the Apothecary turn.

VRE / VRSA "Plasmid Transference" – If you play Resistance Plasmid on VRE or VRSA, you may (immediately, or later) choose another combatant to gain resistance to the same Apothecary combatant that was named when Resistance Plasmid was played. There can only be one Pest combatant benefiting from this ability at any given time. Once chosen, you may not change the recipient of the Transference, but if the Pest combatant benefiting from the Transference is discarded, a new Pest combatant may be chosen during the next Reveal/Play Tricks step.

Healing Blade Game Design by Francis Kong, MD & Arun Mathews, MD
Instructions v2.0 by Brandon Patton
2009 NerdcoreLearning.com All Rights Reserved: instructions reproduced here with permisson.
Healing Blade is a trademark of Nerdcore Learning.

14

DESIGNING CARD AND BOARD GAMES

ALAN PAULL, SURPRISED STARE GAMES, UK

Tony Boydell and I at Surprised Stare Games (http://www.surprisedstaregames.co.uk/) have between us been designing and publishing card and board games for over 50 years. I was fortunate to have some board games published in the 1980s, including a short-lived commercial disaster called *Starship Tycoons* (Paull, 1986); we learn from failure, as much if not more than from success, and I learned an immense amount. I hope that our experiences will help others to enjoy making games, while avoiding some of the traps that earlier travellers have fallen into.

Words of Warning

Game design is not an easy path. Game design is all about creating games that other people enjoy playing. It's not necessarily about designing games that you like, although that can help sometimes. It's not about having ideas for games, nor is it about designing neat mechanics, although both of those can help, too. It's about designing, developing and finishing games that other people can play.

First be clear about your objectives as a game designer. Is it your intention to design a game for sale, for use in the classroom or workshop, or for your own personal enjoyment? If your purpose is not for making sales, then it's much less stressful. Always keep a healthy perspective on your aspirations as a game designer, and don't lose your house on your 'great idea for a game'. There's a very rocky road ahead.

If you're seeking to design games for commercial publication, then immerse yourself in what's already been published and talk to other designers and experienced players. There's really no substitute for speaking to people and getting the advice from old hands. In the UK your local games convention or the annual UK Games Expo (http://www.ukgamesexpo.co.uk/) are good places to start. Will your game add anything to the field? If not, then even if it works as a game, it may not sell. Bear in mind that at the great annual Essen Spiel (http://www.internationalespieltage.de) – probably the largest games-playing festival in the world – some 700 new card and board games are launched each year.

Decide on your market segment (there are many) and likely geographical areas of sale. There are three major segments, simplistically speaking (and bearing in mind that I'm not a marketing specialist): toys and simple games for children, mass market games for the family, and specialist games aimed at hobby gamers. The first two segments are worth billions of pounds per annum and are dominated by large international corporations (Hasbro and Mattel, for example). To break into these markets you'd probably need a very good agent or high-quality corporate contacts. Unless you're wildly lucky or exceptionally talented, an independent game designer is very likely to experience high levels of disappointment operating in these segments. In-house designers and well-known independents with a very strong track record tend to be used by these companies.

The third segment, the hobby games segment, is much smaller, and it's where Surprised Stare Games operates, and where our focus lies in this piece. While there are some large companies (for example Kosmos and Zoch, to mention just two) there are many more small publishers, and in the age of digital publishing and the Internet, it's becoming relatively cheap for small companies to publish card and board games. Even breaking into this smaller world is difficult for an independent designer, because there are so many aspiring and talented game designers out there, including very well known ones like Reiner Knizia (BoardGameGeek, 2013a), and in the UK, Martin Wallace (BoardGameGeek, 2013b) and Richard Breese (BoardGameGeek, 2013c). For every one of the 700 new published designs per year at the Spiel, there are probably ten more that didn't make it. Many of these designs will be perfectly creditable, even good, games that didn't get a lucky break. There are many more designers in the world who have never had a game published than those who have, and many of these unpublished designers produce excellent work. Competition for limited publishing slots is fierce.

So having started with words of discouragement, for those who are still keen, we have some guidelines for the game design and publication process that we've found very useful. These are not hard and fast 'best practice', just our own views about an over-arching process. For a well-researched, but slightly different process, see *Game Design: How to Create Video and Tabletop Games, Start to Finish* by Lewis Pulsipher (2012).

The Six Steps Process

So you've decided that you want to design and perhaps publish card or board games, and you're not discouraged by the Words of Warning? The Six Steps Process is a way to design, develop, sell and produce your games. I don't guarantee that these six steps will make your fortune through game design, but it should start you thinking about how to do it.

- Step 1: Have a good idea that no-one else has had.
- Step 2: Decide on your audience.

- Step 3: Design your game.
- Step 4: Develop your game.
- Step 5: Sell your game design; or
- Step 6: Produce your game yourself.

1. Have a Good Idea that No One Else Has Had

This can be in terms of a central game mechanic, a game system or even a theme. Although many new designers think that this is the hard part, it's not. It's easy to have ideas – they're ten-a-penny – and a game designer who is serious about it should keep records of all of the ideas generated, wherever they come from. It's important to keep a proper perspective about an idea. It may be a great idea, but it's not yet a game, a prototype of a game or even a game concept.

Check carefully that your good idea really is a new one. It's fairly easy to design something that you think no one's done before, only to find that you've designed *High Society* (http://www.boardgamegeek.com/boardgame/220/high-society) or *Modern Art* (http://www.boardgamegeek.com/boardgame/118/modern-art). This point is an important one, because the games market is very competitive and almost numberless games have already been published. If you think you've thought of something new, it's quite likely that it's already been conceived; as an example, I designed a game themed on the idea that aliens were invading the Earth through fast food outlets, only to discover that someone had already published a game using that very theme.

BoardGameGeek website

The prime reference website for exploring the world of board games is BoardGameGeek.com. As at June 2012, it contained information on over 59,000 board games. In addition it has details of designers, players and conventions, as well as blogs, forums and themed lists of games.

---

2. Decide on Your Audience

Are you designing for a mass audience, a small niche, young children, or knowledgeable adults? You'll need an understanding of the complexity of games that your audience can stomach, the themes that they will rave about and the length and predictability of game play that they will tolerate. If there are educational or training objectives, or traditional learning outcomes, how will your game design deliver these? Will your players have a fun and frivolous experience with your game or a satisfying but serious one? Does your audience appreciate abstract games, or is a theme required, or even a model of reality, such as a simulation game?

If you are designing for sale to a publishing house, make sure that you know their current range and brand image. Do they prefer a specific size of games, with constraints on components, complexity and style? Don't design something that competes with their existing products. Do design something that fits with their approach and style.

3. Design Your Game

This part of the process tends to be individualistic. You're moving from the game idea to a working prototype, through personal playtesting to a finished design.

When you create your prototype, don't worry too much about the look of the thing. Your focus should be on making something that works 'well enough', so that you can check that it functions as a game. Don't spend lots of time creating artwork. You may find that the time is wasted if the game doesn't work. If it's enjoyable without snazzy art, then it will be even better when professionally produced. But if it fails without the snazzy art, then it will probably fail with it.

For prototype components, typically, we use spare bits from stocks of unsold games, pieces of paper or card, and materials in the game designer's ubiquitous 'old wooden pieces' cupboard. It's useful to acquire spare pieces, as they can inspire ideas for mechanics, as well as populate your prototypes. I have 12 plastic wolf cubs that I'm sure will form the basis of a game at some point.

You need to flesh out the game mechanics so that it works as a game system, has internal consistency, and is potentially an enjoyable game in your view. Some designers do this in a formal way, writing a design brief and meeting design objectives. Personally I've found that this approach can help, but it's best not to be too rigid about it. Others design very much by feel, relying on their experience and intuition of what works and what doesn't – does this seem about right? However, whatever your approach to design, remember that you're designing for your audience, not for you. Try to remain dispassionate and critical about your own work. Don't be afraid to experiment with entirely new directions during the design process. Successful games have come about through abandoning all of the original ideas, methods and mechanics, leaving only the good stuff for the final design.

Design contains a lot of inspiration and hope, and then a lot of iterative work to find out if the inspiration and hope can be actualised. Sometimes a design might pop up pretty much fully formed; at other times it will be hard graft. Sometimes the game starts with abstract mechanics, sometimes with theme, a story or an historical event.

For all games, the design process consists of iterations of design, make, test, evaluate. Much of your testing will be personal playtesting. Even with a seven-player game, you should be playing a lot of solo sessions.

Figure 14.1 Final published version of *Confucius*, SSG, 2008

At some point during this process you should have a working prototype and some rules, even if the latter are only in your head. When you're reasonably happy with your prototype, or are confident enough to share some parts of your design with others, you should move on to playtesting with critical friends or colleagues. At this stage, it's usually helpful to run the sessions yourself, because you need to know about and record all the rough edges and comments. Keep your expectations low at this point!

It's difficult to over-state the importance of playtesting. You should play the game yourself so much that you become sick of the sight of it. You should play with your own playing groups, if you can do this without alienating them and without deflecting them too much from their own game playing interests. You should also playtest with carefully selected individuals who have the proven ability to give you critical and constructive feedback – even if this feedback is a reality check on the whole project. It's better to acknowledge a failure, learn from it and move on, than to keep flogging a dead horse. There's always another design in the cupboard.

Be careful how you handle playtest comments. All comments are valuable to some degree, particularly about whether or not the game is enjoyable, whether it works well, and whether playtesters want to play it again. Make sure that your playtesters know that you appreciate their comments. However, some players may want to re-design your game in their image. Remember, it's your game, not theirs. You should be digesting their comments on your game and amending the design yourself within your own design parameters, not adopting their solutions.

Then you may ditch the whole thing, or take it on to the next stage.

4. Develop Your Game

Don't miss out this stage! When you think the game is finished, I can pretty much guarantee it isn't, if you haven't gone through the game development process.

Inflict your game on as many different friends as you can. Preferably use a high proportion of people who you trust and who know about game development. These playtesters should be experienced players with well-developed critical eyes.

This is the period when you find out about and modify the 'playability' of the game. You or your favourite game developer friend needs to concentrate on the experience of the players. You must be prepared to sacrifice or change parts of your cherished design in order to get to the point where players will play it multiple times, so being a purist is not a good idea. Do not expect the development process to be quick – it can take a couple of years or more to 'finish' a game (the average lifecycle from idea to finished unpublished game is two to four years). During game development, chunks of mechanics are likely to be trimmed, slashed and burned away. Development isn't finished until everything unnecessary has been removed, leaving only the essentials that will make the game great. And each act of tearing away – or more rarely, sewing on – requires more playtesting to check that the game is the better for it.

For some games, the design can be handed over to a developer, and you can stop at the end of the design process. If you're working with a publishing company, they may insist on this if they like the design – this independent game development process carried out in-house by a publisher may take months or years, and the game may end up with a different title and theme. In one recent example in our designers' group a Hanseatic trading game ended up with a theme about cooking! Once you've handed over your design, your involvement depends on the financiers, and they may or may not want your help.

Game development should involve huge amounts of playtesting with as many different groups as possible. It's important to manage version control, or you'll go mad. Identify and use gaming groups who will give you high-quality, critical feedback. You're looking for all types of feedback. Typical outcomes of playtesting will be notes about what went right, what went wrong, what was enjoyable and what was not so enjoyable. You should also find out whether all elements of the game mechanics worked as you expected, and whether there were ambiguities in your explanation of the rules, be they on paper or verbal.

Figure 14.2 Fairly late playtest version of *Confucius*

During playtesting, you want to know whether the game system can be made to fail (or 'break') using specific strategies, often unexpected or corner-case ones. Use some players who you know will always try to break the game (and if they do, then take that very seriously). Use 'serious' gamers who play at a high level of skill. Use casual social gamers who play just for fun. Pedants, sticklers and seekers of extreme strategies are your friends! Of course, it's also rewarding to receive compliments, and one of the best is, "when can we play it again?"

If you're developing for markets in different countries, use groups in those different countries if possible – we often use English, German and US playing groups.

When you're sick of playtesting and don't want to see your game ever again, take a short break, and then keep going – you haven't finished. The game development process is only finished when the development team, which might just be you, but should include other trusted people too, is happy that the product is as good as it can be.

4a: Writing Rules

Writing rules for games is a technical skill. It's a type of technical writing. As such, it is amenable to a traditional quality process approach. At Surprised Stare Games we have the following process:

- Designer writes the first draft, which could be notes rather than a full rule set.
- In-house team plays the game extensively as part of our normal development, and then our in-house rules writer produces a second more or less comprehensive draft rules set.

- As development continues, the rules will commonly be re-written two or three times from scratch.
- Once the in-house team is satisfied with the game (note: game not yet finished!), we'll produce another draft set of rules, reviewed in-house, for inclusion in prototypes that will be used in our playtest groups. Then the game will be playtested, supervised by members of our team.
- The rules will be revised following playtesting. Up to this stage, we're looking at the draft rules to answer the questions: "Does the game work?" and "Does the text say what we mean?"
- Towards the end of the development process, we re-write the rules again, this time laying them out with pictures and diagrams in a format that is as close to the published one as possible.
- This draft is then shared with our external 'rules experts' – a couple of people who have a good track record for writing rules. Result: a comprehensive draft rules set that we will use with our four or five blind playtest groups (these are not blind people, just people who have not previously had contact with the game!).
- Blind playtesting will usually come up with further suggestions for revisions, so we will have a final review prior to producing what we hope will be the final draft.
- We then playtest the final draft.
- We also (usually alongside final testing) get the rules translated into German, because we usually produce multi-language games – the translation process often picks up English language problems because of the differences between UK English and International English (let alone US English). We're finding this so useful that we're revising our process to push the translation back into the development process rather than leaving it until the end.

As you can see, the rules will have gone through at least 10 drafts over this process, including several re-writes. One of our latest games (*Totemo*) has gone through this full process, although the rules would fit comfortably on four sides of A4. In fact, looking back through our *Totemo* files, I can see 13 versions of the rules. With larger games than this, it's easy to get to dozens of versions.

5. Sell Your Game Design

There are several ways to get your great game into the hands of the players who will appreciate it. If you're happy with a very small number of players, then simply producing it for your friends and family may be sufficient for you. Similarly, if your game is for your own use in an education or training context, then steps five and six of our process here are not very relevant.

For those committed to a commercial venture of some type, try to get a slot at a games publishing company. For a note of realism, bear in mind that most games fall at this hurdle. Even large game companies have only limited publishing slots and receive many, many times more unsolicited game designs. In the hobby game market there is very intense competition, which has pushed up the quality of card and board games to a high level over the past ten years or so. Even well-known game designers receive many rejection slips, so it is important to remain phlegmatic about your chances of success.

When you contact game publishers, take a professional approach. They will want to see a complete, fully working prototype of your game. It doesn't have to have professional-looking (or indeed any) artwork, but it does have to have understandable rules, so that it can be played 'out of the box' without you being in the room. If you can introduce the game personally, that can be an advantage, and many companies attend games fairs (such as the Spiel at Essen, Germany) for this purpose. If they like the game, they will want to take a copy away, so you should always have two copies (one for yourself). They may wish you to sign a disclaimer to protect both parties from conflict over existing similar projects. You should ask the company for a time scale for their evaluation, but don't be surprised if this is several months. You should also check whether they are happy for you to approach other companies while they are evaluating the game; many companies are content for you to present your game to multiple companies simultaneously, while others prefer to have an exclusive look for a period of time.

If you are fortunate enough to have your game accepted, you can expect a contract for a license to produce the game within a specified time scale and geographic area, and/or in one or more languages. Typical royalties are 5 per cent or 6 per cent of the money the company receives from sales (excluding taxes and postage).

Alternatively you may decide to publish the game yourself.

6. Produce Your Game Yourself

Producing your own game yourself is perhaps the most exciting end point to the process! Exciting and risky. If you have progressed carefully through all of the earlier steps, then you may be on the way to some commercial success. However, you'll need to address marketing and production issues that are typical of any modern product, but which are beyond the scope of this article. Our experience at Surprised Stare Games is mainly in production, while our marketing is limited primarily to sales at large games fairs, through our own website, via specialist games shops and specialist games distributors. There are also sources of income through crowd funding (for example, KickStarter – http://www.kickstarter.com/) or more traditional means via bank loans or venture capital.

Figure 14.3 Dual language card game: *Bloody Legacy*, SSG, 2004

Nowadays several production companies offer 'end-to-end' game manufacturing facilities, including all of these specialist areas:

- Printed paper materials, such as rules
- Sourcing or making wooden and other specialist components
- Game board manufacture and printing
- Card and playing card manufacture and printing
- Box manufacture and printing
- Finishing, collation and finally
- Delivery.

Costs are dependent on volumes. Typically a card game is an economic proposition at production runs of 1,500 to 2,000 copies, while 5,000 copies will reduce the unit costs considerably. But it is essential to beware of printing too many – reducing the unit cost doesn't help if you can't sell those you've made, so realistic appreciation of the likely number of sales is essential. In the hobby games market, sales of 1,500 to 2,000 or more copies marks a successful game, with sales of 10,000 plus being the equivalent of blockbusters. With modern specialist short-run processes, we have achieved small profits with quantities as low as 200 to 300, but these very small numbers only work with much of the hard graft of production carried out at little or no monetary cost.

How to Make Money out of Games Design

Tony and I started our independent games company in 2001, and since then we have published ten card and board games, all but one our own designs. For us, as for most games designers, it's a hobby. Although we design, publish and sell our games, we both have full-time jobs in the 'real world'. We also have an additional Step 0 before the first step of the Six-Step Process: we play games ourselves, and besides enjoying ourselves with our game-playing hobby, we gather ideas and experience from other people's work. While we play, we're also (at least subliminally) casting a critical eye over the way that the design has been put together, so that we're always learning through playing.

We now publish one or two games per year, and our products earn enough money to fund the next title. We take no salaries, and we are fortunate that our unpaid production team includes people with skills in rules writing, graphic design, illustration, print production and project management. All profits go back into the company, which means that over the years we have put money into the company rather than reaping any monetary rewards. There's a famous, yet anonymous, quote with which we would concur: "To make a small fortune through designing games, start with a large fortune".

Surprised Stare Games Ltd

http://www.surprisedstaregames.co.uk/
http://www.facebook.com/SurprisedStareGamesLtd

We design and publish games that people want to play again and again; games that are colourful and rich in theme and detail; games that are innovative and, most importantly, fun! Step inside our world . . . we guarantee you will be pleasantly surprised!

Surprised Stare Games is a card and board games design and publishing company based in the UK.

Figure 14.4 SSG's latest game, *Snowdonia*, SSG, 2012

References

BoardGameGeek (2013a). *Reiner-Knizia*. Available at http://www.boardgamegeek.com/boardgamedesigner/2/reiner-knizia (accessed on 20 January 2013).

BoardGameGeek (2013b). *Martin Wallace*. Available at http://www.boardgamegeek.com/boardgamedesigner/6/martin-wallace (accessed on 20 January 2013).

BoardGameGeek (2013c). *Richard Breese*. Available at http://www.boardgamegeek.com/boardgamedesigner/134/richard-breese (accessed on 20 January 2013).

Paull, A (1986). *Starship Tycoons*. Available at http://www.boardgamegeek.com/boardgame/12850/starship-tycoons (accessed on 20 January 2013).

Pulsipher, L. (2012). *Game Design: How to Create Video and Tabletop Games, Start to Finish*. Jefferson NC, USA: McFarland & Co.

ABOUT THE CONTRIBUTORS

In chapter order

Alex Moseley is an Educational Designer and University Teaching Fellow at the University of Leicester, UK, where he has had long experience as both practitioner and researcher of course design and development for higher education. He has particular interests in online and distance education, museum education, student engagement and provision of effective research skills. His principle research area is the use of games for learning, on which he writes, presents and runs workshops. He designed a successful games-based approach to teaching historical research skills; was part of the team behind the first charity ARG, *Operation: Sleeper Cell*; co-chairs the Association for Learning Technology's Games and Learning special interest group (ALTGLSIG); and co-organises the *Let's Change the Game* cross-sector conference.

Nicola Whitton is a Research Fellow at Manchester Metropolitan University (MMU), UK, and a Director of the Technology, Innovation and Play for Learning (TIPL) research group. She holds a doctorate in the use of educational games for learning and has published widely in the field. She has led projects in the use of alternate reality games for student induction, gaming for older adults, and the potential game-building for learning, and is passionate about the potential of play to engage and enthuse learners. More broadly, her research interests encompass learning and teaching innovation and the use of rich media and technology for learning.

Cas Kramer grew up in the Netherlands and loved 'anything science' from an early age. He started his career with a Biology degree at Utrecht University in the Netherlands. He then moved to the United Kingdom to pursue a PhD in Molecular Biology at the University of Nottingham. His scientific interests included filamentous fungi and biological rhythms. Having been a bench scientist for many years he decided to join GENIE, Centre for Excellence in Teaching and Learning (CETL) in Genetics at the University of Leicester, in 2005. In this role he lectures Genetics and Molecular Biology to Biological Sciences and Medical undergraduate students. Moreover, a very important part of his day-to-day job involves outreach to schools and colleges and organising public engagement events. He thoroughly enjoys making science accessible to all members of the general public, irrespective to whether they are 8 or 80 years old!

Nicola Suter-Giorgini is from GENIE, Department of Genetics, University of Leicester, Leicester, United Kingdom.

Karen Moss is from the College of Environmental and Life Sciences (CELS), School of Science and Technology, Nottingham Trent University, Nottingham, United Kingdom.

Eoin Gill and **Sheila Donegan** are from the Centre for the Advancement of Learning of Maths, Science and Technology (CALMAST), Waterford Institute of Technology, Waterford, Ireland.

Fiona Trapani is a Teacher Educator and PhD student at the Melbourne Graduate School of Education at The University of Melbourne, Victoria, Australia. Trained as a secondary science teacher she has taught science in schools across primary and secondary settings, while teaching in pre-service teacher programs for the last 15 years. Liz and Fiona have been friends for many years, since secondary school and continuing today through a passion for teaching and learning using new technologies. She is currently researching game design theory and the types of contributions new and old technologies offer to effective learning experiences in diverse classroom contexts. You can follow Fiona on Twitter @fiona_trapani, or through her blog which focuses on ICT for organisation and learning at http://mypaperlessphd. wordpress.com/

Elizabeth Hinds works as a Primary School Teacher (Learning Advisor) in St Joseph's Primary School, Mernda, Victoria Australia and completed her undergraduate degrees at Australian Catholic University before completing a graduate certificate in Teaching Studies of Asia at Victoria University. Her association with Fiona Trapani began in their teenage years when they befriended each other at secondary school. Elizabeth has worked across a range of schools and settings in a variety of leadership, mentoring and teaching roles. She is passionate about finding authentic ways to personalise learning experiences and deliver curriculum while integrating old and new technologies. She is always looking for new ways to help students to engage in their learning and develop twenty-first-century skills and enjoys working in team-oriented, open and contemporary learning environments. Elizabeth is currently employed at St Joseph's Primary School in Mernda, on the outskirts of Melbourne, Australia. St Joseph's is recognised as an Apple Distinguished School for their use of technology in Teaching and Learning and has hosted educators far and wide for tours about contemporary learning. You can follow Elizabeth on Twitter: @

lizhinds74 if you would like to know more or visit her blog: http://adventures-incontemporarylearning.blogspot.com

Nathalie Charlier is an assistant professor at the Faculty of Pharmaceutical Sciences and co-ordinator of the Teacher Training in Health Sciences Education at the KU Leuven, Belgium. She obtained a BSc and MSc in Pharmaceutical Sciences and her PhD in Medical Sciences. Her current research interests are (i) game-based learning in health science education and (ii) the use of new technologies in education.

Kris Rockwell is CEO of Hybrid Learning Systems. After gaining his MA from Duquesne University, Pittsburgh, Pennsylvania, US, in 1998, Kris went to work for US Airways as the Manager of the Media Production and Support Group (MPSG). At US Airways Kris oversaw the development of the computer-based training system for the Boeing 737–300/400 series aircraft and developed and implemented the data collection tool for the airlines Advanced Qualification Program (AQP). In 2003 Kris founded Hybrid Learning Systems as a company dedicated to developing new and unique solutions for learning applications. Over the past nine years, Kris has worked with customers to implement innovative solutions with a focus on mobile learning and gaming applications. In 2010, Hybrid acquired ImpactGames to further its development in gaming and socially responsible initiatives. Kris' recent work has focused on newer technologies and works to combine a wide variety of technologies and concepts from additive 3D printing to sensors and physical computing.

Alicia Sanchez specializes in the implementation of games and simulations into a variety of learning environments. Leveraging decades of research in Education and Simulations, Alicia's focus lies in the appropriate use of games within curriculum and emerging technologies that continuously redefine the potential of games-based learning options. Alicia started Czarina Games in 2010 to work with organizations who needed help in determining the types of learning games that might be right for them. Czarina Games has consulted to top companies since and has partnered on the launch of two customizable games: *A Game of Phones* and *Gold Stars*. Alicia has published much of her work and has presented at many national and international conferences including the Human Factors and Ergonomics Society, the Society for Industrial/Organizational Psychology, Simulation Interoperability Standards Organisation (SISO), and the Serious Games Summit.

Päivi Marjanen is a development manager at Laurea University of Applied Sciences in Finland. She is also teaching early childhood education. Her research interests are history of education, collaborative learning and tools in children's learning.

Ilkka Mönkkönen teaches communication skills and foreign languages at Laurea University of Applied Sciences in Finland. His research interests comprise linguistics, especially Anglo Saxon prose and Old English syntax, second foreign language learning and communication studies.

Jule Hildmann is a Special Education teacher in her first profession but resigned her position to work full time in promoting social and personal skills in individuals and groups through experiential education. She holds qualifications in various other outdoor activities and as systemic counselor, paramedic and first aid instructor. As train-the-trainer in outdoor and experiential education, she also puts great emphasis on the value of initiative games and 'soft' methods for process facilitation. Consequently, she developed the *SimpleThings* concept of experiential education with simple means. Jule holds a PhD in (Experiential) Education and Psychology and is continuously doing research and producing publications on various topics in this field. Starting August 2013, she is conducting a project on meta skills in facilitators as research fellow at the Outdoor Education Department of the University of Edinburgh, UK.

Sam Ingleson works at the University of Salford, Greater Manchester, UK, and is currently the Programme Leader for MA Creative Education and also Lectures on the BA(Hons) Visual Arts programme. Sam is a multi-media visual artist whose art practice is centred in social engagement and participatory performances. Her core research themes are the exploration of creative space and engagement in the formation of artistic strategies that include makers and performers. Her current interest is collaborating to develop board games that bring groups of people together to celebrate, learn or reflect. Sam is also working on two other projects – *Guns to Goods* working with a local charity Community Alliance for Renewal, Inner South Manchester Area (CARISMA), the police and other external partners on an anti-gun and -gang initiative, recycling gun metal to provide income for mentoring activities in the community (see http://www. gunstogoods.org) and a collaboration with colleagues in nursing to develop the use of arts practices within nurse teaching to improve reflective skills.

Ivar Männamaa is lecturer at the University of Tartu, Viljandi Culture Academy, Estonia. His educational background is in psychology; currently he is a PhD student of educational sciences with a focus on design and implementation of educational simulation games. Ivar has co-designed several educational games and published on this topic. He has initiated and managed different international projects focusing on effective learning environments.

J. Tuomas Harviainen wrote his doctoral dissertation on larps as information systems. While working as a chief information specialist at a Finnish library, he also freelances as a designer of educational and organizational development larps for museums, universities, non-governmental organisations (NGOs) and corporations. His mini-larps have been run in 17 countries and translated into seven languages. In his rare spare time, Harviainen edits the *International Journal of Role-Playing*. Contact: jiituomas@gmail.com

Ritva Savonsaari holds a Master's degree in the French and English languages. She currently teaches English and Spanish to 16–18-year-old students at Lumo senior high school, Vantaa, Finland. She has found games to be an especially useful tool for teaching spoken language skills to students. Her hobbies include fine tea, literature and Japanese flower arrangement. Contact: ritva.savonsaari@eduvantaa.fi

Barbara Ottolini was born and raised in Italy, where she was playing in the Alpine forests. In this environment she developed an early interest in the study of natural phenomena, biology and science, nagging her parents for microscopes, telescopes and every sort of dangerous science kit. She studied Medical Biotechnologies at the University of Milan Bicocca (UNIMIB), Italy, and then moved to Paris for a Master's degree in Genetics. She is currently in the United Kingdom, finalising a PhD in Evolutionary Genetics at the University of Leicester, where she can keep playing with microscopes and dangerous kits. She is very much involved in teaching activities in Leicester, both at the undergraduate and postgraduate levels. She is also actively participating in outreach and public engagement, organised by the GENIE Centre for Excellence in Teaching and Learning. She loves scientific research and is particularly keen in continually finding the funny side of science, always transmitting her enthusiasm to everyone around her.

Claire Hamshire has worked at Manchester Metropolitan University (MMU) since 2003, initially as a senior lecturer in Physiotherapy, and from 2008 as a senior learning and teaching fellow in Technology Enabled Learning. This role combines faculty teaching with a cross-institutional contribution to technology innovation. From this position she has been instrumental in ensuring that MMU put students' perspectives at the centre of teaching and research developments. Her research interests include student engagement, learning technologies and games-based learning. She led the Higher Education Academy (HEA) funded 'easystart' project and has recently completed an NHS North West funded project that explored healthcare student attrition at nine institutions in the North West of England – Staying the Course. She was awarded an HEA National Teaching Fellowship in 2012.

Rachel Forsyth is a principal lecturer in the Centre of Excellence for Learning and Teaching at Manchester Metropolitan University, UK, with a remit to support curriculum and assessment design and innovation. She is co-author of *Identity Crisis: Teaching in HE in the 21st Century* (Trentham Books, 2010). She is interested in the use of games to promote cross-disciplinary discussion and to replace some of the duller elements of essential staff development.

Arun Mathews is a board-certified internist/hospitalist working as chief medical informatics officer (CMIO) of Medical Center Hospital in Odessa, Texas, US, and director of the Texas Tech University Health Sciences Hospitalist Fellowship program. He completed residency training at the John Hopkins University (JHU) affiliated Good Samaritan Hospital in Baltimore, Maryland, and then completed a year of medical informatics research at JHU, evaluating the use of gaming technology in high-acuity clinical environments, and subsequently founded the NerdcoreLearning publishing house, based on this work. Email: arun@nerdcorelearning.com / Twitter: @arunmathewsmd

Alan Paull is no stranger to game design and development, as his games *Siege, Thunderin' Guns* and *City of Sorcerers* were published in the 1980s. This makes him old enough to have played and enjoyed virtually all types of games produced since the late 1960s. He has written numerous articles and game reviews for games magazines, including a solitaire game *Mindmeld*. He also designed, developed and produced *Starship Tycoons*, a trading board game set in space. Alan formed *Surprised Stare Games* with Tony Boydell where he designed *Tara, Seat of Kings*, SSG's first board game, and *Confucius*. He's quite proud of the fact that the abbreviation for Tara, Seat of Kings, TSOK, sounds like Taoiseach, the Irish Prime Minister.

INDEX